The Black
Culture Industry

This insightful study of the relationship between black culture, wealth, and race relations . . . allows the reader to understand better, and more clearly, the nature and evolution of race relations in the United States, and how culture and art can be utilized by wealthy and powerful interests to manage race

James Jennings, Director of the William Monroe Trotter Institute at the University of Massachusetts, author of *The Politics of Black Empowerment*

Ellis Cashmore's book offers an evocative and engaging look inside black cultural industries

Jan Nederveen Pieterse, Institute of Social Studies, Holland, author of *White on Black*

Can there be such a thing as an authentic black culture, when the industry that produces it is controlled by white-owned corporations? Cashmore's account of how black culture has been converted into a commodity throws into question the very idea of an authentic black culture. It shows how blacks have been permitted success within the entertainment industry only on the condition that they conform to whites' stereotypical images, and how black entrepreneurs, when they reach the top of corporate entertainment ladder, have tended to act very much as whites have done in similar circumstances.

Developing a history of black culture from the post-emancipation period to the present – from negro spirituals to rap – Cashmore argues that inflating the value of a commodified "black culture" may actually work against the interests of racial justice, and that its most significant – and pernicious – effect may be in signalling the end of racism while keeping the racial hierarchy essentially intact.

Ellis Cashmore is the author of . . . *and there was television* and *Dictionary of Race and Ethnic Relations*. He has held academic positions at the Universities of Washington, Tampa, Massachusetts, Hong Kong and Aston, England, and is currently Professor of Sociology at Staffordshire University, England.

Routledge books by Ellis Cashmore

. . . and there was television

Making sense of sports

Dictionary of race and ethnic relations

Black sportsmen

Out of order? Policing black people
(with Eugene McLaughlin)

The Black
Culture Industry

Ellis Cashmore

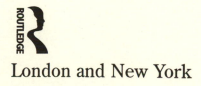

London and New York

First published 1997
by Routledge
11 New Fetter Lane, London EC4P 4EE

Simultaneously published in the USA and
Canada
by Routledge
29 West 35th Street, New York, NY 10001

© 1997 Ellis Cashmore

Typeset in Century Old Style by
Keystroke, Jacaranda Lodge,
Wolverhampton
Printed and bound in Great Britain by
TJ International Ltd, Padstow, Cornwall

*British Library Cataloging in Publication
Data*
A catalog record for this book is available
from the British Library

*Library of Congress Cataloging in
Publication Data*
Cashmore, Ernest.
    The black culture industry / Ellis
Cashmore.
        p.   cm.
    Includes bibliographical references and
index.
    1. United States—Race relations.
2. Afro-Americans—Race identity.
3. Racism—United States—History—
20th century.   4. Afro-American arts.
5. Afro-Americans in mass media.
I. Title.
E185.615.C352 1997
305.896′073—dc21   96–48116
                                  CIP

ISBN 0–415–12082–9 (hbk)
ISBN 0–415–12083–7 (pbk)

Contents

Acknowledgments

The idea on which this book is based came from my friend Chris Rojek and, though I am quite sure the end-product is totally different to the book he had in mind, I am grateful to him for initiating it. Mari Shullaw, my Commissioning Editor at Routledge, has played a constructive and critical role throughout the book's development. Early drafts have been read and criticized by James Jennings, of the University of Massachusetts, Timothy Lukes, of Santa Clara University, Deborah Root, of Bilkent University, Turkey, Jan Pieterse, of the Hague Institute of Social Studies, Holland, and David Jary, of Staffordshire University. Ossie Jones and George Paton, of Aston University, have kept watchful eyes on articles and books I might otherwise have missed. And Amy Shepper, of the University of South Florida, has been absolutely invaluable in assisting my research: whatever would I do without her? I thank them all for their contributions to the book.

**Do you know why the
white man hates you?
Because every time
he sees your face
he sees a mirror of
his crime and his
guilty conscience
can't bear it.**

Malcolm X

**You value things you
can master. Whatever
white men have permitted
us to do we have mastered**

Bernard Vanderstell, in *Drylongso*
by John Langston Gwaltney

Chapter one

Crack in
the Wall

THIRTY YEARS AGO, whites were taught to fear difference. The sight of a black man in a suit was enough to cause alarm in some areas. One of the purposes of segregation was to prevent the potential contamination that might be caused by contact with "others." The others in question were not only different in appearance, language and lifestyle: they were inferior. Neither the moral nor the constitutional imperative behind the separate-but-equal idea had any force at all.

Today, whites embrace the differences that once disturbed them: appreciation and enjoyment have replaced uneasiness. The images whites held of blacks have changed in harmony with changes in aesthetic tastes. What was once disparaged and mocked is now regarded as part of legitimate culture. Any residual menace still lurking in African American practices and pursuits has been domesticated, leaving a black culture capable of being adapted, refined, mass-produced and marketed. Whites not only appreciate black culture: they buy it. Having appropriated music, visual arts and the literature traditionally associated with African Americans, they have put it on the market. Black culture is now open for business. A great many blacks have become rich on the back of it. An even greater number of whites have prospered. This book is about the industry that makes all this possible.

In the course of the book, we will see how black culture has been converted into a commodity, usually in the interests of white-owned corporations; how blacks have been permitted to excel in entertainment only on the condition that they conform to whites' images of blacks; and how blacks themselves, when they rise to the top of the corporate entertainment ladder, have tended to act precisely as whites have in similar circumstances.

One of the myths I hope to expose is that of an unbroken continuum that stretches back from rap music through soul, gospel and negro spirituals to the African-derived slave traditions. This is a melodramatic construction of black culture and one which does no justice to its intricacies or indeed hiatuses. Although impressive as a rallying cry for unity, a "call to consciousness," as the film director Mario van Peebles once put it, the concept of a distinct black cultural tradition is questionable. Cultures, whether African or European in origin, have merged and melded over time and space.

"The history of all cultures is the history of cultural borrowings," writes Edward Said, in his book *Culture and Imperialism*. "Cultures are not impermeable." Western science, for example, borrowed from Arabs, who had, in turn, borrowed from India and Greece. Martin Bernal's *Black Athena* shows how Egyptian and Semitic influences bore on Greek civilizations, though these influences were either obscured or left unacknowledged. Said concludes: "Culture is never just a matter of ownership, of borrowing and lending with absolute debtors and creditors, but rather of appropriations, common experiences, and interdependencies of all kinds among different cultures" (1993: 261–62. Year of publication followed by page numbers quoted will be given in parenthesis throughout the text).

There are rather more appropriations than common experiences and interdependences in the cultures I will look at. My examination will reveal the considerable extent to which whites have intervened in black culture, shaping it, changing it, packaging it, producing it, merchandising it, distributing it, franchising it and turning into any shape that will turn a profit.

"Making black expressiveness a commodity," is how Houston Baker describes the process I am writing about. "Afro-America's exchange power has always been coextensive with its stock of expressive resources," he observes in his *Blues, Ideology, and Afro-American Literature* (1987: 196). Blacks have entered into negotiations with whites, bargaining with their most valuable resource – culture. There are understandable historical reasons for this, many written of by David Levering Lewis in his study of the Harlem Renaissance of the 1920s. After World War I, blacks were denied membership to labor unions, kept out of decent jobs, prevented from participating in the the political process and, generally, marginalized. But, states Lewis: "No exclusionary rules had been laid down regarding a place in the arts. Here was a small crack in the wall of racism, a fissure that was worth trying to widen" (1981: 48). This book, in part, chronicles the attempts to widen that fissure.

In the process of chronicling, I will suggest that inflating the significance of black culture may work against tangible enhancements to the lives of African Americans. The most significant value of black culture may be in providing whites with proof of the end of racism while keeping the racial hierarchy essentially intact. If this is the case, the argument might run like this:

Years ago, the United States was torn by what some called "An American Dilemma," that is, the land of the free was free for only whites, and blacks were profoundly unfree. In 1963, two years before his death, Malcolm X observed: "The white man has a guilt complex and the white people today are so afraid since they know what they have done to the black people in this country" (1971: 115).

The guilt was hardly lessened by the establishment of civil rights because, for years after, nearly four times as many African American families lived below the poverty line as white families, black youths under the age of 20 were four times as likely to die by murder than whites of the same age group, black infants died at twice the rate of white infants, the net worth of a typical black household was about a tenth of that of a typical white household, a black youth's chances of going to prison were better than he or she had of going to a university and, in many states, five to ten times as many blacks as whites between 18 and 30 were imprisoned. The catalog could continue. But blacks were capable of *some* things and whites became mature enough to accept them. Indisputable evidence of this came principally in entertainment and sports, where blacks literally earned fortunes – and the respect of whites. The hatred and racism that pockmarked America has now abated: whites not only recognize that there is a legitimate black culture: they applaud it. And keep this as evidence of the dilemma's resolution.

Discrimination is deplored, its effects regretted. Aspects of the black experience can be integrated into the mainstream and, with the advent of the mass media, consumed without even going near black people. Hit a remote control button and summon the sounds and images of the ghetto. This is culture as the antidote to racism, a way of removing the complexities of history and society from the mind by introducing a painless cure: legitimize black culture, its literature, its religions, its athleticism and, perhaps above all, its music. If this is so, it is time for black culture to be examined with the same kind of cyncism that Theodor Adorno brought to American culture in general. Adorno's most potent argument was that the culture ushered in during late modernity was – and is – manufactured by elites to serve their own interests, often commercially as well as politically motivated ones.

The resemblance between the ways culture and other artefacts of industrial society are produced and distributed was sufficient for Adorno to coin the term *The Culture Industry*. I want to entertain the possibility that black culture is commodified and, at the same time, urge caution about welcoming it as a new basis of power for black people. To do so, I focus on black music, which is virtually synonymous with black culture. In his introduction to *Black Talk* (originally published in 1971) Ben Sidran wrote: "Music is not only a reflection of the values of black culture, but to some extent, the basis upon which it is built" (1995: xxi).

My account of its history and development will accentuate the intrusion of sometimes subtle and conflicting forces in the formation of what we have come to regard as black culture. It will also display the role of entrepreneurs, both black and white, in promoting a culture from which they have sought to profit. And it will open out the meaning of the 1992 track, "Famous and Dandy (like Amos 'n' Andy)" in which the band The Disposable Heroes of HipHoprisy self-reflect that black people can be rented to "perform any feat" (from *Hypocrisy is the Greatest Luxury*, 4th&B'Way™, Island Records).

In an effort to spare him the indignity of wearing handcuffs in front of the world's media and the west Los Angeles paparazzi, the accused was made to wear a concealed electronic belt – reportedly designed to stun him with an electric shock should he try to flee. He arrived in a motorcade of presidential proportions, jurors arriving in a sheriff's department bus usually used for carrying prisoners, shielded from the media by tinted glass and a mobile cordon of 240 police officers. It was February 1995: they were on a field trip, a ritual common to Californian murder trials, the purpose of which is to enable jurors to visualize scenes talked about during trials. The scene in this case was the Brentwood home where Nicole Simpson and her friend Ronald Goodman were found dead. Johnnie Cochrane Jr objected when jurors were denied access to a trophy room. He argued that it was unfair to exclude areas that reflected well on his client. The trial judge agreed, but insisted that a life-sized statue of the accused in football uniform be covered. It was a sheet, though it might just as well have been a sacramental pall that was draped over the icon.

Cochran, LA's leading African American lawyer, led the defense of O. J. Simpson, the ex-football star, sports journalist and movie actor, who was accused of the murder of his former wife and her friend. At times during the trial, Cochran's rhetoric was that of a nonconformist preacher. Robert Shapiro, a white attorney, was Cochran's righthand man. Both attorneys became internationally-known figures in a matter of weeks; yet, they were bit part players in one of the greatest real life dramas.

The Simpson case was America's defining cultural experience of the decade: it claimed the front page of every newspaper in the USA, Britain and probably everywhere else in the world. The television companies gave it gavel-to-gavel coverage and were rewarded with record-breaking viewer ratings. Even the soaps were eased aside to make room for a story that was every bit as involving as *Days of Our Lives* and had an additional dimension – that of race.

While both sets of attorneys publicly announced their intention not to exploit the race issue, one of the defense's strategies was to shake the credibility of Detective Mark Fuhrman, one of the first police officers to arrive at the scene, at first by hinting at his racism. He had, it was alleged, made racist remarks to a psychiatrist. Soon, the entire focus of the case shifted to the detective's racial slurs and it was he rather than the defendant who began to dominate the front pages. The acquittal was widely seen as an expression of outrage at the racism in the Los Angeles Police Department that had been brutally exposed in the Rodney King tapes three years before. The Simpson case unearthed the possibility – however unlikely – that a racist plan had been designed by the LAPD to frame Simpson, an obviously successful millionaire African American.

Without his kind of money, Simpson might have become just another inmate in a prison system already overpopulated by black males: about 32.2 percent of young black American men are in prison, on parole or on probation; in many states, five to ten times as many black men under the age of 30 are in prison as whites. But, Simpson had sufficient funds to hire a top defense team; his legal fees are thought to have been in the region of $10 million.

Time magazine, in its first issue following Simpson's arrest, featured his police mugshot on the front cover. No surprises here: the photograph almost became omnipresent, with virtually every daily and weekly publication making use of the same powerful image. Unshaven black celebrity stares out blankly through hooded eyes, his arrest sheet number BK401397006179 strapped across his chest and "Los Angeles Police: Jail Division" framing the shot. But *Time* added its own Stygian touches. Apart from its headline AN AMERICAN TRAGEDY, it artificially darkened Simpson's face and surrounded it in murky shadow to produce an image that resonated menace.

"No racial implication was intended," the magazine's editor assured 800,000 computer bulletin board readers. The doctored photo was just "a work of art." Not so, answered an assembly of black interest groups led by the National Association for the Advancement of Colored People (NAACP). The cover presented a stereotype that pandered to white racism. Here was the surly black brute, dark, sinister and dangerous, a throwback to the stereotype of years past, when lynching or emasculation were the prescribed methods of taming bestial black males. Even a superficial "reading" of the image revealed a crudely coded message: "Here's OJ, black as sin; no longer someone who entertains whites, whether on the sports field or the screen, but a coveter of a white woman."

Some accused the magazine of a scabrous attempt to crank up circulation figures by appealing to the latent racism of white America. This was the criticism of rival magazine, *Newsweek*, which published the same photograph, but without the additional brushwork. *Time*'s editor, James Gaines, would not apologize for the tampering and actually tried to reverse the tide, by prompting the query: is it not racist to say that being blacker equates to being more sinister?

At the same time as the Simpson hearings, another image of blackness was being relayed around the world via satellite and optic fibers; that of Michael Jackson, who married Lisa-Marie Presley, Scientology devotee and daughter of Elvis. At first, an incredulous media laughed at the very idea. Incomprehensible: the oddest, most famous, yet reclusive rock star in the world getting hitched to the unimaginably wealthy progeny of a once equally famous and equally reclusive white rock star who died dissipated by booze and drugs.

The timing of the wedding was unusual. Jackson, deeply troubled by a dependency on sleeping pills and forced to cancel a world concert tour, was suspected of having molested a 14-year-old LA boy, whom he paid an undisclosed sum, rumored to be over $25 million. Like Simpson, he found that, while money may not whiten, it does buy the kinds of privileges not available to the vast majority of African Americans.

Jackson, of course, was a child prodigy, a singer in the Jackson 5, then the Jacksons, before going solo and breaking records with his bestselling albums and concerts. His popularity was universal and fascination with him grew as he metamorphosed from an African American child, then youth, to a chalky-skinned individual, his face resculpted many times over until its appearance owed more to a surgeon's scalpel than the gene pool. Jackson befriended a chimpanzee, he bought the skeleton of the famed Elephant Man, he slept in an oxygen tent. The public's devotion to him never wavered, despite his idiosyncrasies.

Perhaps his cds and videos carried him; perhaps his flawed and vulnerable private self endeared him to fans. Perhaps even his changing pigmentation – a product of either a skin condition or cosmetic surgery, depending on whose version you favored – won him fans. Whatever the source of his attraction, Jackson was a cultural icon in the strongest sense of the term, a figure who both

5

embodied and formed a constituent part of late twentieth century culture. A black male, born to an African American family, but whose physical form defied any clear ethnic categorization.

Images of blackness are power; the power to frame and affect. The images of Simpson and Jackson presented in the mid-1990s were not just images of black people: they were whites' images, representations created and recreated anew over a period of several hundred years. If Simpson was the brute nigger, Jackson was the black child of countless pictures and posters that circulated in Europe and North America from the seventeenth century and which depicted a white couple scrubbing a black child with soap in a futile attempt to rid him of his blackness. "To labor in vain" was the saying that accompanied the illustration. Jackson's efforts to transmogrify himself were as futile as those of the white couple of yore.

The conventional and always rhetorical question asked is: who are the producers and consumers of these and other images? And the answer is assumed to be obvious. What purposes do they serve? is a related question and here the answer, though not as clear-cut, is still apparent and involves the concept of cultural colonialism. The principal European powers of the past four centuries have divested themselves of the political and economic control they once had over their colonies and the USA has legally granted civil rights to all its citizens, but something else remains as an obstacle to equality of opportunity and treatment. Something far less tangible than the institutional barriers that isolated blacks and retarded their progress in every social sphere.

Jan Pieterse, in his authoritative book, *White on Black*, uses the term "pathos of inequality" to describe the quality of contemporary western culture that excites the thought and emotion of racial hierarchy. In virtually every discourse involving blacks and whites, it is this quality "rather than race or racism in a narrow, shallow sense, which permeates the images of white on black" (1992: 51). The title of Pieterse's work carries the import of his thesis: the historical relationship he is referring to is an imbalanced one, weighted in favor of white colonizers and ex-colonizers who sought to impose images of blacks that they, rather than blacks, had created.

Public representation in a way reflects other interests and images of blacks that elicit a pathos of inequality and serve to stir ideas, not always openly negative ones, but ones which somehow conjure up a sense of hierarchy. The hierarchy in question is pretty much the same one that has endured for 400 years: whites remaining aloft, with subordinate groups of other colors scrambling beneath them. A respectful acknowledgment of blacks' musical gifts, their athletic talent, their lithe, untutored sense of rhythm might seem like a half-compliment. But, it unlocks the same vault of ideas that contains well-worn stereotypes, like the dumb nigger, the selfless domestic worker, or mammy, and the lusty, promiscuous black Venus. All of these contribute the general image of African-originated and -descended groups – whether in the USA, Britain or continental Europe – as *others*, groups that are actually in mainstream culture, yet at the same time not integral parts of it.

None of this is original and the past decade has seen the emergence of a near-consensus regarding the power of imagery. To have cultural power is to have power, period. This includes the ability to define not only images that circulate in culture, but also the content of religious ideas, of art, of electronic media of communication, of popular ideas; all of which influence perceptions and behavior. It follows that having access to the means of changing all of these places one in an advantageous position at a number of levels. One of the consequences of being able to reshape images and ideas, specifically of black people, is the potential to change the racial hierarchy and, so, the pathos of inequality that underpins it. This is why so much store is placed on those African Americans who have assumed some measure of cultural power: people who have control over how representations of blacks are formed and disseminated carry a heavy burden, whether they like it or not.

It used to be that black people who had money and a certain amount of prestige were either sports stars or showbusiness performers. They made comparatively good money and enjoyed a status of sorts, though an apophthegm captures the conditional nature of the status: the only difference between a black shoeshine boy and a black Olympic champion is that the one is a nigger and the other is a fast nigger. The cultural impact of sports and showbiz stars was limited, in the sense that they added new, complementary dimensions to existing stereotypes, rather than undermining them. True, Sugar Ray Robinson was an exceptional fighter, who possessed an almost inhuman mastery of all elements of boxing and was able to prolong his distinguished career well into his thirties. True, Nat King Cole had unrivalled pitch and vocal qualities. But, for all their glory and esteem, they never mounted anything resembling a challenge to existing ideas about blacks. They expanded on older images. Many other champions and entertainers followed them, without affecting the quality of "otherness" that characterized blacks in the eyes of whites.

The problem was crystallized in the career of Muhammad Ali. A boxer of extraordinary technical brilliance, he self-consciously attempted to transcend sports, seizing the opportunities offered to the occupant of sport's most prestigious position, heavyweight champion of the world, to make *ex cathedra* pronouncements on issues that ranged from morality to the military. Even at a distance of some twenty years after his heyday it is still hard to know what to make of the man. Was he a charismatic leader, wise and strong, earnest in his provocative but well-motivated endeavors to shake the US's and possibly the world's black population into realizing its own potential? Or was he just another power-crazed fighter who was naïve enough to think above his station and whose career ended as abjectly as a run-of-the-mill club fighter? Or simply a fallibly human mixture of both?

At the time of Ali's ascent in the 1960s and 1970s, other blacks were also fighting: not in a literal sense this time – they were fighting to get into industries that were historically controlled by whites. The faces of the sports stars and the entertainers who made up what was then an African American elite may have been black; but the promoters, the managers, the executives and the audiences were white. Then at last came an emergent group of black entrepreneurs who could at least approach the kind of positions that carried the power to change images and ideas. Not just performers who stood on stage or ran the length of a football field for the amusement of whites (and audiences would have been predominantly white, of course); but people who were trying to wrest control of industries that dispensed cultural products, like music and sport, and who ultimately should have been able to destabilize the racial hierarchy.

═══════════════

The concept of the racial hierarchy deserves a little explanation. I use it in the same way as Louis Kushnick in the 1980s and, more recently James Jennings. Kushnick's mission was to explain how racism has retarded the progress of both the black and white working class in the USA and Britain in the postwar years (Kushnick, 1981). Jennings describes Kushnick's interpretation of racism as a bribe, whites enjoying psychological privileges and material benefits in exchange for not questioning a set of social arrangements that exploited them slightly less than it did blacks and other ethnic minorities.

Imagine a fir tree with a few small but powerful branches perched near the apex and the majority down towards the base where the shoots fan out; ethnic minorities stand about the trunk of the tree waiting for a chance to shin up. The idea, according to Kushnick, is that whites get to keep their places at the lower levels as long as they keep blacks off the branches completely. This may not even be a conscious process: whites necessarily have privileges; they cannot avoid them. Working class whites "are most afraid of seeing the distance between themselves and the blacks disappear," argues Michel Wierviorka in his *The Arena of Racism*. It is this sharing of relative privilege that "allows whites from different social backgrounds, who, in other circumstances, would be opposed to, or would keep apart from, one another, to come together" (1995: 19, 20).

"Even a cursory examination of academe, entertainment and sports, housing, the military, management of cultural institutions, the corporate sector, or government in the United States reveals that generally blacks serve under, report to, or are held accountable by whites in power," writes Jennings in his *Blacks, Latinos and Asians in Urban America* (1994: 149). "And even in most of the institutions managed by blacks – whether historically black colleges, local social welfare programs, public schools, and other institutions – final authority rests with whites."

The cultural implications of this racial hierarchy are many. The value attached to products coming out of cultural institutions managed – and, we might add to Jennings' point, owned – by whites is correspondingly valued. The products of those few cultural institutions not managed or owned by whites are devalued. At least, that has been the case until recent years, when a warrantable black culture, owned, managed and, in the most general way, controlled by African Americans has developed. This meant that its products were not films, music and other media that used primarily or even exclusively black crews and black actors. As Ada Gay Griffin writes, "They are productions in which the artistic vision is controlled by a person of African descent." Its significance is multifaceted, but, as Griffin notes, "Ultimately, it is about power over the image" (1992: 231).

═══════════════

What exactly is black culture? It is a term we hear a lot about today. We know it is a product and expression of African American and Afro-Caribbean creativity, embodying values, ambitions and orientations unique to black people, whether in the States, Britain or elsewhere in the diaspora. Conventionally, culture is contrasted to nature: we are not born with it, but into it. We acquire it through language and transmit it to future generations, through instruction. In its widest sense, culture is everything we learn from others and pass on to still others. It does not involve instinct, natural propensities or biological dispositions. So, when we talk of black culture, we are not referring to any of the qualities purportedly deriving from black people as a "race" (and I place the word in inverted commas to emphasize my rejection of it as anything other than a mistaken belief). Yet, there is something distinct about black culture and, if it is not anything to do with spurious biology, it must come from experience.

In his classic anticolonial treatise, *Black Skin, White Masks*, Frantz Fanon wrote, "What is often called the black soul is a white man's artefact" (1986: 16). Fanon was making a psychoanalytic point and his purpose in making it was quite different to mine in this book. But, it is a powerful point nevertheless and one I want to retain.

We often hear of the black experience, that is a set of social and historical conditions that all peoples whose ancestors originated in Africa have lived through in one way or another and which unifies them. Struggle: this was the basis of the experience. Racism, in whatever form, whether manifest or covert, imposes limits with which black peoples have to contend. Exile, enslavement and discrimination were all integral parts of the experience and all resonate through the lives of black people, even today.

Out of struggle comes unity of purpose and identity, a sense of resolve and cohesion. This was a popular argument in favor of the black experience and quite logically flowed into arguments about the character of black culture. Amid the different forms of discourse lay something of the essence of blackness, a nucleus created out of struggle. All cultural expressions have at their center this essence of blackness.

It is, as Paul Gilroy acknowledges, "a potent idea" that is "frequently wheeled in when it is necessary to appreciate the things that (potentially) connect black people to one another rather than think seriously about the divisions in the imagined community of the race" (1993: 24). Gilroy's work concerns what he calls *The Black Atlantic*, a "webbed network" comprising elements of African, American, Caribbean and British culture, but without a core essence. Criticizing what he calls "a brute pan-Africanism," Gilroy challenges purified conceptions of black culture as the contemporary expression of a centuries-long tradition.

In one heady passage, Gilroy describes versions of rap music, often accepted as a strong expression of contemporary black culture, as "a culture of compensation that self-consciously salves the misery of the disempowered and subordinated" (1993: 85). And, in another, he broadens this point to include other cultural forms, like song, that "are developed both as a means of transcendence and as a type of compensation for very specific experiences of unfreedom" (1993: 123). In his view, blacks have been denied access to some cultural forms, like literacy; the forms to which they have been granted access, like sport and music, have performed compensatory functions.

In this sense, black soul could well be an artefact of whites: a music forged in the smelter of oppression and exploitation, soul is often seen as the special preserve of blacks, but not always as a compensation for the "experiences of unfreedom," as Gilroy would argue. To this I would add that the very term "black soul" to describe a fusion music that owes much to blues and gospel is a creation of whites; most probably a racist creation too. The depth and intensity of emotion that are associated with black soul are not typically available to whites. Yet they come naturally to blacks. So goes the argument. The inference is clear. (We will cover soul music in Chapter five.)

The same might be said for all black culture: it serves to soothe and heal the weals of racism and, as soon as it begins to take on a recognizable shape as a cultural form, the appellation "black" is slapped on it by whites, who are always willing to market it as a commodity. Once this happens, it is said to embody all manner of exotic qualities that are in the province of black people. Whites can only copy and imitate – like Al Jolson did in the 1920s and Vanilla Ice did in the late 1980s. And like any number of white rap bands did in the mid-1990s.

In his book *The Signifying Monkey* Henry L. Gates examines the African American literary tradition as a "fragmented unity" comprising self-conscious speakers of English who defined their status as "one of profound difference vis-à-vis the rest of society" (1988: 47). Yet, Gates' analysis of the "subtle and perhaps the most profound trace of an extended engagement between two separate and distinct yet profoundly – even inextricably – related orders of meaning" makes no mention of how commercial imperatives intervened in the "engagement." In stressing the role of cultural producers in developing strategies of resistance, Gates shows how black people share creative credit in disrupting racial hierarchies and "inscribing" black culture.

Compatible with this is Houston Baker's work, especially his *Modernism and the Harlem Renaissance* in which he argues: "Afro-American expressive culture appears in its complex continuity and genuine cultural authenticity when it is analyzed according to the model that I have proposed" (1987: 100). My account brings into question both continuity and authenticity. In her *Cannibal Culture*, Deborah Root proposes that we treat the phrase "cultural authenticity" with some cynicism: it is often "a definition imposed from the outside" and so functions in the interests of those who profit from selling commodified versions of culture (1996: 70). We will see how black culture has been subject to such definition and commodification; and how whites profit most from these.

The process of creating commodities out of culture involves strenuous attempts to contain, control and manipulate notions of fidelity: the people who either discover or manufacture authenticity – and this is not as ironical as it sounds – have needed to calibrate their marketing with changing social conditions. We will see how different types of commodification have been suited to different stages in history. Berry Gordy's prescience in spotting social changes, for example, served him well in moving from an owner of a black music label to a prime mover of the black culture industry – Chapters six and seven deal with the transition. With other culture industry chiefs, Gordy shared an ability to shape, present and sell black culture as something genuine.

On the surface, it appears offensive to argue that black culture is, in some way, not an original product, but a construction: it devalues the creativity, denies the fertility of imagination that lay behind many of the expressions that we now popularly regard as black. Still, it should be stressed that there is nothing natural, less still inevitable, about blackness; any more than there is anything natural about whiteness.

As early as page 17 of *The Shaping of Black America*, Lerone Bennett stresses that "the first white colonists [in America] had no concept of themselves as *white* men. The legal documents identified whites as Englishmen and Christians" (1993: 17). The term "white" did not even enter popular usage until the latter part of the seventeenth century. Its associations with guilt, superiority and cultural arrogance came later. Much the same point is made but in far greater detail by Theodore Allen in his book *The Invention of the White Race*, which examines the transformation of English, Irish, Scottish and other European settlers to a single all-inclusive status – whites.

Allen's historical analysis pays particular attention to the experiences of migrant Irish, once victimized and disparaged as degenerate and not amenable to civilizing influences, yet later transformed into defenders of an exploitative order. The Irish were certainly regarded by English colonizers as an inferior racial group (colonization of Ireland took place during the sixteenth century), but were physically indistinct from the English. There were other groups that would today be recognized as white that were readily associated with savagery. But it became expedient to co-opt them into a new inclusive category as a way of shoring up support for the white-controlled slave order.

Correspondingly, neither the word or the status black was in the vocabulary or the culture of the day: the fundamental division of the slave era, at least the early phases, was not between whites and black, but masters and servants. Being black and being held in contempt because of that fact is a relatively recent phenomenon. One of the many interesting features of Bennett's narrative is the emphasis he gives to the common conditions shared by "Negroes or Negers," as they were called, and white indentured servants. "The tasks expected of both were the same and, in the fields, at least, no discrimination seems to have been made in favor of the latter," observes Bennett (1993: 18).

My intention here is not to delve into history: simply to point out that, if the statuses black and white are created and not naturally-endowed, then presumably, the cultures attached to them are similarly built. Bennett alludes to the same metaphor of construction when he writes of "the bridges of self-determination that black people built for themselves" (1993: 310). How these bridges were built, the conditions under which they were assembled and the support they provided, especially in the postwar years, are described in coming chapters.

I do not accept that there is anything natural or given about the gifts, qualities and characteristics that are customarily attributed by both blacks and whites to black culture. Blackness is as artificial as whiteness; they are both arbitrary indicators of status that appear only in recent history and have been passed through successive generations with such consistency that they appear for all intents and purposes (at first, whites' purposes) to be part of the natural order. Even this cursory glance at history suggests that the categories black and white were inventions. The consciousness of color that infuses so many artefacts, like art, music and film, with significance is a product of peculiar historical circumstances. That so much of culture still has prefixes of color is a kind of testimony to the fact that those circumstances have not changed as dramatically as many smugly think.

Chapter two

Once Pain
and Hunger
Have Been
Removed

T HE HISTORIAN JOSEPH BOSKIN writes of the "incongruity of play
and circumstance" that propelled whites toward a conception of blacks that
explained the apparent contradiction between the horrendous conditions in which
slaves lived and their pleasant, comical mien. "It was a conception that attempted
to encompass all the facets of blacks' playfulness: their cheerful and lighthearted
manner, penchant for frivolity, rhythmical movements, unusual mannerisms,
even their patter of language," Boskin observes of the white mentality in the mid-
nineteenth century. "It was an image whose elements were viewed as a blessing
and a curse, one that whites were convinced would serve them well in dealing with
blacks in any environment or circumstance" (1986: 54). For whites, blacks were
the embodiment of humor, "mirthful by nature." In this chapter, we will see how
the image affected the shape and substance of early black culture.

Reheating overcooked dishes rarely produces a satisfactory meal. Doing likewise
with scientific debates has different results. Take the case of Herrnstein and
Murray's book *The Bell Curve* (1994). The debate it joined was started in the
1960s by Arthur Jensen, who soared to international infamy after publishing the
results of his research in a respectable scientific journal, the *Harvard Educational
Review*. The title of the article was "How much can we boost IQ and scholastic
achievement?" Jensen's project had been to unravel the riddle of nature versus
nurture. Are we born with intelligence, or do we acquire it as we grow up? he
asked, though in rather more erudite terms. Specifically, he wanted to test the
intelligence of three groups of children: white, black and Latino. Jensen found
that blacks consistently scored 15 points below whites. Nothing shocking in this:

indeed, it would have been a major surprise had African American children fared any better, given the history of slavery and the denial of civil rights they and their forebears would have endured; the impact of this and other factors on intellectual development is plain enough.

Jensen, though, did not accept that social, cultural or environmental forces, the nurture side of the equation, were the cardinal causes of the persistently low scores of black children. He concluded that genes bore 80 percent of the responsibility for intelligence. Nature, in his experiments, won hands down. Even if, as Jensen stressed, the motives behind the research were all about the spirit of scientific inquiry, the conclusions could not have been designed better for the truth-seeking racist (if that is not an oxymoron). Caucasians are more intelligent than other groups that have been called races and the reason they are lies in the realm of biology. We can do nothing about it: blacks are naturally inferior.

Nobel prize winner William Shockley threw his scalpel into the arena when he proposed that blacks be sterilized to prevent them from passing on their inferior genes. Unlike Jensen, Shockley did not insist that his motives were pure. Few would have believed him anyway.

The notorious article bearing Jensen's findings drew fire from all quarters and, only years later, after several other studies yielding different results, did the debate die down. Few noticed the embers glowing. Years later, in 1994, Richard Herrnstein, who had once suggested members of the working class carried different genes to their middle class counterparts, and Charles Murray, author of the "black underclass" thesis, published their own study. Entitled *The Bell Curve* to convey the parabola formed when plotting the distribution of intelligence in a population, the book strengthened Jensen's suggested link between IQ and race.

Many studies, said the authors, demonstrated about a 15-point difference in the mean scores of black and white Americans. There is also more equivocal evidence that Asians score significantly higher than whites. Herrnstein died while the book was in production, though Murray survived the trauma and robustly defended its argument. Nature may be unfair in its distribution of talent genes, but its does not determine our destinies. *"Differences in IQ don't much matter,"* emphasized Murray. "We put it in italics; if we could we would put it in neon lights."

The riposte was as sharp and resonant as that which followed Jensen. No one was seriously entertaining Murray's meek apology about IQ differences not mattering, nor his insistence that the results told us only about group differences, not individual ones. In the sample studied, there were many blacks who outscored whites. Glib as it sounded, Murray asserted his commitment to individualism: being born to a group that is collectively inferior does not mean the individual should accept his or her own inferiority. They should travel as far as their natural talent will take them along the road to success; this was the gist of Murray's message.

When Jensen's article was published, the United States was in the throes of a series of changes that were to transfigure America's social and political landscape. The civil rights movement led by Martin Luther King had literally marched its way into public prominence figuratively holding a mirror to white America.

This dear, untutored land that created tragedy by either its own ignorance or its own malevolence had turned a nation sundered by slavery into one serrated by class and ethnic divisions. Tormented by the lack of progress that followed the 1954 *Brown v. Board of Education of Topeka* decision to dissolve the legal boundaries that segregated whites and blacks in educational institutions, the States had to negotiate the commission of full civil rights to an African American population openly dissatisfied and prepared, in some instances, to take violently to the streets.

Predictably, the white backlash to desegregation brought an unwelcome reminder that, for many, the traditional institution of slavery was still the favored social arrangement and the segregated society that succeeded it was a move in the wrong direction. The case for desegregating schools had to be fought at local level in many state courtrooms in the south, defenders of the old system resisting the federal injunction to create mixed schooling. One can easily imagine how the Jensen report rained down like manna to this rearguard. It all but mocked the federal government's vision of an integrated society in which black, white and Latino children shared classrooms while their parents peacefully blended into society, producing ethnic diversity, or pluralism.

The melting pot beloved of the 1960s was in fact full of wormwood-laced stew, the main ingredients simmering without ever mixing. Federal laws could change the rules, but they could not change hearts and minds, at least not in the short (and, as it turned out, not in the medium) term. Jensen's report fortified both heart and mind: it supplied scientific credibility to what was previously only an appeal to tradition and a claim about propriety. You can make blacks and whites learn together, work together, even live together; but you cannot create equality, the research confirmed. And the reason for this is hardly anything to do with historical or social circumstances: it is mainly (80 percent) due to nature. In a way, a perverse way perhaps, this cemented what many whites, especially in southern states that had vehemently opposed the Brown decision, had known all along: that blacks were at the foot of the racial hierarchy for no reason more mysterious than nature. They, the white population, were not responsible for the impoverished conditions of blacks, their lack of formal education, their miserable existence at the fringes of society. Blame mother nature.

The quarter-century that elapsed between the Jensen report and the publication of *The Bell Curve* had seen momentous changes both in the objective condition of black people and in the cultural products they created. How about the black image in the white mind? I take this phrase from the title of George Frederickson's authoritative history, *The Black Image in the White Mind: The debate on Afro-American character and destiny, 1817–1914*, first published in 1971. In his introduction to the second edition of the volume, Frederickson defines his subject matter as "the problem of how ideas become instruments of group advantage or domination" (1987: ix).

This involves not just " what whites thought about blacks," but how black thinkers and writers' contributed to the discourse and imagery. In a sense, my project in this book is similar to Frederickson's, except I am interested in the more recent period in which black musicians emphatically contributed to the discourse and imagery. As they did so, an entire industry largely – though not entirely – owned by whites developed and prospered around them. This is what I refer to as the black culture industry and its full significance in the purgation of white guilt will unfold in chapters to come.

I also have additional objectives because, with Pieterse, I agree that there has been and still is a type of reasoning at work which "transforms a negative stereotype into a positive one" (1992: 12). A stigma can become a badge of honor, while remaining a derivative of a stereotype based on simplification, generalization and, at very best, part-truth. We will see evidence of this when we consider African American artists who have been reconstituted as postmodern icons.

Before moving to the specific task, I want to dwell on the epochal period 1787–1837, which overlaps with the era studied by Frederickson, moving then from 1914 to World War II and then to the publication of Jensen's *Harvard Educational Review* article in 1969. I use the term "epochal period" to describe the phase beginning in 1787 because this marked the beginning of the years of making and shaping of what might warrantably be called black America replete with its own distinct culture. During this period, black people assumed the roles of political and cultural leaders and made tentative moves toward the creation of inchoate institutions that could reflect the unique circumstances and problems of black people. The church was pivotal in this process. Yet it developed as a response to the specific conditions of black people and those conditions were dictated by whites possessed of the view that blacks were inferior to themselves. Racism, in other words, was the decisive force in the formation of the black church and by implication of black culture. It is impossible to see black culture without considering the ideas and institutions that permitted its growth.

Late in the eighteenth century and early in the nineteenth, representations of blacks as "others" (I will drop the inverted commas from this point) was strikingly different. Contrary to the popular wisdom that blacks were despised and loathed as subhuman, there was a rough consensus in North America about the desirability of creating a unique and homogeneous republic in which black people would play an integral role. The problem was: blacks were manifestly different and inferior beings, so how could they be changed in such a way as to make them acceptable to whites?

Many times, I have tried to understand the enduring near-global popularity of Michael Jackson. A performer practically since he was old enough to grip a microphone, the youngest member of the Jackson 5 (later, the Jacksons) has almost wilfully defied every convention for achieving innocent-messianic status, getting involved in child molestation allegations, developing obsessional personal habits, refusing to give interviews and, oddest of all, undergoing extensive cosmetic surgery that has almost removed all physical traces of his African Americanism. His albums are unerringly bestsellers, though, for this listener at least, not extravagantly brilliant; his videos are ingenious, but owe more to directors and technical staff than to him; and his performances are works of art that draw admiration rather than awe. Yet, Jackson remains arguably the most significant male icon of the late twentieth century.

My own explanation involves reaching back way before 1969, when the Jackson 5 released their first number one, "I want you back" (number two in Britain). To the sixteenth century, in fact, when illustrations depicting a black child immersed in a tub of soap suds being scrubbed by two zealous whites circulated in Europe. Trying to remove the child's color was, of course, "labor in vain" as the phrase went: it was hard but futile work. Just like trying to civilize, educate, upgrade or assimilate Africans. Their blackness was a visible reminder that they were simply not amenable to the kinds of changes or, more aptly, metamorphoses required to bring them into civilized culture.

The motif came from Jeremiah 13:23: "Can the Ethiopian change his skin, or the leopard his spots?" The answer was, of course, no; and the efforts of the two whites were in vain. Scrub though they might, the child would remain black. Four hundred years ago, they did not have the benefit of cosmetic surgery, otherwise the answer might have been different. Without imputing motives to Jackson, his efforts *appear* to be similar to the scrubbers: to "change his skin."

Might it not at least be feasible to suggest that this exercise has an appeal to many whites, who can admire Jackson, crave his wealth, privilege and status, yet still content themselves with having something he wants, but can never have – whiteness? Perhaps it is Jackson's inability not his considerable ability that provides the source of his extraordinary popularity. His is a largely white following that has grown accustomed to his quirks and oddities. Quirks and oddities, we might add, that could have killed the career of many a performer, especially a black performer. Jackson is different: there is an elaborate mystery about him. He remains the best known, possibly most celebrated and probably most castigated African American ever. He vies with Oprah Winfrey and Bill Cosby as the highest earning black entertainer of the 1990s. He has been allowed to be colossally successful possibly because of his enigmatic but unthreatening presence. Maybe he is the contemporary equivalent of the mythical black boy who wanted to be white, but could never make it.

Interpreting Jackson in this way makes us see an African American icon of today as linked as if by some molecular chain to an entire history of whites' unwillingness or maybe inability to accept blacks as blacks, unless they fall into some prescribed image mold. (Chapter nine is devoted to the Michael Jackson phenomenon.)

The homogeneous culture sought after by many whites at the start of the last century would have been a bleak place for black people, many still mindful of the horrors of slavery, others struggling with the vestiges of a system that enfeebled blacks both economically and mentally. But, there was at least one leading republican scholar, physician and political theorist who thought he had the solution to blacks' problems and, in a bizarre way, the solution resembled Jackson's seeming pursuit of whiteness.

When Dr Benjamin Rush died in 1813, Thomas Jefferson declared: "A better man could not have left us, more benevolent, more learned, of finer genius, or more honest." Let me be plainer: Rush was a racist crank, albeit a well-intentioned racist crank. A fervent advocate of independence and republicanism, Rush welcomed a culture in which all races would be assimilated. As a man of medicine, he offered his prescription for the malady of a racially divided society: change blacks physically and incorporate them in a white republic. In essence, he thought that black people could be "cured" of their condition, a condition he believed derived from a strain of leprosy, and then whitened to the point where they would be indistinguishable from people like himself. Then onward to the new republic.

Details of Rush's remarkable thesis can be found in Ronald Takaki's book *Iron Cages: Race and culture in 19th century America*, from which I draw my information. A committed abolitionist, Rush longed for the day when all America could unite in one healthy republican whole. The trouble was that blacks, in their condition, could not participate. That condition condemned them to an unregulated life in which they would continue to be ruled be their "venereal appetites" and the search for "animal gratification." This was hardly the fault of blacks: their savage abnormality was caused by nature. Still, it was well for whites to avoid physical contact with them as the disease might be infectious. Isolation was a short-term remedy.

But a cure could only be effected by restoring the black skin to its normal, healthy whiteness. Hard physical labor was a helpful method of facilitating the discharge of blackness from the skin: the friction of skin against objects took away color, said Rush, pointing to the palms of black people's hands. But, a more direct method was available: "Depletion, whether by bleeding, purging, or abstinence has been often observed to lessen the black color in negroes" (quoted in Takaki, 1990: 32).

Bloodletting was one way to achieve this. Another was with a session in Rush's apparatus known as "the tranquilliser." This hideous machine was a specially constructed chair into which patients suffering from "diseases of the mind" and related complaints, like blackness, were strapped, their heads and arms locked into secured positions. The seat was like an open commode with a pot. One can almost guess the gory procedure. Veins were sliced open to let blood flow and purgatives were administered. The fact that the recipient needed to be strapped in suggests that the enemas were not delivered with tender, loving care.

Rush's project was bizarre. Or, at least, it seems bizarre from the vantage point of the late 1990s; at the turn of the nineteenth century, it probably seemed a sensible and rational response to a new problem for which there were no established solutions: how to reform blacks and incorporate them into a new republic. Rush's answer was to make them white. Yet it is his conception of the problem that is revealing. Blackness was not just something natural; it was a pathology. And, as such, needed treatment. Here was a view of black people that probably had a wide constituency of support. Their blackness was an undesirable consequence of living in the intolerably hot conditions near the equator, which had changed their skin color, altered their dispositions and imparted a form of leprosy. They should not be scorned or derided, nor even feared; but pitied and benevolently assisted toward some sort of equality. It was different to the type of worldview in which blacks were seen as permanently inferior and there was no escape or redemption from their inferiority.

The brand of paternalism typified or exaggerated by Rush was evident in the plantation societies of nineteenth century America. It was in the interests of whites, as self-proclaimed Christians, to disguise the coercive and exploitative nature of their relationship to blacks by claiming that domination was in the best interests of the oppressed. Blacks, it was accepted, were in a state not only analogous to sickness, but of sickness itself. They were dependent, irresponsible and unable to run their own affairs. Whites were acting in the best interests of blacks, according to this view. (It might be argued that this type of reasoning has affected whites' strategies and policies toward blacks to the present day.)

In this period, the image of blackness underwent something of a shift. The "Negro" had been popularly regarded as a degraded, subhuman creature, lacking in restraint and prone to idleness and dishonesty. All manner of theory purported to link black people with apes. But, as the malignant and minatory aspects of this image receded, a different, more pathetic, but redeemable figure emerged. Here, the recognition was that nature had conspired to plunge blacks down the racial hierarchy, but not necessarily forever. With the assistance of right-thinking whites, they could be cleansed of their accursed blackness.

The colonizationist organizations which began in 1817 were, according to Frederickson, typical of benevolent movements which burgeoned in the late 1820s. Many areas of the north had ended slavery, and manumitted slaves were approached with the kind of anxiety that had been previously reserved for drunkards and infidels: they had some potential for disruption. Idleness, disorderliness and criminality were in prospect. The general orientation of the benevolent movement was to address blacks as "degraded," though not necessarily permanently.

Frederickson examines what he calls the "enlightened philanthropy" of the colonizationists "without finding a single clear and unambiguous assertion of the Negro's inherent and unalterable inferiority to whites" (1987: 12). If blacks were "degraded" and inferior, they could also be "upgraded" and equal. This is a rather different conclusion to the one reached by Jensen and the other IQ testers, of course.

In the minds of whites, the racial hierarchy was never threatened by the idea of blacks' degradation. Even if the position was alterable, the conditions under which change could happen were unlikely to occur; so blacks would continue in their state of total dependence and their inferiority would stick.

We see in the image of black people in this period something of a metaphor. Civilization was the creation and domain of whites, it was thought: Europeans controlled about 35 percent of the world at the start of the eighteenth century. Blacks were manifestly not civilized in whites' eyes: their degradation's source may not have been natural, but its effects were what mattered: these structured the dynamics of relations between whites and blacks. Rush and well-intentioned others of his ilk may have busied themselves speculating on the causes of blacks' condition, but the consequences of it remained: blacks were childlike, prone to appetites and desires and totally ill-equipped to conduct their lives in an orderly fashion. Yet, as the 1800s passed, the interest in causes rather than effects spiralled and the theories of Rush *et al.* came under fire. The conception of blacks as permanently and biologically degraded was linked to what became known inappropriately as scientific racism.

Thomas Jefferson, whose views on blacks were as influential as anybody's, was equivocal on the source of inequality – nature or environment – but crystal clear on the fact that blacks were "inferior to whites both in body and mind." A slave-owner, Jefferson, in the 1800s, publicly struggled with a dilemma that, in some way, affected all white Americans. The question he addressed was, to borrow from Audrey Smedley: "How can the American revolutionists speak of liberty, justice, and the rights of man and still keep large numbers of their fellow human beings in slavery?" (1993: 195).

In her study *Race in North America: Origin and evolution of a worldview*, Smedley argues that racism as an ideology was a response to this type of question; its impact on whites' understanding of blacks was transformative. She writes: "In Jefferson's lifetime, the transformation of Africans and their descendants in the American colonies into subhuman creatures was, to a great extent, completed" (1993: 201). Likening black people to animals was by no means new: long before the science of race in the nineteenth century, fables of the missing link drifted back to Europe from explorers and traders in Africa. Anatomists, biologists and an assortment of other -ists compared notes on the position of blacks in the Great Chain of Being.

A 1774 study by Edward Long, who was an administrator in Jamaica, suggested a threefold division between Europeans, other humans/blacks and orang-utans. "Ludicrous as it may seem I do not think that an oran-outang husband would be any dishonour to an Hottentot female," wrote Long in a provocative and much-quoted argument. Long accentuated the satyriasis of the male of the species, as if to promote a fear that was to persist long after his thesis had been discredited.

In the mid-1800s, a zoo in Antwerp, Belgium, exhibited a pre-pubescent black child, who was not considered so dangerous that he needed to be caged and so was allowed to wander about inside the general enclosure. He was far from the only African to be exhibited in the West during the second half of the century. Animal traders would often add humans to their collections and sell to circuses, fairs and the like. P. V. Bradford and Harvey Blume record how, in 1906, a human boy was housed in the monkey house at the Bronx Zoo and labelled *African homunculus*, "the missing link" (1992). Africans were curiosity pieces: not fearsome, but exotic; not civilized, but safe. But, in the eyes of Europeans, they were closer to beasts than to human beings.

While the evidence collected prior to the mid-nineteenth century was inferential or, at best, circumstantial, it included attempts to stake out permanent differences between blacks and whites. Different colored brains, blood and semen; different shaped skulls and jaws: these were among the ideas circulating. They were to be given scientific respectability by the theories that purported to nail down once and for all the precise causes and character of the differences between blacks and whites.

The clamor for proof of racism began in mid-century. The conventional view is that racism as a fully-formed ideology was a convenient justification for slavery: in other words, if it can be scientifically demonstrated that blacks occupy a position way below that of whites on the racial hierarchy, it removes the pressure to treat them as equals and paves the way for domination, exploitation and open oppression. The alternative view is more subtle and begins from the premise that the slaveowners and all those with a vested interest in slavery had no need to justify their deeds. In the absence of sanctions, moral or material, they simply pursued their own best interests using whatever means were necessary. Racism in the first scenario developed in spite of abolition; in the second because of its success.

Pieterse, a representative of the second view, remarks that "the science of race developed *after* the first battle had been won in the struggle against slavery, with the British prohibition of the slave trade in 1807 . . . The period in which science took shape was also the time when the image of the 'noble negro' was at its most popular and when some of the best 'anti-racial' tracts were published" (1992: 45). The scientific approach to racism was, on this account, a defensive maneuver designed to remind the world of the unbridgeable gulfs between blacks and whites at a time when the lobby to abolish slavery was emphasizing similarities. Of course, blacks are inferior, argued abolitionists; but the reason they are so is the inhuman conditions they are made to endure. Not so, said racists: they are inferior because nature has ordained it that way: slavery is an institution that reflects this reality, not produces it.

During the 1840s and 1850s, a scientific consensus emerged: blacks and whites belonged to two different races. So, the differences between them were innate and not liable to change, whether through education or a session in Dr Rush's chair. All discussions were phrased in terms of race, a concept vague and elastic in its application but loaded with emotion. As Smedley writes: "'Race' as a new and infallible truth had to await the development of a proper substitute for religion, and science became that substitute" (1993: 201). She means that the doctrine of polygenesis had attracted adherents for decades, even centuries, but it was accepted as an article of faith. Basically, its central tenet was that humankind had not been born out of a single act of creation as described in Genesis, but out of many possibly independent acts. Different groups had separate origins; they were different species and their physical and cultural differences were reflections of this. The opposing position was monogenesis, the doctrine that all variants of human beings were descended from a common pair of ancestors.

Polygenesis was very much a minority viewpoint regarded in some quarters as heretical. But, it certainly received a boost from the white males who are now safely enshrined as the figureheads of nineteenth century scientific racism. They came from both Europe and North America. Paul Broca came from France, as did Arthur de Gobineau, whose four-volume *Essays on the Inequality of Human Races*, published between 1853 and 1855, is still regarded as the definitive racist study. Charles Hamilton Smith and Robert Knox led a British school of thought. Josiah Nott and George Robbins Gliddon were active in North America. While there were variations in the theories of these and a great many more writers on the subject, the points of agreement were significant.

On the issue of racial typology, they were mostly agreed that racial types were created and developed separately. Some, like Knox and Nott, maintained that human types were adaptations to specific provinces. As marsupials were peculiar to Australia, so aboriginals were the kind of people who belonged to that territory. It followed that efforts to remove racial types from their natural habitat would eventually prove disastrous. I add this to show that such theories were not transparently thin scientific justifications for slavery: according to this version of racial typology theory, colonialism was never a good idea. Yet, of course, the main phase of European imperialist expansion was to follow.

But, there was an undeniable complementarity between theories that advanced the notion of biologically different types, species or races, and social institutions and practices that maintained a strict and unalterable hierarchy structured by those very categories. "Not only were the institutional arrangements of government and politics in states generally useless in making any indentation upon uncivilized peoples," explains Ivan Hannaford in *Race: The history of an idea in the West*. "But the Negro in particular in the United States and elsewhere was racially fixed in his slavery" (1996: 271). It served the purposes of slaveowners well to believe in an arrangement that virtually commended them to exploit and oppress black people *and* reinforce the idea of whiteness as a reference for superiority. The "white race," remember, was just as much a manufactured phenomenon as the "black race." "Perceptions had to be organized to recognize the differences," writes Bennett, adding: "The so-called differences were not the cause of racism; on the contrary, men seized on the differences and interpreted them in a certain way in order to create racism" (1993: 69).

Blackness had been systematically devalued before the advent of scientific racism. From the fifteenth century, the "dark continent" of Africa was associated with primitivism and danger. Cannibalism and witchcraft were powerful parts of the European iconography of Africa, which was depicted in much literature as a kind of primal dystopia. Africans boasted no monumental architecture highly regarded by Europeans; nor did they use a literate culture in the same way as Europeans. Worse, they favored body decoration over clothes. Africa was seen as material allowed to remain raw, as opposed to Europe which had been transformed by manufacture and construction, both products of the imagination. All suggested a strong link between their blackness and their lack of civilization. If whiteness had connotations of cleanliness, godliness, wholesomeness and light, blackness signified filth, heathenism, sin and ignorance. It was a cipher for all that was bad about western society. One result of this devaluation was that black people's deities were forsaken, their languages forgotten, their music forbidden. The response to these prohibitions was an oral culture that did not lend itself readily to transcription.

Racism from the mid-nineteenth century was premised on a total devalorization of nonwestern life. There was literally no possible way for black people to upgrade themselves, for the message offered them by whites included, as Ellas Shohat and Robert Stam express it in their book *Unthinking Eurocentrism*, "*the denial of difference* and *the denial of sameness*" (1994: 24). Blacks were too unlike white Europeans to be anything but inferior; yet, if they attempted to mimic or emulate whites and did so with some success, they were no longer really "black." They might also have added that mimicry sometimes had its costs. An example from the book *Black Culture and Black Consciousness* by Lawrence Levine illustrates this. Levine recounts the testimony of a freedman in New Orleans: "I was once whipped because I said to my missis, 'My mother sent me.' We were not allowed to call our mammies 'mother.' It made it come too near the way of the white folks" (1978: 139). White language and culture generally, being the language and culture of the masters, may have seemed attractive. It may also have carried associations of freedom, power, privilege and mobility. But ultimately offered no promise of amelioration or change: only punishment and perpetual enslavement.

Whites denuded African cultures to the bone and left blacks with little choice: either they submitted to the unremitting racist association of blackness and badness and accepted their inferiority without reservation, or they remade themselves, constructing an image and culture that resisted white conceptions, yet in a way that did not threaten their physical survival. It was the limitations imposed by racism that drove slaves toward their own culture. While some house servants, artisans and urban slaves may have copied or even emulated the language and culture of the masters, the mass were not so much induced as coerced into creating a culture of their own. It was a culture that was to become the bearer of values, standards and identities, all united by the appellative term, black.

In his book *Behind the Mule: Race and class in African-American politics*, Michael Dawson writes that segregation "caused the development of indigenous black institutions, including political organizations, fraternal organizations, businesses, and – by far the most important *politically* – the black church . . . segregation encouraged the formation of a separate culture" (1994: 60). Dawson adds that membership of a church pointed up the salience of group status and interests, bolstering the value placed on membership of a common culture that persists to the present day. The writer explains this by introducing the concept of a "linked fate": "If one believes that blacks as a group are in a subordinate position, one's belief in the linked fates of individual African Americans should be strengthened" (1994: 80). The black church has had a pivotal role in "the reinforcing of group consciousness and group interests," argues Dawson. It has held this role for over 200 years.

Following the end of the North American war of independence in 1783, many Empire loyalists left America for the Caribbean islands, often taking with them their slaves. Travelling with his master, a British army officer, was George Lisle (sometimes spelled Leile), a lay Baptist preacher who had been exposed to Christian instruction but who had added his own interpretation to produce what became known as Native Baptism. Slavery had probably hindered the diffusion of a detailed knowledge of Christianity to slaves and so stimulated them to formulate their own interpretations. Melville Herskovits, in *The Myth of the Negro Past*, published in 1941, speculated that the most "logical adaptation" for New World slaves was to give their adherence to a form of Christianity which in its ritualism most resembled the type of worship known to them. He wrote: "The Baptist churches had an autonomous organization that was in line with the tradition of local self-direction congenial to African practice." Its emphasis on baptism by total immersion and its tolerance of less restrained behavior than that allowed in other Christian denominations made Baptism perfect. As Herskovits noted, Baptism "at least contained elements not entirely unfamiliar" (1941: 233).

Lisle had founded his fusion church in Williamsburg, Virginia, and, after his exit to Jamaica where his preachings were to play a part in the slave uprising of 1831–32 (Christianity provided a positive justification for action, proclaiming the natural equality of all humans and the illegitimacy of bondage). In America, the church, whose leadership was taken over by Andrew Bryan, showed no comparable revolutionary potential, though from the 1820s it inspired protest and so helped stimulate the self-consciousness of black people; that is to think about themselves as people who had common social conditions and, possibly, a shared destiny.

Religion was one of the few areas available in which blacks could unite and express themselves: its uniqueness lay in its supplication to Christian deities while an abjuring orthodox Christian restraint. As Alexis de Tocqueville wrote in his chronicles *Democracy in America* during the 1830s: "Although they [blacks] are allowed to invoke the same God as the whites, it must be at a different altar and in their own churches, with their own clergy" (1946: 373). Separation, or, more specifically, segregation (the former suggests a voluntary process) fostered syncretism: seeming inconsistencies or incompatibilities of faith were brought together. Here we see the beginnings of Gilroy's culture of compensation which acts like a soothing syrup to take away the bitterness of life for the "disempowered and subordinated" (1993: 85).

It has been suggested by some, Bennett included, that spirituality occupied such a central position in the "African worldview" that it was only logical that it carried over into the culture of slaves and their offspring, so that eventually the church became the "platform from which the whole panorama of Negro life in America was launched" (1993: 117–18). It is an assumption widely shared by writers on black culture convinced of the presence of African humor and temper in contemporary forms; these "Africanisms" are thought to have proximity over space and time; they are kept alive by associations across the generations. In this respect, the church may be regarded as one of the most enduring lineaments of African American culture and one which has its source in the efforts of the oppressed to draw some comfort from a past dismembered by slavery.

In contrast to the Christianity preached by whites, the master class, black churches laid emphasis on apocalyptic visions and heroic interpretations of the scriptures. Direct parallels were found between the epic bondage of the ancient Hebrews and the driven restlessness of black people, exiled and captive, awaiting deliverance. The Old Testament generally was packed with tales that seemed to foretell the destiny of blacks: against all odds, the smaller David slew the formidable Goliath; the world mocked Noah as he patiently worked at his harebrained scheme, an ark that would save him; Jonah gained freedom from his confinement in the belly of the whale through his unerring faith. The meanings were clear.

The beauty of black religion lay in its originality: it borrowed from white Christianity without mimicking it. Mimicry could be painful, as we saw from Levine's illustration. But, by adapting generic Christian precepts and prophecies to the particularities of African American life, a new matrix was cast. The black church as a matrix is a useful trope because the term describes a womb, or place in which something develops, as well as a mold (from the Latin *mater*, mother).

The church unified its believers with the collective effervescence that comes through worship and ritual and so encouraged the kind of self-consciousness that is vital to any culture. It also promoted the networks of peer groups, opened channels of communication and so encouraged the sharing of ideas; again features germane to any culture. While slave religions had made some of these possible, the distinct denominations that grew after 1820 introduced an institutional framework, what Bennett calls the "infrastructure of the black community," which permitted permanence and stability. Both were essential for the mutual affirmation and the transfer of experience.

Secession from white churches accelerated after emancipation, often angering Anglo-Saxon church leaders who, if not appalled by the accentuation of the Old Testament, were horrified at the overtly expressive aspects of worship. Excessive emotionalism, wild dancing, howling and screeching: these were regarded by whites as dangerous tendencies. Levine detects a difference between attitudes in the north and south, southern whites content to let blacks form their own churches and pay the consequences for their deviations; northerners believing that, like errant children who had left home before being fully instructed in the facts of life, they needed to be brought back and re-educated in the proper Christian manner before they made up their own versions. No matter: the churches continued to burgeon, as did the new standards, possibilities and aspirations they fostered.

Music was especially important to the churches. The evangelical music of black Baptist and Methodist churches was one of a number of influences on what became known as the "negro spiritual," which compelled a sense of identification with the Children of Israel. Other influences include West African and white church music; the precise contribution of each is a subject of debate. However the music was constructed, the result was a unique hybrid music that directly addressed and invoked "God," "Lord Jesus," "Savior," "Moses" and so on. Nor was the music restricted to church: it was used at work, and at secular gatherings. But, the church's music was more episodic, ceremonial, decorative and convivial; it also effected a shift in focus away from a concept of heaven on earth to a heaven distinct from the material situation of humans. Spirituals used analogy with biblical situations, but the church music that would cohere into what we now call gospel was predicated on pure faith. The Lord would provide.

Let me remind the reader of the background against which this development took place. The outlines of what was to become scientific racism were drawn after the British abolition of the slave trade in 1807, when the antislavery movement began a worldwide dissemination of propaganda. As the movement picked up speed and the legal status of slavery came to be questioned, those with an interest in its continuation enthusiastically welcomed theories that explained differences between blacks and whites and, indeed, other racial groups as part of a natural hierarchy. Even opponents of slavery and proponents of a free society, like Rush and, more ambivalently, Jefferson, were in their own ways contributors to the racism debate. For all the disagreement about the exact status of blacks, whether bestial, subhuman, childlike or whatever, there was a consensus on their manifest inferiority. This at a time when African Americans were busying themselves in the construction of their own infrastructure on the basis of which to transmit a new image of themselves. The image, as Bennett describes it, was of "Africans separated from Africa and Europeans, who excluded them and mocked their aspirations" (1993: 115).

Such was the churches' growth and the confidence that accompanied it that it was possible in the 1880s, after emancipation, for Reverend J. Benson Hamilton, pastor of the Cornell memorial Methodist Church of New York City, to inveigh against the kind of policies that encouraged mixed congregations. There was nothing unchristian about racial segregation, claimed Hamilton contra his contemporaries who were adding to their flocks. His message was: let blacks have their own established churches and keep out of Anglo-Saxon institutions. A prophet of race war, Hamilton envisaged a black population of 50 million in the southern states alone by 1930. As this element of the population was licentious, intemperate and illiterate, it was preferable to let them have their own churches and leave whites alone.

Perhaps the most significant boost given to this type of theorizing was the publication in 1859 of Charles Darwin's *Origin of Species*, which carried a puzzling subtitle "The Preservation of Favoured Races in the Struggle for Life." Puzzling, that is, for those who wished to apply the theory of natural selection to the human condition as it existed in America. Owing much to a liberal interpretation of Darwinian principles, speculators were prone to visualize a successful adaptation to the environment by civilized races and the elimination – perhaps even extermination – of what Darwin himself had called the "savage races" (an image embellished by the sight of blacks zealously emoting in the type of church assembly whites considered should be solemn).

The "survival of the fittest" model (Herbert Spencer's phrase) was seized on by all sorts of interpreters, all convinced of the futility of philanthropic gestures and of the fate of blacks, now left at the mercy of their own devices. There were several versions of the "They were better off under slavery" argument, many summarized by Frederickson (1987: 228–55). All had the payoff: segregate or quarantine the black race before it becomes a source of contamination and danger to whites. Preparing blacks for full citizenship and participation in society was not remotely near the Darwinian agenda: they would virtually self-destruct anyway. Frederickson may be guilty of exaggerating the influence of Darwin in solidifying racist ideas. We know that, even today, there is resistance to the teaching of evolutionary theory in some southern schools for fear that they will contradict the fundamentalist interpretations of the book of Genesis.

Far less sinister, though more demeaning, was the paternalistic theory popularized prior to emancipation. This went against Darwinian notions in its insistence that whites should take care of blacks. One way of taking care of them was through slavery. Adjectives like enlightened, humane and benevolent would properly describe those slavemasters for whom slaves were but slow-witted children. Slow-witted, but happy and contented. Enter Sambo.

The Sambo stereotype (I shall refrain from dignifying it with a capital "S" from now) has occupied a special place in western culture's pantheon of racist images. It is living proof of the longevity of despicably racist types way beyond their official demise. Possibly starting life as *zambo*, a sixteenth century Spanish word for a bandy-legged person and a type of monkey, the word took on new meanings in mid-nineteenth century America when used to refer to blacks. Joseph Boskin, whose book *Sambo: The rise and demise of an American jester* is the most authoritative historical account of the subject, traces its application to black people to an 1820 publication, *Samboe: or, the African Boy* by an unknown British author. In this, a comical aspect was attached to the name, suggesting something absurd.

Characterizing blacks as sambos meant they were carefree buffoons, devoid of the kind of sensibilities of whites. They grinned a lot, danced a lot and sang a lot. A little evidence goes a long way: this was meant to prove that they were all happy with life and totally committed to their masters. Never mind the backbreaking daily toil in the fields, the habitual lashing of the bullwhip, the wrenching away of loved ones and the total denial of anything resembling a life; blacks were happy in their social and moral void. Just look at them. And the evidence did, in a bizarre way, seem to match up. "Once pain and hunger were removed, the natural state of blacks was one of 'enjoyment'. For as soon as burdens were lifted and working suspended, 'he sings, he seizes his fiddle, he dances'," writes Boskin quoting English geologist Charles Lyell who, in the mid-1800s, observed the fondness of "Negroes" for music and dancing and concluded that this was not due to what he called "external influences."

The reason for this could be expedience. Look unhappy and brooding and it could earn you a beating; beam away and it might make for a slightly less unpleasant life. Also, as Takaki points out in *A Different Mirror*, "they might have been playing the role of loyal and congenial slaves in order to get favors, while keeping their inner selves hidden . . . many slaves wore masks of docility and deference in order to shroud subversive plans" (1993: 115).

Sambo was dramatic evasiveness: as the possibility of abolition encroached, slavemasters artfully invoked a music hall caricature (at least, it would become a music hall caricature) in an attempt to avoid the inevitable. Why end slavery, when the slaves are so happy? asked querulous plantation owners. The slave system afforded slaves a structured environment, which might appear to those who do not know it uncomfortable, though not unbearable. Slaves themselves, however, are quite at home. So went the slaveowners' logic.

The uses of sambo were many: apart from keeping whites amused at the puerility of slaves, the type helped persuade an incredulous outside world that blacks actually benefited from slavery, it assured all but the slaves themselves that obedience was not the result of coercion but of devotion, it partly sold the idea that blacks were incapable of the sophisticated thought of whites and were destined to remain as dependants come what may and it might have convinced many of the plantocracy that blacks, for all their pain, were well under the control of whites. This final point leads Pieterse to call sambo a "cultural talisman" through which masters "sought to choreograph reality" (1992: 153). The sambo artifice was an antidote to the real Denmark Vesey and Nat Turner, who initiated violent uprisings in 1822 and 1831 respectively (both, interestingly, inspired by Christianity). Fearful of more rebellions as rumors of freedom circulated, slave-owners probably indulged in self-delusion. Sambo was too content, too dim and probably too lazy to challenge existing arrangements.

It is rather too easy to dismiss the sambo type as a product purely of white racist imagination, devised by whites, for whites and in the interests of a white-controlled system. Equally, it is misleading to interpret the behavior of blacks who seemed to conform to the type as scheming and manipulative. What also needs attention is the extent to which blacks had options other than to play the part of sambo. Whites, having material, if not moral, power sufficient to dictate the ebb and flow of plantation life, would have had the ability to impose certain conditions. I refer to conditions under which it would have been virtually impossible for slaves to act in any way other than like sambo.

A theatrical performance it might have been, designed, as Takaki suggests, to disguise other motives, like getting favors, plotting subversive action or just getting by. Yet, sambo transferred, becoming a component of black culture: sambo was a way of earning a living for many comics and actors way into the second half of the twentieth century; though they may not have used the word sambo to describe themselves. We will return to this in the next chapter; for now, let us take stock of the fact that the racist grotesques beloved of the plantocracy had effects reaching far beyond the mentalities of those who authored them.

Other stereotypes – or perhaps we should call them archetypes, recurring as they do as motifs through the generations – reflect changing conceptions of blacks and these in turn reflect changing social circumstances. They helped establish contexts in which black culture either flourished or was stunted. As I pointed out previously, images do not so much have power: they *are* power. They can and do affect and shape the quality of relations between groups. It is simply naïve to try to appreciate contemporary black culture without a comprehension of the limits within which it was forced to develop. I will argue in later chapters that today's black culture elicits the pathos of inequality in a way that uncomfortably resembles the past; which is precisely why we need to look so closely at history and see its ligatures with the present.

The sambo type fills us with horror. Not because it is so false, but because it is so disquietingly close to the truth. African Americans have never been able to purge themselves fully of the sambo legacy. Black culture has been expressed through many channels, the principal one being popular entertainment, specifically dance and music. The rhythm and innate talent that advantages blacks in these areas is popularly thought to derive from natural gifts, an inherent disposition to perform and excel. More likely, their sources are far less prosaic; they lie in the obligation slaves were under to entertain slaveowners. The skills cultivated and developed by slaves were not confined to singing and dancing either. Whites made blacks perform for them in a miscellany of demeaning ways, many of which were refined and put to different uses. Blacks were made to compete in footraces, in wrestling and prize fighting, in "whiskey guzzling" contests and other events.

When blacks are praised for their God-given gifts in singing and dancing and their natural ability in sports, we should not forget that these are products of an imposition. But, the legacy of sambo lived on for two reasons. First, blacks were able to use the so-called gifts profitably, if, at first unceremoniously: they became adept at the very activities whites had found so appealing and so escaped some of the drudgery of postslave culture by deftly playing to whites' preferences. Second, as Boskin writes: "It is hard for society to relinquish a funny man, to view him as anything else, especially if that funny man is an entertainer of ironical status" (1986: 120). Blacks may have been consciously playing the roles whites had created for them; they may also have been manipulating images for expedient purposes. But, as subsequent years proved, whites had difficulty in seeing blacks as fit for anything more than singing, dancing, fighting and running, all for their amusement.

Boskin's enlightening passage at the start of this chapter reminds us how useful the "mirthful by nature" conception was in resolving whites' ambivalence. It was *natural* for blacks to be happy whatever the conditions, thought whites. Whites created a character who was funny even as he was horrifying. That character may have existed only in their imaginations, but his effects went far beyond.

Much of the literature on the origins of black culture stresses the durability of African influences and their transmission through the generations, changing through the passage of time without losing the imprint of their source. The roots of the musical and dance traditions are often traced to Africa. I see more promise in locating the sources in slavery. Black culture was not unadulterated by white racism and the images it promulgated. Though distinct in many ways, it was shaped by the contexts in which it developed: as such, it bore many of the values, aspirations and, crucially, perceptions of white society. We can now better understand the earlier point of Levine about the difference in reactions between northern and southern whites to the spread of black churches after emancipation. Both sets of attitudes were critical, though southerners found ample evidence of their belief that sambo was still alive and kicking. They inferred childishness from the exuberant ceremonies, ignorance from the misreading of the scriptures and harmlessness in their religious convictions about the afterlife.

In the northern states, the self-consciousness that came through communal worship was seen by many as the first groping movement toward a new status, perhaps even that of civilized human beings. If this was so, then blacks' style of worship needed to be changed so that it resembled that of whites. The mispronunciations and malapropisms that whites had found so mirthful needed correction. Standards of morality ought to be tightened. Emancipation took place in an atmosphere of rapid urbanization and industrialization, changes that encouraged the view that men (not so much women) were masters of their own destinies. If blacks were to shrug off notions of inferiority and participate fully in the new republic, they would have to develop themselves as individuals rather than members of black communities whose fate was linked.

Within many northern black churches, members were urged to shed the epidermis of slavery by not celebrating traditional slave festivals, like John Canoe or John Kuners, which continued to be observed after emancipation (at least until the turn of the century). The black clergy found such festivals unhelpful reminders of a past they were trying to leave behind. The same group offered instruction in the correct use of English rather than the dialect that had amused slaveowners. A Reverend Paul Pollard told his Baptist following at a state convention in Richmond, Virginia, in 1904, that a class division should be introduced to demarcate those who wished to raise themselves and those who wished to remain tied to their past, according to Levine (1978: 151). Instruction such as this was hardly needed: what homogeneity there had been in the traditional slave communities dissolved over the decades as blacks tried to make the best of their fortunes.

Striving for success in a culture dominated materially by whites, where racism, though not uniform in its impact, was pervasive, thrust black people between "two warring ideals," as the African American scholar W. E. B. Du Bois expressed it in his seminal work, *The Souls of Black Folk*, first published in 1903. Du Bois' thesis was that there are two souls, one American, the other negro. Black people cannot "Africanize" America, but they were warned against "bleaching" their "Negro soul." His warning was one of many issued during the first two decades of the twentieth century, a period when the Ku Klux Klan was in its ascendancy and racism was at its most virulent. The racial hierarchy we touched on in Chapter one had been violated by emancipation and the reaction was severe. New and old archetypes, each one a character from the drama of racial hierarchy, surged across history's stage in the early years of the century. It was a period, as we will see in the next chapter, when black culture was enriched amid the grim continuity of white racism.

Chapter three

Irony to Some,
Theft to Others

T HE PAST MAY WELL BE ANOTHER COUNTRY. But it is still not beyond the clutches of those entrepreneurial colonizers who can turn a penny by capturing some small part of it and dragging it into the present. Witness the medieval restaurants that recreated the courts of King Arthur, or Disney's Celebration, a reconstruction of smalltown USA as it was at the turn of century. Or the House of Blues. This was the invention of Isaac Tigrett, the man behind the Hard Rock Cafés: he wanted to extend his winning formula, this time building a series of themed restaurants based on the blues joints of old. Of course, the resemblances were superficial in the extreme: music systems rather than acoustic guitars brought in the sounds, video monitors portrayed the artists, the drinks were brought to your table by uniformed staff. It was a shameless, perhaps, parasitic attempt to bring culture into the marketplace. By the 1990s, the meanings of blues had migrated a long way.

There is a wicked, unintentional wit about the phrase "separate but equal." Originated in a spirit of well-meaning beneficence, it soon became a paradoxical aphorism describing exactly the opposite of its stated meaning, and ultimately a weak joke. The doctrine that black and white people were and would continue to be separate and should be allowed separate provisions for their development was an outgrowth of a Louisiana court case involving a Mr Plessy, who claimed he was "seven-eighths white," but was not allowed to travel in "whites only" railroad cars on the grounds that he was for all intents and purposes a "negro." The case went to the US Supreme Court which, in 1896, upheld the decision that seating on trains should be segregated, at the same time confirming the constitutionality of segregation. Poll taxes and literacy requirements for suffrage effectively

31

disenfranchised blacks. They were denied access to reasonable educations and jobs; sharecropping was one of the few means of survival. The joke was, of course, that the conditions created were separate alright; yet anything but equal.

Not until 1954 when the watershed *Brown vs Board of Education of Topeka* decision nullified the separate but equal concept and ushered in the desegregation of educational facilities could black people legally lay claim to justice and equality of treatment. The interim period was known as the Jim Crow era, Jim Crow being a common slave name and an archetype not unlike sambo. With no facilities for improving their education, for showing skilful application nor even for protesting (at least not without fear of violent reprisals), blacks were almost compelled to conform to the popular Jim Crow image of them.

During the Jim Crow era, popular entertainers toured America and England in burlesque shows that derided blacks for the amusement of whites. The minstrel show, or the Ethiopian Opera was the most popular entertainment form at the turn of the century, ceding place to vaudeville, theater, then film. It comprised white singers and dancers, their faces blacked up, playing banjos, wisecracking and generally imitating crude caricatures of inoffensive "plantation niggers" or "coons," the popular name for southern blacks. They were foolish, joyous and without a care in the world; and, of course, white audiences loved them for much the same reason as they loved sambo: because they assured them that all was well and there was nothing about which they should feel guilty or afraid.

As blacks broke away from slavery and grew confident in their ability to mix and advance in a white world, the minstrelsy mocked their pretensions. A staple character was the bumptious, mock-important fellow forever embarrassing himself as he tottered along the road to total freedom. It was, of course, farce: blacks, the audience was agreeably reminded, were just not cut out for freedom. But, the black grinning visage with the thick lips and wide eyes was only one aspect of a Janus face, the other being a miserable wretch stuck in the moil of sharecropping, constantly brutalized by the Klan and its affiliates, which, in 1920, had an estimated five million members. This gives some idea of the intensity of hatred or fear of blacks that permeated both north and south.

Joseph Boskin, on whose work I drew in the previous chapter, reckons that, "By the early 1820s, songs and dances by white actors along the eastern seaboard expanded the character of the black" (1986: 74). White performers wore "black" clothes, imitated "black" accents and acted in a ludicrously jolly style. This, according to Boskin, was influential in persuading whites that the sambo was not just a white-invented cartoon, but a reality. A century later, with slavery at an end, the image had undergone only minimal alterations and blacks were still known for their singing, dancing and merrymaking. The difference was that the characterizations had been elevated into a fully fledged theatrical tradition.

One of the most interesting features of the minstrelsy was that black people were rarely given any credit, even for supplying the raw material on which the minstrels worked. Occasionally, whites would claim to have researched their characters by observing southern blacks; one in particular, E. P. Christy, studied the "queer words and simple expressive melodies" of New Orleans blacks in the 1830s. He eventually became leader of the Christy Minstrels, acknowledged as one of the best troupes of the day.

In his history of the nineteenth century minstrel shows, *Blacking Up*, Robert Toll highlights several beliefs, songs, dances and elements of folklore expropriated by minstrels. "The presence of these distinctively Afro-American themes supports the view that minstrels borrowed from black culture," writes Toll (1974: 50). He sees significance in this "because it was the first indication of the powerful influence Afro-American culture would have on the performing arts in America. It does not mean that early minstrels accurately portrayed Negro life or even the cultural elements that they used. They did neither" (1974: 51).

The minstrels specifically stretched and distorted aspects of black culture they deemed useful in such a way as to endorse popular images. Their efforts and initiative were well rewarded. White impresarios, like Charles Callender, J. H. Haverly, George Christy and Sam Hague, an English entrepreneur, mined black culture and came up rich.

Minstrel troupes featuring black performers began to appear in the mid-1850s, one in Philadelphia in 1857, one touring through Massachusetts and New York and another in Ohio in 1858. By the 1860s, they began to rival their white counterparts, their appeal being based on their purported authenticity. The afore-mentioned Hague, in 1866, took a company of ten African American minstrels to tour in England. Hague was the first white owner of an all-black troupe, but it was Charles Callender, a tavern owner, who turned the black minstrelsy into legitimate big business.

As Callender's shows began to draw large crowds and laudatory reviews, his performers asked for more money and were refused. A dispute ended acrimoniously and two of his star entertainers left to form their own company. Many aggrieved others left the troupe, many of them returning after failing to make it in other ventures. Despite at least 27 competitors owned and run by blacks, Callender's company maintained its position as the leading show. By 1875, he had started a second troupe to tour the Midwest, while he kept his main troupe in the more lucrative eastern states. White minstrelsy continued to dominate and Callender's company was the sole black show to challenge them.

In 1878 he sold out to J. H. Haverly, who, with more marketing know-how, took the company from strength to strength. His ploy was to present his minstrels not as entertainers, but as true representatives of plantation "Negroes"; "like animals in a zoo," Toll remarks (1974: 206). The success of the enterprise indicated the perverse amusement whites took in having popular images of uneducated, pitiful and brutish blacks presented, albeit in theatrical form. It also served to legitimize plantation caricatures. We find here an early example of blacks' being *permitted* some measure of commercial success not by passively accepting whites' conceptions but by actively bolstering the idea of white paternity. Flanked by white owners and producers in the wings, the minstrels laid on a costumed performance of such hilarity for whites that it was almost possible to forget the slave days were gone.

But, of course, they were gone and, as if to emphasize this, several blacks ventured into the minstrel business, their minds set on owning, running and producing shows and lining their own pockets instead of whites'. Lew Johnson began his operation in the 1860s and kept afloat for twenty-five years. A smalltime outfit comprising between six and eight players, Johnson's "Black Baby Boy

Minstrels" (one of their many names) was effectively shut out of the big cities but worked the frontier territories with modest success. The bigger companies shied away from places like Wyoming, Utah and Montana where the audiences were notoriously hostile and unruly. Johnson risked it and, in this sense, was something of a pioneer, being the first troupe owner to perform in these and other uncultivated states.

In the same period, another black company owner, Charles Hicks, found getting into the lucrative city markets a problem, so opted for Europe and Australia. Hicks continually challenged white owners, sometimes luring their performers away, sometimes losing out to owners who could offer better money. He ran into trouble in Chicago when he tried to take on the powerful Charles and Gustav Frohman and got squeezed out of the city. Like Johnson, Hicks was pushed out to marginal markets and was forever made to seek out new audiences. He died, fittingly perhaps, in the Pacific island of Java, where he was touring.

The contrasting fortunes of those African Americans who sought to run minstrelsy and those who performed in them was a portent: not for sixty years after Hicks' death in 1902 was a black entrepreneur able to wrest control of a sector of the black culture industry large enough to rival white-owned corporations; in the meantime, many black artists shot to stardom and became formidably successful.

The first of these was Billy Kersands, the highest paid minstrel of the late nineteenth century, whose stardom revolved around his ability to perform with his mouth full of billiard balls, cups and all sorts of objects. His cartoonish contortions and clod-poll manner made him a perfect enactment of sambo. Less of living stereotypes and correspondingly less well paid were Wallace King, a noted tenor balladeer, Horace Weston, a banjo virtuoso, and James Bland a noted singer-songwriter, who gained fame in Europe and reputedly earned, at his peak in the 1880s, $10,000 per year.

Sam Lucas assiduously tried to escape the artistic constraints of the minstrelsy, yet was periodically forced into it by circumstances. His appearance in an 1875 stage production of *Out of Bondage*, a salutary tale of an ex-slave's climb to dignity, was one of many exceptional roles he played. The Frohman brothers were known to seek his services for their minstrel shows, so great was his crowd-pulling power. But, work for someone who avoided types did not come easy and Lucas needed his job as a barber to fall back on. He was involved in the first nonminstrel musical written and produced by blacks, *A Trip to Coontown*, which premiered in 1898 and acted in the 1903 silent movie version of *Uncle Tom's Cabin*.

Perhaps the most intriguing and, for our purposes, most important figure was W. C. Handy, whose serpentine career will be documented at stages throughout this book. He started out as a musician with Mahara's Minstrels in 1896, earning a decent $6 per week plus room and board. In the early years of the twentieth century, Handy transferred from performing to booking, promoting and publishing before going into partnership with Harry Pace to start the Pace and Handy Music Company. Pace later started the Black Swan Phonograph Company, whose bearing on the dissemination of black culture we will examine later. Suffice it here to say that Pace and Handy's influence spans two cultural genres: those of the minstrelsy and the blues.

If the minstrels injured blacks in one sense, they actually helped them in another: by generating widespread interest in black people. Could they really sing and dance like the minstrels? Were they really so funny, so talented, so ridiculous, so happy? Curiosity about the black experience enabled blacks to perform themselves outside the minstrel tradition. Their audiences were not entirely uneducated, of course; though the version of black performance presented by minstrels was aesthetically fraudulent, trivial and lacking in the nuance of the genuine article. There was a bizarre coexistence of African American entertainers and white performers mimicking them, or, more specifically, parodying them. And, if Toll is to be accepted, black performers copying whites copying them.

The thirteenth amendment to the constitution, which outlawed slavery, was ratified in December 1866. It carried no implication that black people were the equal of whites in any respect. Northern whites in the late nineteenth century were wondering what a future without slavery would mean to them. Hordes of dangerous blacks invading job markets and stealing white women? Not if the minstrelsy depictions bore even the vaguest resemblance to reality. Even the genuine black minstrelsy showed black people to be carefree and contented, posing no threat to the existing racial hierarchy at all. In fact, they had a contribution to make: they could actually amuse whites. The plantation mythology lived on; Uncle Toms and sambos were all about. "This distortion," writes Toll, "was an almost inevitable price that blacks had to pay for bringing their culture into the shows" (1974: 243).

But according to some, working within the racist restrictions, black minstrels were able to weave in elements of black culture, particularly music, and this had important consequences. LeRoi Jones, in his book *Blues People*, points out that: "For the first time Negro music was heard on a wider scale throughout the country, and began to exert a tremendous influence on the mainstream of the American entertainment world" (1995: 86). The problem was that, for a long period in the early decades of the twentieth century, blacks were not around to spread that influence; the decline in the popularity of the minstrelsy meant fewer work opportunities in the mainstream of popular entertainment.

A question arises: was the culture that some writers believe was borne by the black minstrels a product purely of the plantation? Lawrence Levine believes that the black performers of the early twentieth century were influenced by and in turn influenced many white southern country singers. "One has only to compare the many folk song collections compiled in this period or the records made by white and black country singers in the 1920s and 1930s to understand the deep pool of shared traditions," he writes (1978: 195). This "black–white musical admixture," as Levine calls it, was not limited to folk song: vaudeville, phonograph records, radio and movies all showed elements of eclecticism.

Levine has an engaging explanation of why, given the fact that, as the century progressed, larger and larger numbers could listen to and probably not escape from the music of the white majority, African American music kept its unique identity and remained distinctive. "In part, of course, this was because a large body of the white music they heard had already been profoundly influenced by black musical styles and thus could be reinterpreted into the black tradition with little strain," writes Levine; "and, in part it was because black Americans have always had a penchant for refashioning the music they borrowed to fit their own aesthetic priorities and social needs" (1978: 196).

So, it became possible for a young Louis Armstrong to be honing his trade, integrating the diverse influences of a bugle-playing pie seller who blew his horn to attract customers, a banana man who sang about the virtues of his fruit and numerous barroom quartets, at the same time as a film played in which the white actor Al Jolson blacked up and portrayed *The Jazz Singer* (first released in 1927). Music and theatrical performance leapt across the kinds of barrier that separated blacks and whites in virtually every other social sphere. Black music drew its influences from many sources, some of which were whites' exaggerated interpretations of them. The longevity of the sambo type as depicted by black actors, many of whom up to quite recently made a handsome career out of it, is evidence of this. But there are plenty of other instances, which we will come on to in later chapters.

"A defusing process" is how Boskin describes the self-mocking fashion of many black actors and theatrical performers, who played out the sambo role, perhaps in slightly revised ways, for the benefit principally but not exclusively of whites; many blacks enjoyed the "inner spoofing." Boskin's observation is that black entertainers were able to draw short of total compliance with the old stereotype, subtly undermining it in a way that was probably more recognizable to blacks than whites. While Boskin does not mention it, a nice example of defusing was the "cakewalk," which was a ridiculous caricature of whites' dancing originally used slyly by black minstrels. It was soon ironized by white minstrels who intended to mock blacks without understanding they were compounding their own indignity.

Boskin cites Eddie Anderson's portrayal of "Rochester," the ostensibly sambo-like butler/valet of white comic Jack Benny in his 1950s television series, as an example of the defusing process. The work of black comic-actors Dick Gregory, Richard Pryor and Eddie Murphy extended the process. Anderson's effect was greatest as he was the first black male to push and stretch the sambo role in front of a national television audience. Anderson clearly felt emboldened to challenge a man who was, in the racial hierarchy of the day, his superior; he often violated the sambo role by outwitting Benny and contributing his own one-liners. "While playing obeisance to the fashionable image, the Rochester figure never fully conformed to it," writes Boskin (1986: 184–85).

This sort of opportunism has not been applauded by some, for obvious reasons, but we should not ignore its impact on the shape of black culture for it suggests how white racism has done two things: set limits to black modes of expression and absorbed black culture into white culture. This became more pronounced as black culture widened its base of appeal; in other words, when whites' fascination with the black cultural experience deepened and broadened. Toll writes that: "Minstrelsy was the first example of the way American popular culture would exploit and manipulate Afro-Americans and their culture to please and benefit white Americans" (1974: 51). The exploitation, he notes, was not limited to the white audiences, who delighted in the portrayals. The "white-owned and -structured shows had the greatest exposure, made the most money, and focused audience expectations on stereotyped images of Negroes. Most of all, they illustrated that when blacks became marketable as entertainers, it was white men who reaped the profits" (1974: 211). This was to be the basic pattern for many more years.

White audiences eventually grew tired of the minstrels, black and white. Public curiosity, concern and interest declined in almost direct relation to the abatement of any threat that the post-emancipation period seemed to hold. Racist-inspired fears were unfounded after all. Yet, the minstrels' impact lasted beyond their own lives. Black people had established a presence in popular entertainment and whites had accepted, perhaps even encouraged, this. Prominence in entertainment was no indicator of equality in whites' eyes. On the contrary, it suggested a raw, untutored and, in all probability, natural predisposition to perform.

"Live" minstrel shows dwindled and vaudeville gained. This offered new opportunities for black musicians, especially those who were prepared to mix drops of mirth into the serious business. Louis Armstrong not only recorded inferior material for the sake of appealing to a white audience, but introduced comic routines into his act. In this sense, he did not stray too far away from the minstrels' maneuvers.

His drummer, Zutty, would dress up in women's clothes and Armstrong in rags. In *Black Talk*, Ben Sidran notes how Armstrong himself was not at all embarrassed by this "prostitution," as Sidran calls it: "The essential point to be grasped is that the black musician, and the Negro in general, did not see himself as other than *gaining* on the white culture . . . he didn't mind acting a little foolish as long as it was in the name of progress" (1995: 70). Armstrong's preparedness to play up to expectations assured him a white audience eager to accommodate a black person who confirmed the sambo type. He ventured into and remained in the mainstream for the rest of his career.

White audiences, in warming to the minstrel shows, effectively reduced the suffering and abjection of black people to a series of amusing tableaux. They could enjoy the sight and sounds of African Americans, or their imitators, without actually considering the social experiences of the performers and their peers. This depersonalization or even dehumanization was – and maybe still is – characteristic of whites' appreciation of black culture.

Minstrel shows were, of course, a commercial venture: the culture they embodied was not separable from the business structure that made them possible. This was also true of the artefacts and genres of black culture that followed. Deborah Root raises the question of whether cultures that are subject to commodification are able to exist outside capital (1996: 25). The minstrelsy would not; it was strictly a commercial phenomenon, largely though not exclusively owned, controlled and run by whites for consumption by other whites.

Yet, there was one cultural domain occupied by blacks that seemed inviolable. No matter how you dressed it up, blues music was about as far removed from the perennially upbeat songs of the grinning minstrels as you could get. But, in the 1920s, when people like Handy and Pace were building publishing and phonographic recording companies, blues singers were offered the chance to immortalize their music and, in the process, make money for aspiring entrepreneurs.

Blues was the first style or expression that was universally acknowledged as being an integer of black culture; something genuine, whole and untouched by white influences. There are those, like William Barlow, who, in *"Looking up at Down": The emergence of blues culture*, argues that: "The blues . . . were an amalgam of African and European musical practices – a mix of African cross-rhythms, blue notes, and vocal techniques with European harmony and ballad forms" (1989: 7). His is but one of many histories of the music's formation and development (see, for example, Berry, 1986; Cone, 1991; Booth, 1991). While interpretations differ, all agree that the music grew out of the collective work of the first generation of blacks after emancipation. They had not directly experienced slavery, but their lives remained oppressively harsh and unpromising. The music they played externalized feelings of hopelessness and depression; the topics they sang about were sickness, imprisonment, alcohol, drugs, work and the segregation forced by Jim Crow.

This was a secular music: it avoided the churches' spiritual music which gloried in God's salvation and ecstatically encouraged the journey to the promised land in terms that generally avoided the more unpleasant aspects of life on earth. "Negro spirituals" which were in the 1930s displaced by gospel as the dominant religious music, conveyed the kind of hope offered by the church, particularly the Baptist church. Blues offered no such thing: only realism. Levine offers a nice distinction by quoting the singer Mahalia Jackson, who refused to give up gospel music even though blues music would have given her a better living: "Blues are the songs of despair, but gospel songs are the songs of hope. When you sing them you are delivered of your burden" (1978: 174).

It was, of course, a temporary deliverance. But it did not diminish the importance that religious music had held for black people since slave times and beyond. The spirituals together with the evangelical Baptist and Methodist music of the eighteenth and nineteenth centuries were clearly the expressions of captivity. Biblical imagery, especially that of the Children of Israel, was invoked as if to affirm the deliverance that would surely arrive if not in this life, then after. The dramatic momentum of religiously inspired gospel carried the singer away from the practicalities of the present toward some future salvation or even to a mythic arcadian past.

Gospel never had much commercial potential. Its live performance in a crowded church was shot through with an untrammelled passion: singers conveyed an energy smashing against the rocks of the tumultuous world outside. Gospel was essentially to be experienced, not listened to. We will see later that the importance of gospel to the black culture industry did not become apparent until the 1950s when its practitioners began to blend it with other musical forms. Attempts to industrialize pure gospel yielded limited success. In 1939, a phonographic recording of "Rock me" by Sister Rosetta sold respectably enough, though there were few record labels interested in gospel. On the other hand, there were a number of independent companies zealously trying to sign up blues bands; some of them, like Chess, grew to national prominence as a result.

Unlike gospel, blues was profoundly irreligious. It was also engimatic. What did the color refer to? A sea into which we might stare, pondering its hidden depths, or a sky full of expectation and promise? The former was more appropriate. Musically, the blue notes are the neutral or flattened pitches occurring at the major and minor points of the third and seventh degrees of the scale. But, the connotations of depression and despair were much more resonant. As such, it had specific relevance to blacks: it documented a distinctly black secular experience. Yet it would probably not have rated a mention save for a historian's reference, were it not for white audiences.

It is irony to some, theft to others, cultural syncretism to still others: the fact remains that African American culture fascinates whites and, without such a fascination, its destiny might have been to be overlooked. The minstrelsy took to whites an insight into black culture that was at once satiric and reverent. While it derided blacks, it also paid them an almost unwitting respect. It opened many eyes to the fact that blacks actually had a culture. It may have borne little resemblance to the one portrayed by the blacked-up minstrels; but it did recognize *something*.

Blues, for the most part, resisted such parody. There was nothing to laugh at: its central narrative was misery and pain. It was also highly individual. Unlike, early African American musical forms, blues was usually performed solo and without antiphony (i.e. a choral response). This suggests to Levine "new forms of self-conception." These features distinguished blues as what Levine describes as "the most typically American music Afro-Americans had yet created". As such, it "represented a major degree of acculturation to the individualized ethos of the larger society" (1978: 221). West African influences may be there for some to detect, but there can be no denying that blues was very much part of an American consciousness, an adjustment of individuals to the here-and-now.

While gospel music emphasized fellowship, camaraderie and the immersion of the individual in the community, blues focused on personal emotions and anxieties, the singer adding his or her own inflexions to 12-bar, three-line formats that were structurally very similar to each other. It was the first black-originated music that allowed, even forced, the artist to imprint his or her own individuality on the number. It was the singer not the song that gave blues its emotional power, conviction and, ultimately, commercial appeal. When Gertrude "Ma" Rainey, Trixie Smith or Blind Lemon Jefferson sang, there was an almost palpable bond with audiences. Their experiences were shared, making them all participants in the action.

For all its intrinsic character, the enduring success of blues as a cultural and commercial form came from without: the phonographic recording ensured a wide audience across the United States. In this sense, the experience of blues was an embryo of the whole black culture industry: authentic, original and loaded with virtuosity; yet exploitable and ultimately dependent on white culture for its production, dissemination and its recognition as a legitimate cultural product. "It had begun as early as the 1920s," writes Gerri Hirshey. "Scouts and field engineers were being sent out by white companies to find and record black singers down South" (1994: 60).

The widespread popularity of folk or country blues, as the unrecorded music was called, accelerated the incorporation of black music into the marketplace. Record company entrepreneurs saw the blues as a new musical fad they could exploit, their idea being to transform the blues performance into a mass-produced commodity that could be sold back to black and hopefully some white consumers.

The mechanical reproduction of the music on discs made it available to far greater numbers of people than ever before and, if the immediacy and authenticity of the blues performance suffered, its potential to reach a large audience on a regular basis was considerably enhanced. Local, rural and later urban blues cultures were infused with new songs and styles to an extent that was never before possible, giving a broader definition of the music. Aspiring blues musicians in the 1920s actually learned from recordings rather than performances. The early black culture industry, in spite of its other more overtly commercial intentions, played a progressive role in the support of an African American art form.

Authenticity was a selling feature of blues and it was a term imposed on a living culture: it functioned as an ideal for the early entrepreneurs peddling commodified versions of the music. But, even accepting that the term was capable of being turned into a merchandising ploy, was blues an "authentic" culture?

In their book *From Blues to Rock*, David Hatch and Stephen Millward provide evidence of "musical integration" in the midst of strict segregation. The field recordings often featured black and white musicians playing together, producing "a great deal of interracial borrowing." Folk blues, on this account, was not quite the pure black aesthetic form many assume it to be: "The constant interplay between ragtime, blues and boogie and the relatively large number of white musicians playing in black styles, narrowed the dividing line between black and white musical practices" (1990: 28).

Hatch and Millward defy the usual interpretation of blues as an unalloyed African American cultural form. At the time when entrepreneurs were spotting the commercial potential of blues, the music itself lacked an identity distinct from other forms, many practiced by whites. Much of the work now classed as blues was musically indistinguishable from the output of white performers. Only when the music underwent a commodification did it acquire the shibboleth, black. And, when it did, its commercializers found it useful to occlude its diverse ethnic history.

"The idea of blues as a form of music that could be used to entertain people on a professional basis i.e., that people would actually pay to see and hear blues performed, was a revelation," writes LeRoi Jones. "And it was this revelation that gave large impetus to the concept of the 'race' record" (1995: 98). "Race records" were commercial recordings aimed initially at the African American market. OKeh, a label owned by Columbia Records, which used it exclusively to sell to "Negroes," is customarily credited with the breakthrough, Mamie Smith's "You can't keep a good man down" backed by "That thing called love." OKeh's second recording, another Mamie Smith number, "Crazy blues" sold at a rate of 8,000 copies a week in 1920. Estimates of its overall sales vary, the highest being one million copies; but it seems they sold almost exclusively to black customers. As Donald Bogle writes of the period in *Brown Sugar*: "The music industry realized there was a whole new market for records" (1980: 27).

OKeh's inspiration was a black saloon pianist, Perry Bradford, who worked with Mamie Smith and, in 1920, cajoled the small New York record company into taking what was then a big risk. Bradford, who was also the secretary of vaudeville performer Bert Williams, wrote Smith's first few records. Considering the black population numbered only 15 million, sales of blues recordings were astonishing: up to six million per year in the 1920s. Bessie Smith's version of "Down hearted blues" alone sold 750,000 in 1923 and her total *oeuvre* sold between six and ten million copies. The media potentates at Columbia saw dollar signs and bought the label, keeping it as a low priority toehold in the African American market until 1962 when it brought in Carl Davis to retool it for the rock-'n'roll boom. Columbia shut down the operation in 1966.

In 1927, Victor, or RCA-Victor as it became after 1929, appointed Ralph Peer, who had worked in the field for OKeh, to head up its folk-blues operations, and he signed the likes of Blind Willie McTell and Jimmie Rodgers, the celebrated white country musician. Chicago-based Paramount released records by Ida Cox and Alberta Hunter: the company employed a black recording director, Mayo Williams, whose expertise in writing the copy for the mail order advertisements contributed to the label's success.

The embryonic record industry was effectively a duopoly, comprising Victor and Columbia, most of the smaller record companies being owned by whites. Some exceptions, like the New-York-based Black Swan Phonograph Company, were started by black Americans, in this case, Harry H. Pace, one-time partner of the previously-mentioned W. C. Handy, an itinerant minstrel then band leader turned entrepreneur. Handy's first band was sponsored by a black fraternal organization in Clarksdale, Mississippi. While touring, he became familiar with the blues and suspected that it might have commercial possibilities. He began to create his own arrangements of folk numbers and perform them with his own band. The success of his band took him to Memphis, where he published his first blues in sheet music form in 1912. This venture was to be the flagship of what later became a recording company.

Teaming up with entrepreneur Pace, Handy formed a music publishing business, specializing in African American songwriters' sheet music. It was the first company of its kind. Pace spent most of his time in Atlanta, where he had an insurance business, leaving Handy in New York to make decisions over music. In 1920, Pace joined his partner in New York and a year later branched off to start his own company.

The Black Swan Phonograph Company, as Pace called the venture, prided itself on the authenticity of its products. It derided others in its advertising during the early 1920s, announcing that "Others are only passing for colored." Obviously, this was not a record company interested only in white buyers: like other independent labels, its records were classed as "race records" and sold in black neighborhoods. Having W. E. B. Du Bois on its board of directors obviously helped credibility.

The company's fortunes were quite interesting: after early success with the more scabrous blues, it ventured toward a smoother product, Ethel Waters becoming its house torch singer. Pace refused to let Waters sing the blues, insisting that she record ballads. In 1922, Pace made an arrangement with Olympic

Records which allowed his company to use its more sophisticated production equipment. Part of the deal made Black Swan reissue older Olympic recordings by white artists under new names that sounded "black." Pace also decided to emphasize classical music performed by black artists, at the same time cutting back on the number of blues releases. It was a move designed to widen its market and it failed: sales dipped and the company was sold to Paramount, by then one of the major players in the industry. Black Swan's founder maintained his clutch of other successful companies and remained one of the most successful black entrepreneurs of the period.

The emergent industry created work opportunities for blacks: as talent scouts and agents as well as recording artists. It also effected a modification in the market's approach to African Americans. True, their mean income was well below that of whites and many were fearfully impoverished; but they managed to find some part of their disposable income to spend on records and so were consumers worth pursuing. The black leader Marcus Garvey singled out Pace for severe criticism in this respect. In his book *Keep Cool*, Ted Vincent reproduces Garvey's description of Pace: "A business exploiter who endeavors to appeal to the patriotism of the race by selling us commodities at a higher rate than are charged in the ordinary . . . markets" (1995: 104).

But the transformation of a folk music into a commercial product had negative consequences too and these were pretty much the same ones that Theodor Adorno bemoaned in his critique of *The Culture Industry*. Record companies tended to replicate past success with formulaic numbers, conventional arrangements and bowdlerized lyrics. There were two interpretations of this. On one hand, the content and the character of blues was diluted as a predictable simulacrum of the real thing came to dominate the record market. On the other, one could argue that the catalyzing effects of the record companies produced an entirely new musical form, one that reshaped the contours of blues, without losing its narrative thrust. This transformation became more pronounced in the 1940s when some record companies insisted on straightening out the ragged edges of blues and adding the precision of electric instruments.

These very small independent recording companies stood no chance of challenging the dominance of the big corporations, few of which had any interest in black music. Five of the six major record corporations (Capitol, Columbia, Decca, Mercury, MGM and RCA) had totally ignored minority markets: not only blacks, but rural whites in southern states. White middle class consumers were the most sought-after group. The six and their ally the American Society of Composers, Artists and Publishers (Ascap) were not interested in anything that had African American origins.

Ascap had at first condemned jazz, then relented after white musicians began to incorporate it into popular songs. It then turned on "race music" or, after its rechristening in the late 1940s, rhythm'n'blues. Black music was seen as vulgar and primitive. Much as whites saw black people themselves. The term jazz, or "jass," was applied to denote the music as trivial. Miles Davis once pointed out that "Jazz is a white man's word." Black performers who appealed to whites did so by adopting white styles and characteristics. Nat King Cole, Sarah Vaughan and the Mills Brothers are examples.

Many black musicians responded to this by going "underground," developing structures and techniques that were both unconventional and unfamiliar. Jazz innovators, such as Lester Young, Charlie Parker and Dizzy Gillespie, emerged from the 1940s, though the full value of their contribution was to be realized only much later. Their distinct approach became known as bebop. In contrast to African Americans who were doing their utmost to convince white audiences of their acceptability, the radical jazz musicians adopted an "I don't care if you listen to my music or not" approach, as Sidran puts it. Any musician who identified with this form of jazz "refused to play the stereotyped role of *entertainer*, which he associated with 'Uncle Tomism'" (1995: 105).

Earlier jazz artists, many inspired by the New Orleans ensembles of the 1920s, in particular the Original Dixieland Jazz Band, had established a basis of mutuality, according to Jones, who contrasts whites' empathic attempts to play like blacks with the blackface minstrels who sought only to burlesque blacks: "White jazz musicians," writes Jones, "wanted to play the music because they thought it emotionally and intellectually fulfilling" (1995: 150). Other writers saw the chemistry of jazz differently. Writing in the 1920s and 1930s, Alain Locke lamented the disintegration of what he took to be a truly creative, innovatory culture actualized in the "golden age of jazz" in the early 1920s. Locke specified the beginning of the end as 1926 when there appeared a "flood of popularity and profit," as he puts it in his book *The Negro and His Music*, first published in 1926. Locke argued that the musicians, both black and white, were true artists. The corrupting influences of commercialism were to blame for the transformation of expressiveness into a fashion that went the way of all other fashions.

Ted Vincent's more recent analysis of the Jazz Age, *Keep Cool*, locates early jazz as a black initiative, both creatively and financially: "The Jazz Age Black music in Chicago appears to have been mostly under the control of African-Americans from 1918 into late 1921 or early 1922" (1995: 70). After this, white interests arrived and grew increasingly parasitic. Like Locke, he believes the concentrated essence of this culture was "watered down" as commercialism took over. The Jazz Age gave way to a more popular, bowdlerized jazz, practised by as many whites as blacks and consumed by many more whites than blacks.

Jazz's center of gravity moved north to Chicago and the music lost its brassy drive, reed instruments coming much more to the fore following Young. While some writers, Jones included, interpret jazz as at root an African American phenomenon, there is a case for arguing that white Chicago musicians – Benny Goodman, Gene Krupa, Bud Freeman *et al.* – were as influential as Armstrong, Joe Oliver, Jimmie Noone and the other black artists in refining jazz into a freer and expressive medium. Another and probably more important function served by white musicians was in changing public tastes: simply by being white they ensured a wider audience than their black counterparts. Without this change in emphasis, individualists who themselves were to refine and perhaps redefine the music would not have found an audience to entertain or, in some cases, to snub.

John Coltrane, Miles Davis and others turned their backs on audiences as if to signify their defiance and intention not to become entertainers, at least not in the conventional sense. The style they created was known as *cool* and it was a significant development: previously, black culture had been seen as amusing yet harmless. The cool ethic informed a self-conscious turning away from playing or performing simply for the entertainment of whites. This is what the minstrels were about, of course. Cool jazz musicians did not want to extend this tradition: they played for themselves and for each other and, if whites were willing to pay to watch, so be it. There were no concessions; there was no acting up to stereotypes. Being cool implied a rejection of the values that had ensured the subjugation of blacks, politically and culturally. It conveyed a covert anger which if ever made overt would draw retribution from white society. Instead, musicians detached themselves from their audiences and created a manner, a posture, an argot even a "look," all recognizable to those who shared their orientation, yet invisible to outsiders, known as squares.

Heroin became integral to the aura of cool. Its users included many jazz musicians who coalesced into a junkie subculture and so reinforced the sense of isolation from mainstream society, while promoting an in-group of users and dealers. Sidran believes the drug was well suited to cool musicians, as it suppressed emotional excesses and allayed anxieties (1995: 113).

Charlie Parker had used heroin since he was 12 years old and was one of countless jazz players and aficionados who became dependent on and were ultimately destroyed by the drug. "These musicians were less secular stars than quasi-religious figures, and their fans often referred to them with godly reverence," writes Nelson George (1988: 25).

If artists wishing to break into the mainstream were playing the whites' game, cool musicians decided the game was not worth playing. They remained almost arrogantly outside the musical establishment, attracting little interest from the record corporations. Like most gestures of defiance that start life among a circle of like-minded rebels, cool became appropriated by both blacks and whites who were fascinated perhaps not by the politics of cool so much as by the external appearance, its image. To look unflappable in the face of turmoil, to prefix and suffix sentences with "man" or "baby," to talk with a hip-sounding slur that made you sound as if you were on heroin, to wear apparel with a certain looseness; to walk with a distinct swagger; all these were features of cool that were soon seized by what Norman Mailer once called "the white negro" and that were eventually dissipated. Jack Kerouac and the beat generation of which he was part embraced many of the idioms and some of the values inherent in cool. Even today, we use the term without reflecting on its source in African American culture and on its eventual ramifications. Sidran concludes that the disaffection behind the cool movement was much the same as that behind the much more overt expressions of the 1960s, as we will see in Chapter eight.

Jones disagrees with this interpretation, suggesting that, Davis apart, most of the musicians associated with cool were actually white. He praises the efforts of Cecil Taylor, Ornette Coleman and others who veered away from the some-times intricate and oblique tangent of cool jazz with its elaborate and often baroque lyricism. They gave back to jazz "its valid separation from, and anarchic disregard of Western popular forms" and argues that, in introducing what he terms jagged, exciting rhythms, Taylor and others "restored the hegemony of blues as the most important basic form in Afro-American music" (1995: 225). Jazz, in its cool incarnation, was a sophisticated and relatively inaccessible form, followed by devotees, many middle class whites who were attracted by the subterranean character of the music and the qualities it embodied.

Contemporary blues, by contrast, being simpler in construction and more accessible, had little white following and probably even less of a black middle class one. (By the 1940s there had emerged a fledgling group scathingly called by E. Franklin Frazier the *Black Bourgeoisie*.) One of the principal reasons for whites' lack of enthusiasm is that they rarely had the chance to listen to any blues. It was played on hardly any radio stations. Still, the music interested many record entrepreneurs in much the same way as it had interested impresarios and, radio stations or not, there was money to be made.

Independent companies like Chess, Sun and Atlantic – which will be covered in the coming pages – were given their opportunities almost by accident. In 1940 when Broadcast Music Inc. (BMI) was created by radio station owners, its purpose was to license music that Ascap would not. Both organizations licensed songs for airplay, collected royalties and distributed proceeds to the copyright owners. Unlike Ascap, BMI was willing to let any songwriter or publisher, regardless of ethnic background, join. A dramatic boycott of radio stations by Ascap backfired in 1941 when the stations simply turned to BMI for its songs. Hence listeners were familiarized with music previously only available to blacks. Interest grew and independent record companies were encouraged to seek more zealously for African American talent. Out of this search came some of the standard-bearers of Chicago blues and, later, rock'n'roll.

The independent record labels were absolutely crucial in the development and dissemination of black cultural product. The market they envisaged was not primarily white, so it was not thought necessary to make artistic concessions to the potential audience. All the same: "Profit, not prosperity was most often the motive," Gerri Hirshey quotes Leonard Chess, founder of Chess Records, as saying. Once asked why his company made so many 78s – the brittle wax 7-inch-diameter records that were replaced by the more convenient and smaller vinyl 45 revolutions per minute discs – Chess replied with blunt patronizing honesty: "Because the black folks down South like the big records." It took another twenty years before a major record company owned by African Americans was able to sell its product to a white market.

The majority of the independent labels were owned by whites, many Jewish; of those owned by blacks, only two made significant impacts, according to Nelson George (1988). They were the Houston-based Peacock, started in 1949 by Don Robey, which, for a while, recorded Little Richard; and Vee-Jay, which began trading three years later and had bases in Chicago and Gary, Indiana and boasted the services of John Lee Hooker. (Hooker never really adapted to the sleeker, more disciplined ways of other Chicago blues players, but his unfussy approach proved more durable and he continued to tour in the mid-1990s when a septuagenarian.) We will return to these two small but important companies in chapters to come.

Chess, more than any other label, was also able to capitalize on the north-ward migration of blacks. Many, like Blind Lemon Jefferson, from Texas, settled in Chicago. In fact, Lemon – now acknowledged as a seminal blues musician and inspiration behind countless contemporary bands – signed with another label, Paramount Records, a small company, but one with extensive mail order sales that gave it a market in the rural areas where blues were most popular. In 1926, the year after Lemon's move, Paramount released eight phonographic recordings of his music. Buoyed by their success, the company busily set about signing other hitherto unknown southern blues players, including Blind Blake, Sam Collins and Son House.

Expeditions from the north quickly followed, though some record companies, like Columbia and Victor, took whole recording units with them in order to make the records *in situ*. That meant going into bars, farm houses, even homes to capture the raw texture of what remained a rural art form. And, as if to reinforce the sovereignty of the artist, production was strictly a passive affair. The choice of numbers, takes, accompaniment and indeed all the major decisions that conventionally rest with production engineers were made by the musicians themselves. One hesitates before hailing blues as a "true" original: a musical form that was plucked whole from its natural environment and consumed without modification. Yet it does appear to be a cultural product that found its way into people's homes plain and ungarnished.

Chess stuck to its hands-off policy, even in the 1950s, when many other commercial companies had spotted potential and were wooing white markets. By the time of his death in 1968, the founder Leonard Chess had accumulated one of the most influential back catalogs in music history. Its value is not only as a chronicle of unassimilated black music to be preserved for posterity; but as evidence of the significant parts played by whites in the shaping, promotion and, ultimately, industrialization of black culture. It also reminds us of African Americans' pivotal role in the development of a music from which they were subsequently excluded.

The great integrative dynamic that brought blacks to the record industry was, of course, money. Record industry owners were nothing if not pragmatists; true they may have had an ear for the blues and gospel that black people produced so purely, but, more relevantly, they found black artists cheap. Two observations, the first from Robert "Bumps" Blackwell who worked at Specialty Records, an independent label based in Hollywood, California, owned by Art Rupe: "I felt the reason some companies dealt with black artists was because black guys wouldn't sue" (quoted in White, 1984). The second follows from this and concerns the kinds of contract that the label owners would typically offer black artists. Specialty's contract with Little Richard, the rock'n'roll artist, was an improvement on the one Richard had with Peacock – which he considered exploitative.

Yet Specialty's was hardly generous. The artist would receive 5 percent of 90 percent of the retail price of a record (in the early 1950s, 49 cents a copy). This meant the performer could expect about 4 cents per sale plus a broadcast fee calculated on the number of radio airplays; this could be 1 or 2 cents. If an artist also wrote the song, he or she would receive 2 percent "mechanical rights" on every copy sold, in addition to royalty and broadcast fees. But the serious money lay in publishing the music. At Specialty, Rupe owned the publishing company that bought Richard's and other artists' songs. As Charles White relates: "He [Rupe] leased them to his own record company at one-half rate, which cut Richard's share of the mechanicals to half a cent" (1984: 57).

"It didn't matter how many records you sold if you were black," said Richard himself. "The publishing rights were sold to the record label before the record was released. 'Tutti Frutti' [a big seller] was sold to Speciality for $50" (quoted in White, 1984: 58).

As many publishing companies owned the record companies, they licensed their songs at whatever rate they wanted and the artists under contract effectively lost out big. Rupe's habit of licensing numbers to himself at half-rate became a known case, only because Richard kicked up a fuss about it in later years when he was a big star. Remember: this was an improvement on the deal he had with his previous label – which may have been more typical of the ones of most blues and gospel artists. Lacking in formal education, it is probable that most artists were unable to read the contracts, anyway, less still retain the services of an attorney if they felt dissatisfied.

The independent record company owners were no white philanthropists zealously seeking to speed the recognition of a genuine piece of black culture. Theirs was an improbable, but highly productive venture in which white entrepreneurship (or greed) interacted with black impoverishment. The result was an asymmetrical relationship. In this relationship, blacks made some money, many whites made more. But the outcome of the relationship was a commercial product. Like other genres, blues represents a triumph of marketing as much as anything else. And, as if further proof was needed, we should close this chapter with an observation on the relaunch of blues.

Much of the initial popularity had gone by the 1950s as a fondness for fast fretwork and flashier licks dragged blues away from its instrumentally sparse origins and turned it into other forms, like rhythm'n'blues and rock'n'-roll. Incongruously, blues thrived in Britain, where white bands like Blues Incorporated, John Mayall's Bluesbreakers and the Yardbirds attracted a following in the 1960s. Cream was the product of three white British musicians, Eric Clapton, Jack Bruce and Ginger Baker, who got together in 1966. Cream's use of blues material was quite brazen: the band's albums were filled with compositions from Chicago and Mississippi Delta bluesmen. The first, *Fresh Cream*, made little impact in the States, but *Disraeli Gears* and *Wheels of Fire* were both commercial successes. The latter, which reached number one in the US in 1968, featured extended versions of Willie Dixon's "Spoonful" and Robert Johnson's "Crossroads." The tracks typified Cream's use, as opposed to recreation, of blues: the basic structure was an all-purpose showcase for the band's improvisational talents. In this, Cream's approach owed as much to jazz. Hatch and Millward believe that Cream, in bringing blues into popular currency, "inspired curiosity as to the music's origins" (1990: 106). We might add that the main beneficiaries of this new interest were the likes of Led Zeppelin, the Butterfield Blues Band and Canned Heat; all white artists.

But, in the 1990s, the sales of black artists' blues records picked up, Hooker's work especially leading a veritable second coming. Some might point to the decade of the 1990s as valuing simplicity and authenticity over complexity and artificiality: this, it might be argued, was the perfect context for blues. Others might favor a more commercial perspective: the distinct aura of danger and ineffable cool associated with the devil's music were picked up as desirable qualities by advertisers wishing their products to have what they called a usp (unique selling point). Hooker's work was used under all manner of British television commercials, including ads for heart drugs, bluejeans and beer. Sales of Hooker's records perked up and re-releases of other artists' work multiplied. Blues, in short, became a *fin de siècle* marketing instrument.

It was also a means through which whites could remind themselves of the misery of blacks without actually punishing themselves for the sins of their forebears. As Daniel Lieberfeld writes in his "Million-dollar juke joint": "Because of blues culture's commercialization and accompanying loss of social context, the white imagination ignores or romanticizes the poverty, violence, and endurance that bred and fed the blues" (1995: 220). He cites the House of Blues, the restaurant chain mentioned at the start of this chapter, as a prime example of "a blues theme park." This will offend purists, but there again, few cultural forms escape commodification; at least, not the cultural forms we have heard about.

In contrast to jazz, blues was all openness and innocence: it told of drifting, dreaming and being down and out. Perhaps there was something reassuring to whites about a black population so close to despair yet prepared to sing about it like the minstrels once did. If this is so, there was nothing reassuring about jazz, certainly not in its cool form: musicians like Davis played as if they might jab fingers in your eyes if you asked for an autograph. Unsurprisingly, it offered little temptation to entrepreneurs looking for a way into the white market. At least not until the 1960s when the true virtuosity of black jazz musicians was more fully appreciated. Meanwhile, blues was open for business. The single most influential company in fashioning blues into a culture industry was Chess Records. Its development is worth recording in detail; which is the idea of the next chapter.

Chapter four

White Boss
in a Black
Industry

DESPITE THE HISTORICAL SIMILARITY of their experiences and the urgings of African American scholars, blacks and Jews in the United States have rarely, if ever, manifested anything resembling an alliance. There is, in fact, a long and virulent streak of antisemitism among black Americans. Dating back to the 1920s, when the whites with whom poor northern city blacks were most likely to have direct contact were Jewish landlords, store owners or social workers, the antipathy reared politically in Marcus Garvey's United Negro Improvement Association. This organization all but scapegoated Jews for the injustices perpetrated by whites in general.

The unbroken streak continued through the 1990s, when Nation of Islam leader Louis Farrakhan and his followers expounded a theory of enslavement in which Jews were key conspirators. Even the liberal Democrat Jesse Jackson, in an unguarded moment, let slip a remark about "kike city" (New York). The reasons for this and an evaluation of its consequences are to be found in *Blacks and Jews* (1994) edited by Paul Berman, which concludes, among other things, that the sharedness of poverty and discrimination has bred racial hostility rather than comradeship.

In the 1920s and 1930s, Jews scrambled away from persecution in Eastern Europe, finding refuge wherever they could. Many made for Ellis Island and, from there, to the major metropolitan areas of the north, where the chances of work were most promising. These were also the industrial centers to which southern blacks headed primarily in search of jobs, but also to escape the persistent racism of Jim Crow. Racism may not have been so overt in the north, but its effects were comparable. Denied access to places in educational institutions, quality housing and decent jobs, blacks slid toward the poverty trap. The whites with whom poor blacks were most likely to have contact were often Jewish landlords or store owners. They became living reminders, perhaps even symbols, of the exploitation faced daily. But Jews were also excluded at every turn; their response was to start their own institutions in an attempt to become self-sufficient. Entrepreneurs took advantage of money-lending facilities created by and for Jews.

The seeds of many commercial empires, including the Hollywood film industry, were sown in this period. Unlike many other enterprises, "there were no social barriers in a business as new and faintly disreputable as the movies were," writes Neal Gabler in his book, *An Empire of Their Own* which has the subtitle "How the Jews invented Hollywood." In a passage that could easily be applied to the music industry, Gabler reflects: "There were none of the impediments imposed by loftier professions and more firmly entrenched businesses to keep Jews and other undesirables out" (1988: 5).

Lazer Shmuel Chez migrated to the United States in 1928, following his father, who had left Poland some years before and settled, like thousands of others, in Chicago. After working for his father, a scrap dealer, Leonard Chess, as he Anglicized himself, tried his hand at a few small business ventures before opening a bar with his older brother, Phil. By the 1940s, the brothers owned a string of bars, the main one being the Macomba. Black artists, such as Ella Fitzgerald, Billie Holiday and Lionel Hampton performed at the club. The Macomba's house singer, Andrew Tibbs, attracted some interest from record scouts outside Chicago, and the Chess brothers, in an effort to preempt them, booked some time at Universal recordings studios and made a record of "Union man blues." Tibbs had written it on a brown shopping bag. It was released in 1947 on the Aristocrat label, which the Chess brothers created.

At first, Leonard schlepped his taperecorder around the taverns and juke joints of Chicago in an attempt to cull talent for the label. Pete Golkin, author of "Blacks, whites and blues: The story of Chess Records," writes that: "Leonard began trips to the South in 1950, logging 'five thousand miles every three months' to distribute his product from the trunk of his car and search for new artists" (1989a: 26). He found mostly solo bluesmen, one of whom was McKinley Morganfield, better known as Muddy Waters. Waters had been an itinerant player in the south whose music was made distinctive by his copious use of slide guitar. He made arguably the most successful adaptation to electric guitar and accompanying rhythm sections; so much so that his music is now regarded as the clearest example of what became known as Chicago blues. His recording of "Feel like going home/I can't be satisfied" gave Aristocrat its first commercial success, selling thousands, mainly to blacks in Chicago and in the South.

By the 1940s, the market for phonographs and wax records was encouraging for entrepreneurs like Chess. Rural blacks who had migrated to northern cities had more money than ever before and, though still far, far from affluent, had some disposable income to spend on music. The wartime industry's boom attracted southern blacks and Caribbeans who crowded into already crowded urban neighborhoods. There was also steadily growing interest among whites, the war having thrown many together with blacks in defense plants in places like Detroit, Chicago and LA and opened up their musical tastes. But there were also different reactions from whites. In December 1946, the Chicago Housing Authority assigned a few black families to a new housing project in a hitherto all-white area on the city's southwest side. They lasted only two weeks; white residents stoned them, beat them and, generally, made their life hell. A year later, a similar move to integrate neighborhoods collapsed in the face of a white riot; and, despite a Supreme Court ruling that racially restrictive covenants were unenforceable, Chicago's housing policy changed to concentrate on constructing exclusively black projects in black districts. Although blacks' input to the workforce was welcomed by Chicago's industries, their presence as neighbors was resisted.

This type of mentality was reflected in the popular media. Few radio stations played black music, so the jukebox was the main source for blues and there were about 300,000 jukeboxes in the USA by the early 1950s. It was a small market but sufficient to keep the Chess brothers afloat and Waters more than any other artist kept sales up. Waters was later to reflect favorably on Leonard Chess: "He did a lot for me, putting out the first record and everything, and we had a good relationship with one another" (quoted in Golkin, 1989a: 25). "I didn't even sign no contract with him. It was just 'I belongs to the Chess family'."

Such fond recollections were few and far between, however, and many of the blues players who recorded with Aristocrat complained of Chess' exploitative approach. Jimmie Bell, for example, still insists Chess cheated him out of $200,000 in royalties. Willie Mabon stormed into Chess' office with a loaded pistol after receiving a $3,700 royalty check for his 1952 hit record "I don't know." Chess was forced to take cover in the packing room. Jerry Wexler, of Atlantic records, whose critical importance to the black culture industry will be examined in the next chapter, observed that "maybe" Chess did not pay his musicians everything they were due; "but he recorded them, that's what's important" (quoted in Golkin, 1989a: 29).

There seems little doubt that Leonard Chess and his brother were not in business for altruisic reasons. The previous quote about giving black folks what they want captures his approach. Yet, Wexler's point is a strong one. The Chess brothers taught themselves how to produce and gambled with then unknown and relatively obscure artists like Howlin' Wolf and John Lee Hooker, both now recognized as central figures in the blues pantheon.

Leonard was, by all accounts, aware of his artistic limitations, but intuitively brought out the best in his musicians. Odie Payne, a studio drummer, recounted how Leonard's idiosyncratic methods worked: "Chess would sit there with his eyes closed in the booth. If it hit him, he'd say 'that's it, man', but I heard him many times, 'Man, you got to make me feel it'" (quoted in Golkin, 1989a: 27). The artist would reply: "I doing the best I can," to which Chess would bark back: "Yeah, but I don't feel nothing." Payne moaned: "He'd work you to death." On one occasion, Leonard, exasperated at one of his drummers' failure to find the right beat, jumped in himself and lent an untutored hand. Known for his hands-off approach in early years, Leonard took a much more active part in production as the label gained recognition.

With its widening distribution network, the label would sell the records of other companies. A notable success came with "Rocket 88" made by Jackie Brenston, with guitar played by Ike Turner. This sold one million copies and, in the eyes of many, set an agenda for later rock artists. The fuzzball electric guitar played by Turner on this track has been emulated countless times. Rock folklore has it that the sound was achieved by default: Turner had damaged his amplifier and performed on-the-spot repairs which distorted the clarity of his guitar.

Aristocrat became the Chess label in 1952, plying its trade mostly in the south with its "race records," as recordings by black artists were listed by the music trade publications. Leonard continued to tour the southern states personally, scouting and selling records to stores and jukebox operators. One of his key contacts was Alan Freed, a Cleveland-based disc jockey who worked originally under the name "Moondog" and who enthused over Chess records in his radio shows. He became instrumental in not only spreading the good word about Chess, but in raising awareness about black music. Freed became embroiled in a scandal over bribery in 1955. It involved a bluesy number that Leonard Chess felt needed a bigger beat and a financial boost.

By the end of 1954, Chess was no longer a struggling blues label: it had achieved its best financial year, Muddy Waters' "Hoochie coochie man" selling 4,000 units in one week alone. Chess' distribution had expanded so that it could now sell to a national market. It outgrew its offices and moved to larger studios. Its reputation meant that blues players actually came to Chicago rather than Leonard having to go to them. In 1955, Chuck Berry, from St Louis, arrived at the Chess offices with a wire recorder and played Leonard some of his material. It was too country and western flavored for Chess, but one piece called "Ida Red" appealed to Leonard so he suggested a rewrite and produced a recording of it under the name "Maybelline." The original treatment had been rejected by both Capitol and Mercury.

Berry might have been a bit of a greenhorn when he first recorded his number. It had been rewritten prior to recording and Berry was surprised to find that he was only co-credited on the royalty payments, his co-writers being Russ Fratto, an associate of the Chess brothers, and Alan Freed. He also claimed he knew nothing of the business arrangement between Chess and Freed, the dj receiving payments for promoting the record. This "payola" method, as it was called, guaranteed airplay and virtually guaranteed sales. The stranglehold of the major labels and Ascap was so great that, as Donald Mabry points out, "R & B and rock'n'roll would never be played on radio (and thus records sold) were it not for bribery on the part of the independents" (1990: 416).

"Maybelline" was a commercial success and gained Berry national exposure. Chess angered Berry just as he had many other artists and Berry, frustrated at receiving what he considered the short end of the royalties, threatened to set up his own publishing company. Music publishing has for long been one of the most lucrative areas in the culture industry and involves the exploitation of song copyrights. The owner of a copyright typically earns royalties each time a song is broadcast or performed, regardless of the artist.

Berry, the writer of his own numbers, would have received songwriting royalties on his own numbers and, later, when many of his compositions, like "Memphis, Tennessee" and "Roll over Beethoven," were recorded by other artists. In chapters to come, we will see how publishing was a recurrent issue, often engendering disputes between black artists and their record labels. Berry clearly wanted the additional income to be gained from publishing. Whether he had a genuine gripe or was just naïve about a business that was growing fiercer by the year we cannot be sure. What is certain is that his record sales on the Chess label helped elevate Berry to international stardom. Thirty years after the release of his first record, Chuck Berry was still touring and performing to sellouts.

Berry had walked into a studio specializing in blues with a country and western number and emerged as pioneer of what became known as rhythm'-n'blues (r'n'b), an uptempo variant of blues with guitar riffs that attacked rather than defended the vocalist. Bo Diddley, a contemporary of Berry on the Chess label who was also soured by Chess' wheelings and dealings, once interpreted r'n'b as "rip-off and bullshit." But the fact that we know the name Bo Diddley is not due solely to white Texan Buddy Holly, who covered Diddley's compositions: Chess made and sold his records.

In one light, the Chess brothers were operators; in another, they were following the logic of the then burgeoning record industry. They bought radio stations and "bought" other stations' djs. They pushed black artists in an industry that was dominated by whites, many of whom drew inspiration from blacks. "The entertainment industry has traditionally relied on white performers to provide black styles with their entry into the 'mainstream'," writes Charles Shaar Murray in his *Crosstown Traffic*. The idea was to "render them acceptable to white audiences, and ultimately to disarm them"(1989: 86). But, Chess' music was always fully armed. And, we should remind ourselves that the brothers were natural risk-takers. Donald Mabry, in his history of another independent label Ace Records, points out that: "At least 90 and perhaps 95 percent of records lost money in the 1950s, so the probability of never recovering advances was quite high" (1990: 443).

The payola case was another example of the Chesses' preparedness to do what it took to get their artists played. When a federal trades commission ordered a number of record labels to stop paying djs, Leonard Chess refused to sign a cease and desist order, arguing that it was standard practice in the industry. Unlike some other record companies, Chess was quite open about its dealings. In fact, the company's venture into buying radio stations was an almost brazen attempt to promote Chess records. The brothers bought stations in Flint, Michigan, and Chicago, the latter being called WVON – the Voice of the Negro. Through the decade of the 1950s, Chess continued to sell primarily to blacks, its specialty remaining the single release.

If any event prefigured Chess' future, it was Berry's arrest in 1959 for violating the Mann Act by transporting a minor across a state border (Jack Johnson was previously the most celebrated black man who fell foul of this law). The market had changed substantially in the second half of the 1950s. White artists were appropriating black music, "disarming" it (to use Murray's term) and selling it by the millions. There was also a change of emphasis in the market: long-playing records, either 9 inch or 12 inch diameter, became popular, and, though Chess released compilations of their numbers, its stock-in-trade was the blues single and it was ill-equipped to compete with the corporations or even the newer independents, like Atlantic and Stax, which we will cover in the next chapter.

Exacerbating the problems of Chess and, for that matter, all independents, were the chastening effects of the payola scam: new legislation prevented independents inducing djs with sweeteners and so strengthened the position of the major players of the record industry. Media cross-ownership meant that record companies had interests in radio and, later, television. They could virtually blot out smaller contenders. Chess' response was to shrug off the family atmosphere and become more businesslike in their dealing with musicians. The proliferation of radio stations operating on the FM wave meant more exposure, but it also meant a more systematic approach to marketing: as many as 3,000 promotional copies had to be sent out, press parties needed to be arranged, appearances had to be made.

Television had also made its impact. In 1950, 10 percent of US homes had a set. Five years later, this had leapt to 67 percent. And the trend continued so that, by 1963, 90 percent of all homes had at least one television set. The record industry's growth was tied to this. Popular music, abbreviated to just "pop," unlike earlier music forms, was not sold on sound alone; image was equally, perhaps more, important. Murray's point about "rendering" black music styles to make them more acceptable to whites is a valid one, but it misses the significance of vision. It was not just the minimally altered sounds that made white versions acceptable: potential consumers in the late 1950s could see artists performing the numbers. Seeing white fashion spread Pat Boone preening as he smoothed over Little Richard's "Long tall Sally" was evidently more attractive to audiences than the sight of Richard himself manically tearing his way through his own numbers.

Set against this, Berry's commercial success may seem puzzling. But, recall that Berry was a country or hillbilly singer when he first met Leonard Chess, so his style and diction was quite different from blues players. His skin was pale and hair conked (chemically straightened). In his 1987 autobiography, he reveals how his promotional photographs were airbrushed to give the impression he was white and how promoters would often book him on this assumption. On television, makeup made it possible for Berry to pass as white, though even he saw some of his originals picked up by whites. The Beach Boys' "Surfin' USA," for example, owes much to Berry's "Sweet little sixteen."

As a mainstay of the Chess label, Berry became almost synonymous with Chess. His legal problems did not help the company negotiate a shifting market.

The 1960s were difficult times for Chess, which persisted with old-style blues rather than recruiting the newer mutations that were becoming popular. In a show of symbolic submission, the brothers sold out to a California company, General Recorded Tape (GRT) for about $10 million. In 1969, this was a handsome sum for a floundering independent outfit. There were other contributory factors, like Leonard's worsening heart condition and his run-ins with Jesse Jackson's Chicago-based organization, which pressed Chess to hire more black staff. Jackson's argument was (and, for that matter, still is) that companies that profit by the talent of blacks, whether sports stars or entertainers, should appoint and promote more black people behind the scenes. Chess tried to accommodate Jackson's demands, but admitted: "It was going to be hard to be a white boss in a black industry" (quoted in Golkin, 1989b: 28).

Within a year of the sale, Leonard had a heart attack while driving and died in the resulting accident. Shortly after his death, GRT fired all the former Chess staff that had been rehired after the buy-out. Phil Chess left in 1971, as did Leonard's son. GRT moved the Chess studios from Chicago to New York. For many, it was like moving the Vatican to Milan and, to no one's surprise, the company folded in 1979. The Chess catalog – still revered – went to the Sugar Hill and then MCA labels. Muddy Waters moved to CBS and had several successful albums before his death in 1983. Chuck Berry went through a rocky patch after his release from prison, but, in 1972, enjoyed the most commercially successful record of his career with an icky *double entendre* novelty number called "My ding-a-ling," which was about as far away from his sforzando "Roll over Beethoven" and "Johnny B. Goode" as he could get.

The consensus view is that Leonard was the prime mover of Chess, Phil handling the administration of the label and its subsidiaries, like Checker. Reviled as a sharp operator by some, respected as indefatigable promoter of black culture by others, his impact was undeniably huge. His resolution in sticking to a "purer" form of blues as opposed to the more gospel-influenced soul of his counterparts at labels like Atlantic, was part of his undoing. But, during the 1940s and 1950s, Chess' achievements are remarkable. At a time when the record industry was an oligopoly divided among six main corporations which produced music largely by and exclusively for whites, small regional labels like Chess were almost bound to fail. Chess made life harder for himself by keying his products to the tastes of African Americans, whose size in the total population and mean incomes made them unattractive to most entrepreneurs.

No doubt Chess was out for himself; but in feathering his own nest, he created opportunities for black musicians, primed interest in their music and helped shape that music into cultural product. Chess strove for authenticity, but was quite willing to muddle his way through the complexities of production in an effort to get what he *felt* was quality. History suggests his intuition served him well: Chess' titles make up a treasure chest. It also reminds us of the trickiness in trying to discern which of Chess' motives was uppermost – his search for music of substance or his self-interest? Or whether it is a proper question at all.

Demarcating between the two presupposes that something lay beyond Chess' enterprise: a culture raw and untainted by commercial interests. Once committed to the big wax discs, blues and its successors lost their authenticity and became counterfeit versions produced for profits; and white men's profits at that. At least, that is one argument. Another is that blues may have existed as a living culture, rich in meaning for performers and audiences alike prior to the encroachments of the Chesses and their kind. But it was no less authentic, rich or meaningful as a result of becoming merchandise: just different.

At various points in his career, Chess intersected with figures who were like lightning conductors of the times, each transmitting social currents or dynamics of the age. His somewhat sleazy dealings with Alan Freed were touched on earlier; Freed's own role in the development of black culture deserves greater attention. As does that of Sam Phillips, the owner of Sun Records, another independent label with which Chess had links. During the 1960s, Chess became a benefactor of many organizations and causes, among them the Southern Christian Leadership Conference. Around his office in Chicago, he hung pictures of himself with the leader of this movement, Martin Luther King. We will consider the roles of these three key characters next.

Alan Freed does not appear on anybody's list of great influences on black culture, but we see and hear him everywhere. His detractors have accused him of being self-serving and exploitative of blacks; but the effects of his work on the promotion of black music are beyond doubt.

Sometime in the early 1950s, a white Cleveland record store owner noticed that his young white customers were progressively buying more "race records" by artists such as LaVern Baker, Ivory Joe Hunter and others on independent labels like Chess. He mentioned this to Freed, then a dj at a local radio station WJW. There were isolated examples of white djs who played black music; Zena Sears at the Georgia state-owned station WGST was one, LA-based Hunter Hancock was another. Freed's *Moondog Show* soon began integrating black music into its programs and to good effect: ratings shot up and sponsorship money poured into his station. The money was a useful antidote to the threats he received on account of his becoming an overnight "nigger lover."

Freed maintained that it was during this phase he "invented" the term rock-'n'roll in an attempt to avoid accusations of being a "race music station"; he also rejected the then current term rhythm'n'blues, which was a virtual euphemism. To rock or to roll, he later explained, were two common terms for sex in the blues vocabulary; presumably, as in "rock me, baby/rock me all night long" and "he stole that diamon' ring/for some of Betty's jelly roll." Hence the compound had rather more meaning for those familiar with the genre than for uninitiated whites. It is interesting that, if this version of the term's origins is accepted, rock'n'roll referred exclusively to black music; within a few years, blacks had been all but pushed out of the genre.

Freed moved to radio WINS, New York, in 1954, changing the name of his 7–11pm show to *Rock'n'Roll Party*. In the interim, he busied himself organizing concerts. Segregation still held sway and the concerts, whose audiences were mixed, were decried by the die-hard racists of Cleveland, a segregated Midwest city. As if by default his impact was to desegregate audiences, drawing to his radio shows and concerts both blacks and whites, though not in equal measures. Freed courted whites: there were more of them and they had more money. And if they thrilled to black music and Freed had access to it, it made good business sense to go with the market.

It is unclear whether Freed was motivated by anything other than profit. His involvement in the payola scandal of 1962 seemed to confirm his dedication to mammon. Floyd Mutrux's 1978 film *American Hot Wax* depicts Freed as a benevolent, if flawed, patron of black music, whose downfall was the result of an organized attempt by conservative groups to discredit him. The movie, which focuses on the hostile response to Freed's presence in New York, recreates a period in which the embrace of black music was seen as a lurch toward primitivism. The attack on the music was personalized and Freed was singled out as the culprit; it proved to be the first step in a sharp descent. In 1960, he was charged with commercial bribery; he pled guilty in court. But the hounding continued and, in 1964, he was indicted on charges of income tax evasion. Freed died penniless the following year.

Motives aside, there is no denying the importance of Freed's combination: a white man with a white following, playing black music. He refused to play white cover versions of blacks' originals and called white djs who did so "anti-Negro." But, it is one of those injustices of history that he, rather than any of the other djs who were specializing in black music, is credited with being the single most influential carrier of black culture to mainstream audiences.

Rufus Thomas had been playing blues and gospel on radio WDIA in Memphis since the 1940s and, as such, could lay legitimate claim to being the first black dj to play black music for black listeners; there was limited interest in black music among local whites. WDIA was known as "The Mother Station of the Negroes." Thomas was something of a jack-of-all-trades: a vaudeville entertainer turned impresario and talent scout, he also recorded "Bearcat" for Sun Records in 1953 and had a number of international successes, especially with his "Walkin' the dog" in 1962 on the Stax label. Being black, Thomas was unable to gain the kind of acceptance available to white djs at the time.

Mabry calls djs "gatekeepers of the marketplace" and, for this reason, we need to reiterate the importance of Freed and others to the growth of the black culture industry. Convincing djs that they should play a record was crucial to the record's success. The domino effect meant that several stations across the state and perhaps nationally would also play the record. Airplay in big markets, like New York, LA, Chicago or Philadelphia, could make the difference to a record's commercial success or failure. So, the 100-plus independent labels scattered across the country all scrambling for a share of a tiny cake, were dependent on the favors of djs.

Thomas' station, WDIA, was owned by two white entrepreneurs, Bert Ferguson and John Pepper, who, in 1948, decided to turn an ailing country music radio station into one which specialized in "race music," soon to be r'n'b. They hired an assortment of djs, included Nat Dee, formerly Professor Nathaniel D. Williams, and Maurice Hulbert Junior aka Maurice the Mood Man. Before he became blues ace B. B. King, Riley B. King was a WDIA dj, who used his radio show to advertise his own gigs.

Another Memphis station boasted Dewey Phillips who, like Freed, earned himself the epithet "nigger lover": a white dj who played black music. His station, WHBG, was created as a result of WDIA's success. The paradox of Phillips was that, as a white, he could hold down a job, even while trying, in an almost minstrel-like way, to sound black.

The Sun studios in Memphis was like a factory's smelter shop, where the ores of blues, gospel, country and rockabilly were melted down and their extracts turned into records. The original venture was started in 1950 by Sam Phillips, who opened a small studio for recording southern blues artists, like Howlin' Wolf and Junior Parker, then selling the recordings to labels like Chess. Three years later, Phillips decided to promote and distribute his own recordings under the Sun label.

Artistically, Phillips is regarded as a great eclectic who recognized no categories and urged his artists to blend as many elements as they could into their music. For example, traditional southern blues eschewed the kind of electric guitars and drums Phillips wanted on his records. Acoustic pick-and-slapping and a stomping foot were much favored by bluesmen like John Lee Hooker (who stuck resolutely to this for his career). "Memphis blues was harsh and aggressive – and it existed alongside white country music," writes Dave Rogers in his book *Rock'n'Roll*. "Some musicians were beginning to mix the two together and Phillips uged them to sing and play in a rougher manner" (1982: 36).

Phillips had mostly black artists, but is known to have craved a singer who could combine the qualities he had pursued in the studio with an image acceptable to the white market. "If I could find a white man who had the negro sound and the negro feel, I could made a billion dollars," he is often quoted as saying. In 1954, he recorded a number written by blues artist Arthur "Big Boy" Crudup by a white bluegrass singer. Elvis Presley's version of "That's all right, mama" was his first single and, of course, the launchpad for a career of historic proportions. Presley's "Lawdy Miss Clawdy" was a re-recording of a Lloyd Price single. "Hound dog" was a cleaned-up version of Willie Mae "Big Mama" Thornton's Peacock Records single, which was a number one on the "race music" charts in 1953. Originally a blues number that expressed the rage of a woman throwing a gigolo out of her house, "Hound dog" was copied by other artists, black and white, and prompted Rufus Thomas to make his "Bearcat (the answer to Hound dog)", a blatant cash-in written by Phillips; so blatant that Don Robey, of Peacock, sued him for infringement of copyright. (We will cover Robey and his Peacock label in Chapter six.) Whether you view Presley as a parasite on black music or as someone who stimulated worldwide interest in it, there is no doubt about the fact that Phillips created a wonderfully encompassing concept: a white boy with the looks and manner of a Dean or a Brando, but who sang with the emotion of a Waters or a Hooker.

"With Elvis, the label changed," writes Greil Marcus. "Blues vanished almost completely; Phillips went for the main chance, which meant white boys who could sing country rock" (1976: 259). Presley left Sun in 1955, RCA paying Phillips the then sizeable amount of $35,000 for the unused portion of Presley's contract. Phillips continued to prosper from other white artists, like Roy Orbison and Jerry Lee Lewis.

Ike Turner started as a scout for Phillips. He began performing with his band the Rhythm Kings, later to become the Ike and Tina Turner Review, the idea being that "Tina" was an interchangeable female lead singer rather than one person. Annie Mae Bullock became one of those Tinas and went on to retain the name for the rest of her celebrated career. Ike's career was considerably less celebrated: after a number of hits, Tina made "River deep, mountain high" and, later, left the band. Ike drifted into the wilderness, serving a prison sentence for cocaine violations and returned to showbusiness with only modest success. His recording of "Rocket 88," mentioned earlier, was retrospectively considered a milestone.

Some believe Ike Turner self-destructed on booze and dope binges. His alleged beatings of Tina may not have helped his career either. But, there are more glaring reasons why he and, for that matter, half a dozen other black musicians, who were melding the hillbilly country sounds of southern whites with blues, were outshone by Presley and other white mimics, like Gene Vincent, Eddie Cochran and Jerry Lee Lewis (who worked with Phillips on the Sun label).

Like the other independents, Sun was made to crawl in the 1960s. With the major corporations asserting their dominance, many smaller labels were obliged to sell their catalogs or just go out of business. The popularity of British bands across the States also proved to be a problem. Few of the independents had the money to sign them; the corporations did. Phillips ducked out and switched his attention to the then new Holiday Inn chain of motels.

For all his ruthlessness, Leonard Chess was beneficent when it came to minority organizations. He gave generously to the Israel Bond effort, the Chicago Youth Commission and the National Association for the Advancement of Colored People (NAACP), of which he was a life member. He was named 1966's "Man of the Year" by the Chicago Urban League, for working "to establish equal opportunities and equal results for Negroes and other minorities in this city." Chess used the medium of radio WVON, which he owned, to promote self-sufficiency among African Americans. "Don't sit back and wait for a quart of milk," he once bade his listeners. "You're as good as the next guy." This sat uncomfortably with the stories of many Chess musicians who claimed he had cheated them of royalties; their interpretation of his actions was cynical: he got great publicity from his philanthropy.

We still need to reckon with the fact that Chess was a Jewish migrant in a society officially committed to becoming the world's melting pot, but unofficially a witch's caldron that spat as it came to the boil. Boiling point arrived in the 1960s when virtually every major city experienced rioting. Prior to this, resistance to racial inequality mounted steadily. As a benefactor of the Southern Christian Leadership Conference, Chess came to meet its head, Martin Luther King. Whatever Chess' motives, his own background experiences of migration, anti-semitism and ghetto life would have given him a certain affinity with the social condition of blacks. Travelling to Chicago in 1928, Chess was part of a gigantic demographic movement to the USA's northern cities. By 1930, over two million blacks from the south had migrated north in search of work and better housing. It was known as the Great Migration.

Southern blacks and East Europeans alike would have found employment as laborers and semiskilled operatives in packing houses, steel mills and automobile factories. Many Jewish migrants and their offspring worked in the textile trade. Many others, like Chess, began their own businesses; a practice that contributed to the time-honored stereotype of the Jew as a self-interested, acquisitive, if not miserly, entrepreneur, always ready to exploit others for a profit.

The comparisons between the Jewish and the black diasporas are striking. Both groups have epic histories of driven rootlessness, scattered about the globe, denied civil liberties and subject to abominable violence. In the United States, the Jewish response from the 1930s was to build commercial empires, the results of which we see in media corporations, the film industry and other institutions in which Jews are prominent. Theirs was progress by stealth. Much more dramatic was the civil rights movement which culminated in the legal dissolution of the separate but equal doctrine.

On May 17, 1954, a couple of months before Elvis recorded "That's all right, mama," Judge Earl Warren of the US Supreme Court delivered a ruling that was to transform North America: "We conclude, unanimously, that in the field of public education the doctrine of 'separate but equal' has no place." It was 164 years after the principle behind segregation had been established and, during that time, the United States had been two nations, each with its own facilities, institutions and cultures. The case of *Brown v Board of Education of Topeka* had challenged that principle through the courts, insisting that separate schools were unconstitutional and inherently unequal. Once won, the verdict prepared the way for the dissolution of America's version of the caste system. Any jubilation was short-lived. Not only was the pace at which schools desegregated agonizingly slow, but whites, especially those in southern states, reacted with such fury that many must have wondered whether the decision was the blessing it seemed.

The catalog of atrocities in the aftermath of *Brown* included the lynching on barbed wire of 14-year-old Emmett Till in 1955. In the same year, Rosa Parks, a black woman, refused to give up her seat on a segregated bus in Montgomery, Alabama, and inadvertently set in motion a chain of events that was to lead to the civil rights movement and, ultimately, the passing of civil rights legislation. The incident so inflamed local African Americans that they brought the NAACP into the picture and organized a boycott of the buses. What violence there was came from whites. In December 1956 the Supreme Court ordered Montgomery to desegregate its buses; it was a victory that gave impetus to a movement founded on a single issue but which was soon to widen its scope.

Within a month, black ministers from various cities formed the Southern Christian Leadership Conference (SCLC) and commissioned King to organize a coherent campaign for greater equality. The strategy pursued at Montgomery was duplicated by blacks across the States: inspired by Martin Luther King – himself inspired by Gandhi – blacks practised nonviolent disobedience as a way of making their demands known. They staged sit-ins, jail-ins, marches; all designed to dramatize their situation without recourse to violence.

The severity of white resistance to civil rights campaigners made it clear that racism was not the type of phenomenon that would disappear as a result of legislation. Its status as part of North American culture ensured its longevity. There were too many whites, especially in the south, who were deeply committed to the view that blacks' proper place was back on the plantation. The fact that they were there in the first place was evidence less of rapacious whites' greed, more of divine ordination. Racism was not a mere convenience to justify the oppression that held sway in the south: it was a genuinely-held conviction that racial inequality was part of the unfolding manifest destiny of Anglo-Saxons. Civil rights legislation from this perspective was a perversion. Its implications were to be resisted.

The condition of black artists had much in common with the position of all blacks: stuck on the margins and denied access to the mainstream culture. Even when, in the mid-1950s, black music surged in popularity, it was mostly bowdlerized by white artists. Only from the mid-1960s, after the passing of civil rights laws, did black music, especially performed by black artists, become truly acclaimed as a legitimate cultural form. But, through the 1950s, when Chess, Phillips, Freed and others were in their own ways disseminating black-originated music, America was, to use Andrew Hacker's book title, *Two Nations*. Such was their separateness that it was barely conceivable that whites could tolerate, let alone appreciate, a culture that was produced by a manifestly inferior "race" that was prone to mediocrity in all aspects of civilized life.

The civil rights laws of 1964 and 1965 did not lay waste to racism. King was never naïve enough to think it would. As he once said: "Maybe you can't legislate morality . . . but you can regulate behavior" (quoted in Williams, 1987: 168). When he was assassinated in 1968, he left others to pursue the hidden connection between morality and behavior. But, during his last few years, King was able to witness something resembling a nonprejudicial intelligence. Black Americans were credited with a cultural expression that was for once spared the devaluation that had undermined their other music. This was something greeted without sneers, winks or groans: it was a genuine article, divinely poetic with the power of a juggernaut. The élan that made it special always escaped whites. No matter how hard they tried to emulate it, they could never capture the amalgam of sacred and secular that became known as soul. Whether this genuinely was an untutored product of gospel spirituality mixed with blues profanity is open to question; for there is evidence that soul was subject to crucial white interventions during its creation.

Chapter five

Armed to
the Teeth

PICTURE THIS: three males, one a Turk, one a Jew, the other an African American, are driving south into Louisiana in the late 1940s. They reach New Orleans, where they ignore "coloreds only" signs, sometimes at their peril, and drop into juke joints, bars, dance clubs, pool halls, anywhere they hear music. Incongruously, they sit, rapt, listening to barrelhouse pianists like Henry Roeland Byrd, or Professor Longhair as he is best known, and Blind Willie McTell, who has been singing the blues and occasionally religious numbers since the 1920s. No drums, no rhythm section, no electric guitars: the bluesmen down here stomp their feet to keep a beat; they pick and scratch rather than strum their guitars. A bass croak issues from these players. The two whites are going to try to persuade Byrd, McTell and other swamp blues players to record for their fledgling record label. Their success in drawing them away from the bayou will be the basis of their *grand projet*: to build a record company based on black music. Meanwhile, the black male is jotting down notes as he listens to the music; his job is to find a way of committing what is at root an oral music form to paper. He will transcribe and later recreate on record music that is characterized by its untrammelled spontaneity. The end-product of the three men's and their artists' labors will be known as soul music.

The Atlantic label was pivotal in establishing black music's respectability; commercial respectability, that is. In creating an independent record company specializing in not exactly obscure, but frequently overlooked music, Atlantic developed a worldwide market for black culture. The two white males responsible for the Atlantic label came from very different backgrounds.

Ahmet Ertegun was the son of a Turkish ambassador based in Washington, DC. The youngest of two brothers, he developed a precocious interest in jazz. While other children might be playing ball, Ertegun would be tuning into BBC radio's World Service in an effort to find a few bars from the Hot Club de Paris or other European venues where jazz was performed.

As soon as he was old enough, the well-heeled Ertegun began to frequent jazz clubs, hobnobbing with the likes of Duke Ellington. He would invite musicians to the Turkish embassy where dinner parties would climax with performances. Segregation ensured that the performances were the only integrated shows available. Sometime in the mid-1940s, Ertegun met a married couple, Herb and Miriam Abrahamson, who matched his enthusiasm for jazz. Herb had some experience with producing records, having worked at National Records, and Ertegun proposed that they start their own label. The year in which they started, 1947, saw record sales reach 325 million in the United States. It augured well for a new venture.

Their first few releases were nondescript jazz numbers, like "The adventures of Bronco Bob." Jazz, being a genre that owed much to improvisation, had no tradition of recordings. The Atlantic label, as Ertegun and Abrahamson called it, had its first hit in 1948 with a more blues-oriented number by "Stick" McGhee, brother of Brownie, famed of the blues partnership Sonny Terry and Brownie McGhee. Bizarrely-titled "Drinkin' wine, spo-dee-o-dee," the record gave Atlantic valuable leverage with other African American artists and, over the next five years, Atlantic signed Ray Charles, Ruth Brown, Joe Turner and LaVern Baker, all of whom were to make significant contributions to the label's commercial and artistic success. Atlantic Records regularly appeared in the *Billboard* magazine's list of bestselling "race records." (*Billboard* began using the term "rhythm and blues" instead of "race" music in 1949.)

The sojourn in New Orleans was productive, though not all Atlantic signings were well disposed to the touring that was essential to backing up a record release. Professor Longhair, widely acknowledged as the most influential blues pianist of his day, refused to leave Louisiana and died penniless in 1980 shortly after the release of his *Crawfish Fiesta* album. After an initial visit, Ertegun recruited Jesse Stone as Atlantic's chief arranger and took him along to capture on paper some of the authenticity of the southern blues. Stone had been in the music business since the 1920s, working as a songwriter and, at one time, a band leader. At first, he was not a fan of blues, regarding it as too primitive and backward for his tastes; but he applied the lessons he had learned over the years and stuck to his task of trying to convey some of the authenticity of black music.

The project Ertegun and Abrahamson saw before them was to act merely as a conduit for black music. They were probably not aware of the shaping influences they would have on that music. They wanted it pure and untainted; they sought the opinion of artists rather than imposing their own; they recorded material that was unheard of outside their artists' repertoire. Yet their influence, in particular Ertegun's, was greater than either could have imagined. For instance, there is a story about Ruth Brown, who signed with Atlantic in 1950 with the intention of singing like Doris Day, the blonde actor/singer who sang light and sweet ballads for the delectation of whites. The Atlantic owners would have none of it: they made her explore her full range, ripping into blues numbers Doris Day would have shrunk from. Her breakthrough came in 1953 with the commercial success of "(Mama) He treats your daughter mean," a straightforward 12-bar sung with the kind of power few females could summon. Brown was one of many singers whose style was refined so as to make it sound rawer, more authentic, more soulful to relatively untutored white ears. And that was only one of a number of paradoxes.

Ray Charles' style was based too consciously on other artists for Atlantic's tastes. In his *Sweet Soul Music*, Peter Guralnick writes of Charles' early recordings: "Each one evinces a precise enunciation, a cool, rather brittle presence, a precocious sophistication that is virtually indistinguishable from that of a Nat Cole or Charles Brown hit of the period" (1986: 53). Charles consciously tried to emulate Cole and had some success with the approach, scoring a couple of decent-selling records on the Swing Time label, for which he signed in 1949. But he was encouraged by Ertegun and Stone to develop a more explosive approach, such as that used by a "shouter" in the black churches (the role of the shouter, who exclaims emotionally at religious worship, dates back to the Old Testament-based slave religions). Ertegun added horns to Charles' backing band, giving him a brassier sound. Charles' adaptation was memorable: after joining Atlantic in 1953, his blend of gospel emotion with blues piano thrust him to the fore of what later became known as soul. Again, Atlantic had worked the oracle, digging out talent and molding it, without losing the earthy originality that distinguished its products. Charles was once described as singing Jesus' tunes with the devil's words.

The recordings were done in an impromptu studio in Atlantic's offices. Desks were piled on one another, floorspace was cleared and recording equipment was wheeled in. Needless to say, the sounds were not polished, but that was exactly the effect desired. Ertegun was dismissive of the predominantly white recordings that were available. Crooners and balladeers, he believed, were not what the market wanted. This, remember, was at a time, when rock'n'roll had yet to materialize.

Yet, for all their commitment to authenticity, Atlantic's bosses were not averse to writing numbers for their artists. Abrahamson was experienced in record production; Ertegun learned on the wing. He learned to write songs in pretty much the same way. Bereft of decent compositions to record and without the money to buy published music for his performers, he took to being a songsmith. His technique was not dissimilar to the one later employed by Michael Jackson, who sang his numbers into a taperecorder. Finding his way into a recording booth in Times Square, Ertegun would either hum or sing his composition, take his recording to the artist and let the artist add his or her own interpretation. Artists like the Clovers, the Drifters and Joe Turner all had commercial successes written by Ertegun, or "A. Nugetre" (spell it backwards) as he sometimes used to credit himself, and his associates at Atlantic.

Ertegun worked out a novel deal with two Jewish songwriters, Jerry Leiber and Mike Stoller, who had written Big Mama Thornton's "Hound dog" in the early 1950s. They had come to Ertegun's attention through the Robins, a band that recorded on Spark Records, Leiber and Stoller's own label. Two members of the Robins became the core of a new band, the Coasters, which had a series of successful singles between 1957 and 1961. Under the terms of the agreement with Atlantic, Leiber and Stoller wrote and produced music and sold the finished product. This worked so satisfactorily for Atlantic that Ertegun later extended the arrangement to another record label in Memphis.

Nothing is guaranteed to enhance appeal more than a ban, so when Memphis' chief of police declared an Atlantic record by Clyde McPhatter too lewd to be played on jukeboxes, the company were delighted. "Honey love" actually had a tame lyric, but references to "I want it" and the like drew the wrath of some in the bible belt states. Jesse Stone's "Shake, rattle and roll," recorded for Atlantic by Joe Turner, had to be cleaned up for radio, though its double-coded text left few in doubt about its sexual meanings. Even the expurgated version contained the reference to a "one-eyed cat" who lurks in sea food stores. The number itself was less a coherent piece than a collection of old blues verses strung together.

The irony was that this particular number was one of many, many others that were plundered by rival record companies and re-recorded by white artists. Despite Atlantic's demonstrable success at slicing into the white market using black artists, the import of their enterprise was seen differently by white record executives.

So, if a black blues figure from the 1930s, like Big Joe Turner, could gain commercial respectability with a song, imagine what a white singer, no matter how mediocre, could do with it. And Bill Haley *was* mediocre. Haley and his Comets (as his all-white band was called) were an audacious project: recording poor imitations of black originals, they were promoted as forerunners of a new youth-based musical form called rock'n'roll. Their "Shake, rattle and roll," a watered-down affair, formed part of an extended-play record, which, of course, outsold Turner's many times over.

It was one of a spate of cover versions, these being copies of black recordings by white artists. The usual pattern was for the cover to eclipse the original and become a commercial success. Georgia Gibbs had a hit with "Tweedle dee" which was Atlantic artist LaVern Baker's "Tweedlee dee" minus an "e". "Shaboom" by the all-white Crewcuts started life as an Atlantic record by the Chord Cats. In retrospect, the covers were rather weak, sanitized copies and history has not served them well. Tom Dowd, who worked as sound engineer for Atlantic, was an independent operator who was often asked by Mercury and other labels to record numbers he had made first for Atlantic. And, as if to underline the blatant mimicry involved, he would actually take along the original to duplicate the sound as closely as possible.

The most blatant purveyor of what became known as "whitebread" was Pat Boone who scored hits with, among others, Fats Domino's "Ain't that a shame" and Little Richard's "Long tall Sally" and "Tutti frutti." Domino was also outdone by Ricky Nelson, who, in 1957, recorded his "I'm walking" on the same label as Domino, but with far greater commercial success.

While black writers and artists scraped along from one record to the next on independent labels, the corporations snapped up the likes of Haley and projected them as a pioneers: in 1955 Haley outsold all other records with his "Rock around the clock" (30 million copies), which was featured in the film *Blackboard Jungle*.

Other whites were not so derivative, though their efforts in the mid-1950s established something of a pattern. We might remind ourselves of Murray's point about the "disarming" of black music by white performers in their efforts to get mainstream success (1989: 86).

Atlantic, despite its integrity in relation to, not to say reliance on, black music, was not averse to to such a process. It discovered Bobby Darin and had him "render" black styles on such numbers as "Splish splash." Darin, though, had a lounge singer's demeanor and a voice that was too syrupy for Atlantic. Abrahamson, returning after a spell in military service, worked at roughening Darin, but with little success. His lack of progress may have hastened his departure from the label.

Abrahamson's temporary absence from the company's operations left a gap which Ertegun filled with Jerry Wexler, a New-York-born son of a German-Czech Jewish migrant, who joined Atlantic in 1953. Wexler's influence grew steadily and this may have had something to do with Abrahamson's decision to sell his interest in the label. Wexler was a committed eclectic: he wanted to fuse as many different genres as he could. As we saw in Chapter four, Sam Phillips had successfully fused blues music with a country and western sound in a 1954 release. Atlantic took an interest in Presley, Ertegun travelling to Memphis in 1955 in an effort to buy his contract from Sun. He could muster only $25,000 and so lost out to RCA Victor which bid $35,000.

With Presley came a whole parade of white rock'n'roll artists, like Gene Vincent, Eddie Cochran, Jerry Lee Lewis and Buddy Holly. Their backgrounds were in country, but there were obvious black influences. They were the keys to unlocking the vault of the white market. Atlantic, Chess, Sun and the other record companies that had specialized in black music had never quite prised their way in. By the mid-1950s, white singers, mostly males, eclipsed all others. But, while their success obscured the source of their music and they profited inordinately, their own exposure had the effect of priming a large and mainly white market for blacks' music. Reluctant as we might be to acknowledge it, the later rise of people like Little Richard, Bo Diddley, Chuck Berry and Fats Domino owed something to white rock'n'roll, which, in turn, owed a debt to blacks – another example of the "cultural borrowing" mentioned in Chapter one. It might have been said of white audiences in the mid-1950s that they, to use the words of Alice Walker, "want what you got, but they don't want you."

In Chapter two, we noted the emergence of gospel from its origins in the black churches of the south and how its appeal lay in participation rather than listening: it was an active performance music. So, apart from a few phonographic recordings in the 1930s, its commercial aspect was never exploited. In the 1950s, with the rise of rock'n'roll and a greater than ever interest in black music, a genuine industrialization began: gospel's emotional influences were integrated into newly popularized – and, of course, totally secular – blues to produce a beguiling synthesis.

The fortunes of black music do not interlock like the components of a puzzle cube. Neat as it would be, gospel did not coalesce easily with blues: rather, there was a frottage-like process, gospel rubbing against the uneven surface of blues music to form the basis of a new cultural expression. Segregation ensured that both gospel and blues artists had to scrape a living on what was called the "chitlin' circuit" (a term derived from chitterling, the smaller intestines of pigs, which were leftovers from whites' tables given to slaves). Playing in coloreds-only clubs and bars meant no exposure to white audiences and little possibility of anything but menial pay. Singers who had learned their trade in church halls would occasionally secularize their acts and attract the attentions of record companies. Atlantic, being a proven label specializing in black artists, was able to promote the likes of Ray Charles and Wilson Pickett, both products of church choirs. Pickett's signature screams and yelps could have been drawn straight from a revivalist meeting.

Charles' church background tutored him in gospel harmonies, structure, bar length and improvisational skills. His touring on the road with blues musicians, such as Guitar Slim, furthered his education in how to break out of a gospel manner without losing the emotion that distinguished him from all others in the 1950s. Charles drew the wrath of the church for serving up the fire and brimstone on Atlantic. But, from 1954, when he, with Jerry Wexler, made a negro spiritual into "I got a woman," Charles catalyzed a development that was to be known loosely as soul. Atlantic, thanks to Charles and the others who came under his influence, was *the* soul label.

Singing with barely controlled passion and an accompanying female chorus, the Raelettes, Charles became an unlikely standard-bearer of a new black culture, the first to wade from the tributaries into the mainstream. African American artists and the music they practised were long acknowledged as influences. Some black artists had crossed over completely: Nat King Cole and Louis Armstrong, for example, had achieved an almost perfect integration at a time when most blacks could not even drink at the same water fountain as whites. Charles was different in that he conformed to no established image.

The black artists who had made the transition, however incomplete, to the popular market did so as individuals willing to make accommodations to white tastes. They were not promoted as bearers of black culture. "Black entertainers were decorative and not necessarily emancipated figures," writes Pieterse. "The figure of the black waiter or bartender melts easily into that of the black performer: the bartender's tuxedo is the same as that of the night-club musician" (1992: 141).

Cole remained strictly within safe limits: he whitened his face specifically for his own television series, sang duets with whites and drifted easily into the mainstream. Too easily for the likes of many television viewers and sponsors of his show: the series was cancelled. Armstrong came out of the jazz age of the 1920s and1930s, when whites would happily attend New York's Cotton Club and enjoy black musicians in the knowledge that they would never have to eat in the same restaurant as them. A large avuncular man with glaring eyes and a mild manner, Armstrong endorsed laxatives as if to underline his purgative role: to rid whites of any doubts about blacks' contentment with life. Black people might be being lynched by posses of racists at a rate of 55 per year; but, while Armstrong was up there playing sidekick to Bing Crosby *et al.*, there was evidence that all was well.

In contrast to males, whose success was contingent on their being sexless and hence unthreatening, Josephine Baker was portrayed as the ultimate test of a man's libido. Erotic, outrageous and even vulgar by 1920s standards, Baker was the complete Black Venus. She lived up to this imagery, performing with a wild lack of inhibition, on one notable occasion appearing topless. Baker's natural successor was Dorothy Dandridge, who, in the 1950s, starred in several Hollywood movies, always as the lusty screen vamp. In fact she was actually a serious actor bundled into musicals such as *Carmen Jones* and *Porgy and Bess*. Frustrated at her career, she committed suicide at 42. If Dandridge struggled to escape stereotyping, Eartha Kitt embraced it, though with conniving irony. The other image available to African American females wishing to make an impression on whites was the direct descendant of slave lore, the mammy. Hattie McDaniel's portrayal in the 1939 production of *Gone with the Wind* was exemplary. In Chapter seven, we will examine how Diana Ross was able to defy both images.

But Charles was part of a cultural shake-up in the mid-1950s: he fitted no recognized category for blacks. He wrote his own music, sang it in his own style and did not ham it up for white audiences. One wonders whether the fact that he was blind was a factor in his success. Pieterse extends an idea originally suggested by Beth Day, that blacks who are "permitted" by white society to be successful are "bright children" no matter how old. Their brilliance is acknowledged, but they should not challenge the paternity of the white society that produced them and gave them their big chance. The only black male figure welcome in white society is, in this view, an emasculated one. Did Charles' blindness make him a symbolic eunuch in the mind of whites? We might ask the same question of Stevie Wonder, also blind and also possessed of a unique brilliance.

If Charles served unwittingly as a cipher for white America, it does not diminish his stature as an artist or his importance as an interpreter of music rooted in gospel culture. In 1958, he made an album entitled *The Genius of Ray Charles* and no one accused it of hyperbole. Still in his twenties, he bridged the pulpit and the bar stool. Many church leaders berated him: for them, it was sacrilege to use church music for such secular ends. And Charles would not so much praise the Lord as invoke him to express his lust for women: "Lord have mercy!" or "Hallelujah, I love her so."

"By secularizing gospel and thereby implicitly transferring the concept of transcendent salvation into the real world, Ray Charles articulated a potent political metaphor," writes Murray, perhaps exaggerating his point, "one of an attainable heaven on earth" (1989: 159). Murray believes that, in replacing the individualism of blues with the community spirit of gospel, Charles' music implicitly lauded collective action. The commercial success of Charles' records and his appearances on national television were certainly accompanied by a rising sense of confidence among many sectors of the black population. The civil rights movement was in its ascent and the dream of the dissolution of segregation and drastic improvements in the conditions of blacks was turning into a possibility. It was not Charles, but one of his contemporaries, Sam Cooke, another former gospel singer, who was to record the anthem of the time, his "A change is gonna come." Interestingly, both Charles and Cooke (who was also damned by the church) lost their black followings as their commercial power grew; their careers were sustained by their massive appeal to whites, which, in turn, was assisted by the promotional efforts of white companies, RCA in Cooke's case. Charles went to Los Angeles after a heroin bust in 1958 and he left Atlantic six months after the release of his "What'd I say" in 1959 to sign a deal with ABC-Paramount .

In leaving Atlantic, Charles gave up the personal attention for an arrangement that included greater royalty rates, profit-sharing, a production deal and part-ownership of his own masters; he eventually got his own record label with the benefit of distribution through the ABC network. It was, in its day, a staggeringly good deal and one arguably not bettered by a black performer until Stevie Wonder struck his megadeal with Motown. Charles found unprecedented success as he shuttled between gospel-soul and country numbers. He became, as Hatch and Millward put it, "acceptable to country music followers and large numbers of the white adult record-buyers" (1990: 90).

Earlier in the book, I described the African American churches that took shape in the first part of the nineteenth century as a cultural matrix, allowing the development of later forms. The influence of the church is evident in the music of all those who followed Charles, including a miscellany of white musicians specializing in soul – and these proliferated in the 1960s. Atlantic, having Charles and a clutch of others on its books, was very much at the fore. Ertegun and Wexler sensed the commercial potential of the emergent genre, but were also aware that the days of rough-and-ready recordings designed to capture the aura of the blues were approaching an end. Production played an increasingly significant part, especially when bigger sounds, incorporating brass and strings became popular.

Ertegun and Wexler preempted the new emphasis by linking with another record label, Stax, which had started business in an East Memphis garage in 1957 and later graduated to an unoccupied movie theater. The business relationship between the two record companies turned out to be an artistic wedding made in heaven. Atlantic had the infrastructure, know-how and distribution outlets to make commercially successful music; Stax had artists capable of redefining black culture.

Like Atlantic, Stax specialized in black artists. Also, like Atlantic, it was owned by whites. Prior to the link-up, its main clientele was black. It made perfect sense for Stax to segue into what was a bone fide mass market with a seeming appetite for black music. In 1962, when Stax's house band Booker T. and the MGs, which had both black and white members, had an international million-seller with their instrumental "Green onions," it signalled the start of the label's extraordinarily productive coalition with Atlantic.

Before this, the company had struggled. Jim Stewart and his sister Estelle Axton (hence St + Ax from their family names) founded the company as Satellite Records, but did not produce any hit records. From Atlantic's point of view, Stax had an impressive assembly of black singers and mainly, though not exclusively, white musicians, one of whom, Steve Cropper, became one of the most celebrated soul guitarists of his time. Cropper and Donald Dunn were the two white members of Booker T. and the MGs (for Memphis Group), which worked for the

Stax studio, and they appeared as the house band for dance gigs at the movie theater. The operation also had a retail record store attached to it. Stewart, as producer, would make records at night and sell them from the store during the day. At the same time, he managed to hold down a regular day job at a bank.

The philosophy behind Stax was to record what Stewart called community music: not the type of slick black music that was beginning to emerge from Detroit, nor the blues which was too rambling and untidy; but a sound that genuinely reflected what the black people of Memphis were playing. It was a sharp, electric sound, unfussy but with plenty of the ardent power associated with gospel. Bluesmen appeared – incorrectly, as it turned out – to be a dying breed. Rock'n'roll had brought in a new order. Stax wanted to build on the production techniques of rock'n'roll, yet create something redolent of black authenticity.

Both Stax and Atlantic had made their mark artistically; but neither had made the all-important crossover. At the time of the link-up, Charles was still the only black artist who had achieved anything resembling mass popularity without either camouflaging his blackness or conforming to a trite stereotype. Stax's vision was not so grand as Atlantic's. But Charles' success had convinced Ertegun and Wexler that their market was shifting as quickly as the country itself. America was in flux.

Blacks were becoming impatient: there was little evidence of the brave new world promised by the *Brown* decision of 1954. Far from ushering in a new era of integrated schools, the case had elicited a violent backlash from whites prepared to battle for the maintenance of segregated facilities. The intransigence of whites was often dramatic, as in Little Rock, Arkansas, where the National Guard had to be called in to restore order after state government refused to comply with the federal government's directive to desegregate its schools. In 1957, state governor Orval Faubus came into conflict with President Dwight Eisenhower after Elizabeth Eckford, a black student, tried to enrol at an all-white central high school. Inflamed by the action, whites thronged about the school in an effort to prevent her. State troops were eventually sent in to ensure her safety. Eckford approached the school amid shouts of "Lynch her!" from the white mob. It was one of many violent incidents of the late 1950s and it illustrated the ferocity with which whites clung to racist institutions.

Schooling was one of the two main issues of the day, the other being voting rights. For years, authorities had used many devious means to keep blacks from exercising their right to vote. Until 1954, the Mississippi state constitution stipulated that, to qualify to vote, a person had to able to "read or interpret" that document. Because more and more blacks had been learning to read, however, the state legislature changed the requirement from "read or interpret" to "read *and* interpret." That provision allowed white registrars to judge arbitrarily whether a black person met the test. Needless to say, blacks usually failed. There were instances of blacks with doctorates failing the test. A central effort of the civil rights movement was to encourage African Americans to vote in defiance of white attempts to prevent them. In 1962, a coalition of groups came together to form the Council of Federated Organizations, which had two goals: to demonstrate that, despite racist claims, blacks did want to vote; and to assist blacks in the practice of casting their vote.

Between 1960 and 1962, about 50,000 people had in some way contributed to the civil rights campaign, either sitting in at segregated lunch counters, standing in at movie theaters, kneeling in at churches or even wading in at beaches. There were about 3,600 arrests in an 18-month period. As the momentum gathered, more and more whites became involved. Without doubt, the most radical faction of the whole civil rights movement was the Student Nonviolent Coordinating Committee (SNCC), established in 1960, which became a significant force in its own right. The early 1960s were years of inquiry. Some were asking: what will it take before blacks gain genuine equality? Others: will blacks ever gain equality? Still others: why should blacks expect equality?

It was against this kind of background that Atlantic and Stax made their forays into a market they believed was changing. Severe as the retaliation against civil rights was, there was still support among young whites. Whites marched with civil rights protesters, sat in with them, and, in many cases, suffered with them. The nation was dividing; evidence of this was on television screens virtually every night. Young whites were detaching themselves from old allegiances and aligning themselves with blacks.

If Ertegun had been the brains of Atlantic in the 1950s, Wexler took that mantle in the early 1960s. He first became aware of Stewart and Axton through a number called "'Cause I love you" by Rufus and Carla Thomas, released in 1960, which sold over 15,000 copies in the south. Atlantic and Satellite, as the original Stewart/Axton label was called, shared a distributor in Memphis and they were able to come up with an arrangement whereby Atlantic leased the record for $1,000; that is, Wexler bought the master tape, pressed more records and paid Stewart and Axford a tiny amount for every copy sold. Soon after, Carla Thomas had a national hit record of her own with "Gee whiz." Atlantic was delighted: Wexler could enforce his agreement to distribute all Satellite product and Stewart was in no position to resist. Stax was not big enough to expand without a distribution deal and Atlantic was able to offer that and much more.

Wexler's method was to mine for talent in the north, then send his best singers south to work with Stewart, Cropper and others at Stax. Wexler eventually moved most of the recording out of Memphis to Muscle Shoals, Alabama, previously known for country music. Almost all the session musicians here were white. But the early Memphis sessions proved to be paradigms of soul. In particular, the work of former church shouter Wilson Pickett established Atlantic/Stax as a world force.

Pickett was a singer with a New-York-based band called the Falcons before 1965 when he moved to Memphis, where he met with Cropper. Together they wrote and made a number called "In the midnight hour." According to Cropper, they threw the song together "In about an hour"; according to Pickett, he alone wrote the song (Hirshey, 1994: 309). Like many of the dealings of the independent labels, there were disputes over authorship. Wexler contrived to give the number a distinctive backbeat.

The worldwide success of "In the midnight hour" encouraged Wexler to use Cropper with Pickett again. "634–5789" was another hit; this time Cropper had written with African American Eddie Floyd, who had hit records in his own right, the biggest being "Knock on wood." Pickett's brace was complemented by a series of hit records, including "Land of 1000 dances," and "Mustang Sally," though none matched the sales of the first hit. "In the midnight hour" effectively did what Ertegun and Wexler had planned when they combined with Stax: it changed the composition of their potential market. Young whites were stirred by black music that was not as somber as blues, nor as joyous as gospel: this was music they could dance to. Yet it still had that element of pained artistry seemingly unique to blacks. It was a quality notoriously difficult to pin down or define. It seemed to derive from the shrieking audible at black churches and the continual references to "Mercy" and "Good God, ya'll" suggested something confessional: pouring out one's soul.

Other artists followed Pickett from New York to work with Cropper. The most lastingly successful was Aretha Franklin, daughter of a Detroit-based clergyman, who had been performing professionally since the age of 14, but with little recognition. Her periods with Chess and then Columbia proved fruitless, but Wexler took her to Muscle Shoals in 1966 and assigned her to producer Tom Dowd, who roughened up her previously soft edges. Like Pickett, Franklin had started her singing in church, but she recorded show tunes, ballads and even Al Jolson's "Rock-a-bye your baby with a Dixie melody" before moving to Atlantic. Her much-lauded "natural" voice was actually a fastidiously refined product; she was known to make detailed notes as part of her preparations, even jotting down when to include her "spontaneous" exclamations, like "Wow!" There was some irony in her love songs which were reinterpreted in such a way as to give them historical and social value: 1968's "Think," for example, featured a bracing appeal for "freedom," seemingly on behalf of a black population seeking precisely that. And her 1967 version of Otis Redding's "Respect" was widely read as a demand for property often denied blacks.

The Atlantic roster grew, with Ben E. King and Don Covay contributing to a genre that became recognized as perhaps the most essential of essential black musics. Given the composition of the market, the status was conferred mainly by whites. Most of the songs were written or co-written by Cropper, who also produced many of the numbers, with Wexler producing others, and white musicians backed the singers on virtually all the Atlantic/Stax collaborations. White producer Rick Hall was responsible for most of the Muscle Shoals output. The product was groundbreaking in its day and stands the test of time, as is evidenced by countless soul acts that still tour the USA and Europe.

Soul was difficult to categorize musically. Its lyrics were no different from those of other music: eulogies to women, boasts about male sexual prowess, exhortations to dance. Musically, there were as many differences among soul tracks as there were between them and others. What gave soul its distinct quality was the vocalization. Atlantic's singers were mostly familiar with gospel and were encouraged to use this in their inflexions, modulation, shading and progression: uninhibited, they would approach some numbers with a romping bravado, others with pathos. Whereas many other black artists, particularly from the blues genre, would sound imperious and aloof, soul singers conveyed the sense of vulnerability associated with church singers submitting themselves to God. Exclamations, yelps and whoops were tossed into numbers, giving the impression that the singers were delving deep into themselves to find the words, failing, then just despairing to the Lord. After Pickett's success, Atlantic singers grew even more expressive.

This sometimes led to overwrought performances. Two artists who exemplified this were Otis Redding and James Brown, both now enshrined in the soul canon. Redding, toward the end of his life, was an international star, who made full use of his status. Famous for forgetting his lyrics and just improvising, Redding admitted to lack of preparation, his belief being that soul was "the way you feel." His histrionic wails and exultations may have sounded soulful, but they were more likely ad-libs when he forgot the words. Even Wexler accused him of "oversouling," as he called it.

Redding, who was from Macon, Georgia, was introduced to Wexler by a white impresario, Phil Walden, who had managed black r'n'b bands since he was a teenager. Walden built a complete organization with scouting divisions and a record company, Capricorn Records, which he founded with Wexler. He had managed Redding as a solo artist and, before that, as a singer in Little Willie and the Mighty Panthers. Walden kept Redding busy at blacks-only clubs, but not busy enough to go professional fulltime. So, he worked at all kinds of jobs prior to 1962 when Walden asked him to drive him and one of his bands to the Memphis studios of Stax. While on a break, Redding dropped on a microphone and gave a sample of what he could do. Cropper and Booker T. were in attendance and heard enough to convince them that Redding had something to offer. They cut the first of 17 straight singles and started Redding's career.

Redding specialized in ballads, like "That's how strong my love is" and "Pain in my heart" without much success. Then, in 1965, Wexler decided to up his tempo with a track called "Respect." By then, "soul" had become a recognized category in the music papers and the single sold well enough to make an appearance in the soul charts. Unlike Pickett and a handful of others before him, Redding was working on a scarred surface. Soul was no longer the preserve of Atlantic/Stax: a rival, more commercially successful record company in Detroit was grinding out black music with the consistency of a factory and many English bands were retexturing black music and calling it their own. The Animals were adept at this. Many early 1960s Beatles tracks had r'n'b or Motown origins. The Rolling Stones' early recordings included Chuck Berry's "Come on," Slim Harpo's "I'm a king bee" and Muddy Waters' "I just wanna make love to you." Redding symbolically returned the compliment when he recorded a fierce version of the Stones' "Satisfaction" in 1966.

By 1967, Redding was one of the top selling recording artists in the world. He far outsold any other black recording artist and could lay legitimate claim to being the top male singer in Britain, soul being immensely popular with white British youth. Ray Charles had been the first black singer to cross over, but his exposure was never as great as Redding's. The 1967 Monterey Festival confirmed Redding as an international pop star, not just a soul singer. At the height of his popularity, Redding was killed in a plane crash.

During his life, Redding was regarded as the premier soul artist and, in terms of record sales and large concert appearances, he actually was. He was succeeded by James Brown, who, while no match for Redding in vocal emotionality, could physically outperform any artist. Brown became known for his theatrical delerium:

he would thrill audiences by going into mock ecstasies, falling to the floor and shaking while the band played. If Redding's gift was to disclose his feelings through his voice, Brown's was to achieve much the same effect through his body.

Like Redding, Brown was a southerner, hailing from Augusta, Georgia. His early musical career was interrupted by a spell in prison, but he resumed in the 1950s, opening for bluesmen and, later, rock'n'roll bands. Among the many white-owned independent labels was King, based in Cincinnatti and run by Syd Nathan and his A & R man Ralph Bass. They recorded Brown's "Please, please, please" which sold well enough for Nathan and Bass to extend Brown and his band, the Famous Flames, a contract. This was the subject of a later dispute which went all the way to the Supreme Court. Brown, having established himself with Nathan's label, wanted to move to Mercury, one of the six major corporate record companies. Nathan contended that he was still contractually bound to King. The odd ruling was that: yes, as a singer, he was, *but* as the leader of a band, he was free to record with Mercury. Polygram later bought both companies and so restored Brown whole.

Brown defied time, extending his active career over three decades. His *oeuvre* was reappraised in the late 1980s when rap music came to the fore: one of Brown's techniques of rupturing the rhythm, or cutting, became a staple of hiphop. But, in the 1960s, Brown's contribution was different. As Cornel West reflects in his *Keeping Faith*: "James Brown's 'Say It Loud, I'm Black and I'm Proud' became an exemplary – and healthy – expression of the cultural reversal of alienating Anglo-American ideals of beauty and behavior." Yet, this reversal "was principally a 'new' black middle class phenomenon" (1993: 283). West believes that most working class African Americans were listening to the romantic love songs being produced on the Motown label, rather than the craggy soul sounds of Brown *et al*.

A different view is offered by Ben Sidran in *Black Talk*: "'Soul' music was important not just as a musical idiom, but also as a black-defined, black-accepted means of *actively* involving the mass base of Negroes. It was, in fact, the 'self-definition' Stokely Carmichael was to call for later through cultural action rather than verbalized terms" (1995: 126).

Exactly which sections of the African American population were actively involved in soul is uncertain. Soul definitely enabled a fuller participation in the entertainment business for black people, who were previously admitted to the mainstream as caucasian affectors or stereotypes, albeit gifted ones. Soul singers did not conform to either of these. And they did play important parts in introducing black music to an international mass audience. This may have been, indeed probably was, the main agendum of Wexler and company. In keeping to this agendum, they swapped old stereotypes for a brand new one: the Soul Man, visceral, virile, but a little bit vacuous. Personifying these characteristics was Stax's most durable performer, Isaac Hayes.

There is a song on Isaac Hayes' 1971 album *Black Moses* called "Ike's rap 2." It is the first passage of a medley and lasts a couple of minutes. A dull descending bass and organ surrender to ascending strings and a mellifluous piano before

Hayes' throaty voice, crushed and penitent, breaks through, pleading to an imaginary woman to whom so many of his songs were addressed: "I can't sleep," he tells her, "Can't even eat." It is pure Hayes: submissive, contrite, yet always terribly dangerous, sexually and physically. In the 1990s, lines from the track were sampled independently by Tricky and Portishead. They were by no means the only fragments of Hayes' work to be used in the 1990s; he probably runs James Brown a close second as the most sampled artist of all time.

Like virtually all other soul singers, Hayes began singing in church. Son of a Tennessee sharecropper, Hayes as a child lived with relatives in Memphis. He toured the churches of the American south, singing bass with a gospel ensemble called the Morning Stars. He then transferred to Calvin Valentine and the Swing Cats, a blues band, and then to the Teen Tones, a vocal group specializing in doowop (a cappella music sung in close harmony by groups of black males). His next venture was an r'n'b group called Sir Isaac and the Doodads. Chastened after a flop recording in 1962, he took a job with Stax as a session musician playing keyboards. The first session he worked augured well: he backed Otis Redding in 1965 when he recorded "Respect," "Satisfaction" and "I've been loving you too long," all commercial successes.

At Stax, Hayes met and began an artistically productive relationship with David Porter, with whom he wrote and produced literally hundreds of numbers, including the hits of Sam and Dave, such as "Soul man" and "Hold on, I'm coming." Hayes and Porter formed a prolific partnership pushing out an average of 26 albums a year. They were the force behind much of Stax's work between 1965 and 1970. Hayes made a solo album which bombed, but, in 1969 he tried again with *Hot Buttered Soul*. By now, the Stax sound had been copied, then the copies had been copied to the point where it had become tiresome. Hayes' efforts were adventurously different: his numbers were suave, seductive and, as the title of his album indicated, smooth. In particular, his long and meandering version of white country singer Glen Campbell's "By the time I get to Phoenix" evidenced an artist enmeshed in two genres: it includes a long rap passage that almost anticipates developments twenty years later. The album is generously garnished with Hayes' love-play monologues directed at a woman he is about to fill with delight. It is immodest, erotic, even priapic.

Two albums on, Hayes was invited to write the score for the Gordon Parks movie *Shaft*, which was to become the most successful of what are now called blaxploitation films. The ingredients of blaxploitation were basic: tough black cop, decorative but brainless women, dangerous dope dealers, lots of good-humored gore and even better-humored sex. Whatever Hayes did after 1971, he will always be remembered as the man who played and sang the *Shaft* theme. Hayes won an Oscar for writing the film score. In the movie, John Shaft, played by Richard Roundtree, was the perfect bad mother: slickly macho and not given to long-term relationships; a line in the song described him (recalling James Brown) as a "sex machine." Hayes, because of his stud caricature, was linked with this image. He played to it, appearing in films, like *Truck Turner* and *Three Tough Guys*, and tv shows, like *The Rockford Files*, as pretty much the same type, usually laden with gold jewelry. As Donald Bogle puts it in his encyclopedia *Blacks in American Film and Television*: "Hayes decided he wanted *to be Shaft*.

And therein his problem may have begun" (1988: 223). It was as if an old stereotype had returned in a parodic form; except the blaxploitation films were meant to be serious.

Hayes' career went into sharp ascent at the same time as Stax went into descent. In fact, without Hayes, Stax was doomed. His last album for the label was *Joy* released in 1973 to coincide with his appearances in two concert movies *Wattstax* and *Save the Children*. When Hayes left in 1974 to sign for ABC Records, Stax slid into oblivion, going bankrupt the following year. The dangers of becoming too tightly linked to blaxploitation became apparent when Hayes, after huge success in the early 1970s, nosedived into bankruptcy. Several comeback attempts failed, though, in 1995, he released his best-received album for years, *Branded*.

Like the social context in which he operated, Hayes was alive with menace. He revived the old stereotype of the buck nigger possessed of exceptional sexual hardware and the willingness to use it, and added to this an anger that seemed to reflect the changing mood of black people. Shortly before the assassination of Martin Luther King in 1968 at a motel that Hayes had frequently used, incidentally, many African Americans had turned away from his policy of gradual, nonviolent strategies of accommodation. Instead, many became more receptive to the messages of black power advocates, like Bobby Seales and Huey Newton, and leaders of the Nation of Islam, including Elijah Muhammad and King's *alter ego* Malcolm X. King, it seemed to some, was striving for an impossible goal: to gain blacks entry into a culture that simply did not want them. Both the message and the man were alien to them. As Wilson Moses observes in *Black Messiahs and Uncle Toms* "They did not see how it would be possible for any self-respecting black man to live in the South without carrying a gun and using it at least once a day" (1993: 209). After King's death, living anywhere seemed to carry much the same condition.

Hayes was *bad*. For this he deserved respect. He cut an image perfectly suited to the times: shaven head, draped in gold chains, he sneered instead of smiling and looked like he fed on young children. When LeRoi Jones wrote "soul is a form of social aggression," he could have had Hayes in mind (1995: 219). Hayes' danger was implicit, of course; he never spoke out against white control, nor applauded the efforts of the Black Panthers. His music, far from espousing Black Power, was mostly about love, the stock-in-trade of most soul. Yet, somehow, he captured the spirit of badness when it was a positive virtue. Who wanted to behave in a way acceptable to whites? For many blacks, whites would never accept blacks, anyway; so they might just as well expose, even exaggerate their intentions to get even.

Riots in practically every major US city in the 1965–67 period had signalled a different mood in the ghettos. The rise of Malcolm X and the Nation of Islam, which preached separatism and black independence, was further evidence of an anger that was spreading across America. Without ever endorsing this, Hayes was able to capitalize on its dramatic possibilities. He looked and sounded as if he carried that gun and used it daily.

As interest in soul faded, so did Hayes' career. His albums sold less and film parts dried up. He went broke. Yet, such was his name and his synonymity with the "bad motherfucker," that he enjoyed a renascent period in the early 1990s in the wake of the mannered militancy that accompanied the commodification of Malcolm X.

In October 1967, Atlantic announced an "agreement in principle" with Warner Brothers–Seven Arts: under the terms of the agreement, Atlantic would be absorbed into the media conglomerate for $20 million plus stock options. Ertegun and Wexler were to stay on, but as employees rather than owners. The Stax liaison ended. It was a sharp blow for Stax, as it meant that all Jim Stewart's and Estelle Axton's records and the unreleased Stax masters were owned by Warners. "In their initial excitement at being hooked up with Atlantic, I don't think it even occurred to them to question the eventual ownership of the masters," observes Guralnick in *Sweet Soul Music* (1986). Stewart, who did most of the negotiating with Atlantic, expressed surprise that his life's artistic and commercial investment was being ripped from him. Wexler admitted to Guralnick that "it was a loaded deal" but: "The name of the game was whatever the traffic would bear" (1986: 357).

Stax had no leverage: just its good name. Negotiations with Atlantic proved unproductive and eventually Stax decided to sell its publishing company East/West to Gulf + Western for $2.88 million plus G + W stock. This caused a further rift inside Stax as Stewart wanted 20 percent of the stock granted to Axton and himself to be devolved to Al Bell, who had been faithful to him throughout the label's history; Axton refused on the grounds that she wanted to give up some of her shares to Steve Cropper. In the end, Bell and Cropper received 10 percent ownership of the publishing. By May 1968, a deal with G + W's Paramount Music Division was finalized and Stax began to issue records again, no longer independent, no longer linked with Atlantic and, of course, bereft of Otis Redding. But it adapted: with Axton sliding away, Stewart and Bell became driving forces, "aided" by the ambiguous presence of Johnny Baylor (some believe he was more a hindrance than a help), who joined Stax after he clinched a distribution deal for his label Koko and became an increasingly strong influence in the administration of the organization.

Some of the low-key strategies that had characterized early Stax went by the wayside as Stewart embraced the corporate approach, at one point staging a huge sales convention in Memphis that would have been unthinkable in the days of Pickett and Redding. Hayes' arrival was a case of perfect timing and, as we have seen, his input became crucial to Stax's existence in the early 1970s. Ironically perhaps, his *Hot Buttered Soul* was recorded when Hayes was under contract as a writer only, not as an artist. He agreed to sign a contract, but Stax's usual production deal was not operable at the time of the cut, and production credits, which were ordinarily shared by six producers, did not apply. This meant that the usual producers got nothing.

In 1970s, the Stax story took another turn when Stewart and Bell borrowed money from Deutsche Grammophon and repurchased the company from G + W. But, by 1972, Stewart had tired of the operation and Bell, with help from Columbia, bought him out. With Atlantic moving out of the soul territory and into the domain of white American bands, like Vanilla Fudge, and British rock bands such as Led Zeppelin, Stax remained one of the leading purveyors of black music. While its roster could not match that of Motown, which boasted among others the Temptations, the Miracles, and Martha and the Vandellas, Stax had Hayes, the Staple Singers, Johnnie Taylor and the Soul Children to keep its album sales up. It also sprung subsidiary labels, one of which recorded the first album of comic Richard Pryor, *That Nigger's Crazy*.

While Bell was the titular head of Stax, we should not equate his position with that of Berry Gordy, another African American head of a record label who had been uncompromising in his plan to stay independent of the corporations; at least until 1988. Bell established a distribution arrangement with Columbia, in which he received $6 million as a low interest loan for "expansion." He then used some of this money to buy out Stewart, but found it expedient to keep Stewart on as president, presumably for the sake of continuity. Bell's contact at Columbia was Clive Davis, who also set up the deal behind the *Wattstax* movie of 1973. Bell may not have held the financial reins, but the arrangement was so weighted in Stax's favor it was almost too good to be true. In fact, it was too good to be true. Stax was paid on products delivered, not sales: the more units it made, the more money it made. Whether the records sold or not, Stax benefited to the tune of $2 per album.

The peculiarity of this agreement did not come fully to light until spring 1973 when Davis was dismissed and CBS reappraised the situation, deciding that $1.20 per album was a more realistic figure. Angered by the reduction, Bell claimed the spirit of the agreement with Davis had been violated, though he had no document to support it. Within months, the Internal Revenue Service began an investigation into Stax's financial operations. This revealed lavish amounts of money being spent on salaries and homes for staff and artists and on signing fees. The disclosure was quickly followed by news of a second investigation, this time into the activities of two Stax vice-presidents. Bell reacted by announcing the start of a new Truth label that would be completely independent of Columbia.

Hayes' departure was the end for Stax. For long, the label's main bread-winner, Hayes was moved to sue when a $270,000 check bounced. The financial miasma at Stax was now fully apparent. A federal grand jury examined Stax's books and prevented it from distributing independently of Columbia. Their staff stopped getting paid. The company's bank, Union Planters' National Bank, propped up the label, audited Stax and concluded that it appeared to generate up to $14 million per annum in revenues. Expenses seemed to be accounting for all of that and then some. At this point, Stewart re-entered the fray: he had the strongest emotional investment in the label, having co-founded it sixteen years before, and was prepared to plunge his personal funds (estimated at $4–6 million) into Stax in a rescue attempt. "I never cut my losses. I had plenty of money, I was wealthy," Stewart told Guralnick. "I just lost everything' (1986: 391).

It got even uglier: on September 8, 1975, Bell was indicted, along with an employee of the Union Planters' National Bank, for "conspiring to obtain more than $18 million in fraudulent bank loans." Bell was acquitted, but the bank's employee, who was already serving time for another conviction, was found guilty on two counts. Stax was collapsing around him and Bell fled to Little Rock,

Arkansas, where he earned a living as a freelance producer. Stewart saw it through to the bitter end, finally arriving at the studio on January 12, 1976 to find himself locked out; a federal bankruptcy court had ordered Stax's closure. Also in 1976, Hayes filed for bankruptcy, listing debts of $6–9 million.

By bizarre coincidence, Axton, who had bailed out early and kept some money, struck gold in the same year. As she approached her seventieth birthday, she produced a novelty record featuring Donald-Duck-style quacks and a silly chorus. The track was "Disco duck" and it sold six million worldwide. Soul it wasn't.

Murray believes that: "The black entertainer succeeds with the white audience either by embodying an aspect of blackness with which that audience feels comfortable, or else by appearing almost tangential to the black community: thus rendered unaffiliated, 'universal'" (1989: 79). Soul artists succeeded via the former route: by possessing and articulating a special quality that only blacks could have. White soul was an oxymoron. It was often said that soul was a feeling; if you did not feel it, you could not sing it. "White is then not 'right,' as the old blues had it," writes Jones, "but a liability, since the culture of white precludes the possession of the Negro 'soul'" (1995: 219).

Yet, questions remain. The mysterious origins of the term have never been adequately explicated. "Race music"/blues/r'n'b/soul seemed to belong to the same continuum, the next stage of which was funk. Certainly, there are some continuities, though the discontinuities are arguably more important. Sidran argues that soul constituted a break with other musical genres. "It was one origin of a cultural self-improvement program," he claims, adding that: "It was armed with the confidence of this new positive attitude that the black culture had emerged from its underground status in America to confront a white authority structure already beleaguered with negative and repressive infighting" (1995: 126–27).

We can accept this, yet add further observations about the synchrony of soul and social upheavals of the 1960s. Ertegun and Wexler were skilful operators as well as devotees of black music. Their contribution was not only in finding talent, but in surrounding it with the right musicians, refining it, producing it, packaging it and selling it. It is not clear whether "soul" was originally anything more than a brilliant marketing ploy designed to advance a positive attribute of black people at an appropriate moment in history. It was after all a time when the civil rights movement was holding a mirror to America, reflecting aspects of itself and its history that were painful to acknowledge. "The music was interpreted by listeners in the idealistic sixties as an honest and artistically authentic expression of a Black musical and cultural aesthetic," writes Paul Friedlander, in his book, *Rock and Roll: A social history.* "Paradoxically, this music was produced by an integrated studio band and by white-owned labels" (1996: 172).

And the paradox has other dimensions. In attributing to black artists a "gift" not accessible to whites, did the likes of Wexler, Stewart, Nathan and the whole entourage of whites who promoted soul create an "other"? Whites have been fascinated by otherness. "The allure of the exotic is fundamental to the appeal blues culture holds for the mainstream," writes Lieberfeld, whose work on the commodification of blues we touched on in Chapter three (1995: 219). In listening to blues, whites are made to feel "party to something primal and uninhibited," he argues. We might broaden his point to include many other musical forms, before and after blues, all of which had the effect of insinuating whites into a world which was at once strange but entrancing, perilous but beckoning.

In *Unthinking Eurocentrism*, Ella Shohat and Robert Stam write of the process that underlay this and other maneuvers: "animalization" was originally part of the colonialists' attempts to make the differences between conquering whites and those whom they conquered seem natural, rather than cultural. "Animalization forms part of the larger, more diffuse mechanism of naturalization: the reduction of the cultural to the biological, the tendency to associate the colonized with the vegetative and the instinctual rather than with the learned and the cultural". The mechanism is not confined to the past. "The animalizing trope surreptitiously haunts present-day media discourse," write Shohat and Stam (1994: 138).

Soul was helped to its legendary status by the prime movers of the black culture industry, ably abetted by artists eager to advance their careers. It was not something that could be learned, nor was it something available to whites, not in the 1960s anyway. Presumably then it was natural and specific to African Americans. Looked at this way, soul was as much part of the animalization favored by nineteenth century colonialists to justify their superiority over all the peoples they conquered. By emphasizing the natural or instinctive worth of the conquered, they derogated their cultural or intellectual value. Soul, like the "race music" that preceded it, made sense only in opposition to white music and the cerebral qualities it was thought to contain.

Chapter six

Furthest from
the Money

WILSON JEREMIAH MOSES has written of Nat Turner, the inspirer and leader of the 1831 slave rebellion, that, at the apogee of his influence, he had reached "an advanced stage of acculturation." The phrase comes from Moses' book *Black Messiahs and Uncle Toms*. "The basis of Turner's control over the other blacks," argues Moses, "was his understanding of the dominant culture, his mastery of the white man's language and religion, symbolized by his ability to read and interpret the Bible" (1993: 64). Turner's leverage derived from his ability to move chameleon-like between two cultures. And this was made possible by his *understanding* of whites.

Berry Gordy also had a handle on white culture. He also understood it well enough to sense the market possibilities of producing black music and selling it to whites. Taking an $800 loan, Gordy turned it into a culture industry that realized $61 million when he sold it to the MCA corporation in 1988. In the process, he became the first African American with serious clout in the black culture industry.

Gordy had power, but he was certainly not the first African American entrepreneur to trade in culture. Prior to his ascent, many other blacks had tried their hand at businesses specializing in music. By way of a prologue to Gordy's enterprise, we will trace some early African American efforts at exploiting the commercial potential of black music.

The improbable success of impresarios such as Charles Hicks during the second half of the nineteenth century was due to the popularity of black minstrel shows. We saw in Chapter three how fortunes faded in the early 1900s. Sherman Dudley was a performer who transferred from the stage to the offices: in 1913, he started his own booking agency, specializing in black acts. Even the stars of the minstrelsy were dropping out of showbusiness for lack of work. Dudley's mission was to create a circuit of seven theaters on the east coast and rotate his acts around them. As he held the leases on the theaters and handled the booking of the acts, he controlled a virtually self-contained operation, at least until 1919 when he linked up with white theater-owners in an attempt to widen the scope of the circuit.

In the 1920s, W. C. Handy and Harry H. Pace were among a number of black entrepreneurs who began their own sheet music companies, then expanded into other branches, such as record labels. Handy began his career as a black minstrel in the 1890s. The troupe in which he worked seems to have inspired him in his later projects. Robert Toll, who interviewed Handy for his book *Blacking Up*, explains: "Emphasizing their authenticity as Negroes and claiming to be exslaves, black minstrels became the acknowledged minstrel experts at portraying plantation material" (1974: 196). He points out that the claim was not necessarily accurate, as black minstrels, to be commercially successful, too often resorted to the kinds of stereotype popularized by whites. But, for Handy and other ambitious African Americans, "Minstrelsy was one of the few opportunities for mobility" (1974: 223). Of his experience in the minstrels, Handy told Toll: "It had thrown me into contact with a wistful but aspiring generation of dusky singers and musicians. It had taught me a way of life I still consider the only one for me" (1974: 229).

His performing days over, Handy went on to trade on his showbusiness expertise, partnering Pace in publishing and booking. We saw in Chapter three that Pace owned the Black Swan Phonograph Company which sold itself on being the authentic black music record company, completely owned and staffed by black people and with exclusively black artists. It was, according to its own advertising, the "only bonafide Racial Company making talking machine records." The company was based in New York and handled the pressing of its own records at the Pace Phonograph Manufacturing Corporation.

Pace had been involved in civil rights struggles, having joined the NAACP shortly after the organization's founding in 1910. Already established in banking and insurance, he sensed the potential of a black-owned company when he underwrote the sheet music venture. The principals of the record industry, Victor, Paramount and Emerson, showed little or no interest in black artists.

Pace's Black Swan, like Gordy's company, was ultimately sold to a white-owned record corporation, in this case Paramount (the deal was concluded in 1924), a move motivated by the lack of a distribution network, itself a problem shared by Gordy in the early years of his company's history.

We noticed earlier how the blues record industry was laid waste in the 1940s and reborn in the 1950s. The rebirth was brought about by a number of factors, not least of which was the zeal of white businesses to capitalize on an emerging African American market. But the record industry also provided opportunities for black prospective entrepreneurs. Nelson George, in his book *The Death of Rhythm & Blues*, writes that: "One of the things that defined the R & B world, one that separated it from most other American businesses, was the ability of blacks to form businesses and profit from a product their own people created" (1988: 31). He gives potted histories of two ventures, one started by Don Robey, a smalltime wheeler-dealer, whose businesses began thriving after he started Peacock Records in 1949. Renowned as a ruthless, strictly-business type, he had no ambitions worthier than earning a pile of money; and he achieved that, often to the chagrin of his artists – one of whom accused Robey of cheating him out of royalties and received a kick to the body so powerful it gave him a hernia. The artist was Little Richard; there is no account of his complaining a second time.

In *The Life and Times of Little Richard, The Quasar of Rock*, Charles White quotes Richard on Robey: "He was a black guy that looked like a white guy . . . He was so possessive. He would control the very breath that you breathed." Robey regarded all his artists in the same way.

Less successful, in fact a commercial failure, was Bobby Robinson, who kept all sorts of music-related businesses nested one within another. Robinson's career is a catalog of missed opportunities: at one time or another he either had or was offered contracts with Gladys Knight, King Curtis, Otis Redding, Lee Dorsey and Grandmaster Flash, all of whom became stars. His Red Robin label boasted many recognizable names, but most of them achieved their status with other companies. Aesthetically, Red Robin products were solid: Robinson had an ear for the doowop outfits that proliferated in the 1950s and, while the records themselves sold respectably, few artists in this genre established an identity. Robinson's impatience and reluctance to work through an artist's lean periods contributed to his own leanness and his company, though long-running, never ranked alongside Atlantic, Chess, Sun or, for that matter, Peacock.

Walter "Dootsie" Williams was the leader of the Harlem Dukes band in the 1940s. When gigging at the Brown Sisters' Harlem Club, he noticed the younger members of the audience seemed to warm to the new doowop vocal groups and decided to start his own Dootone Records. He began cutting groups at a garage recording studio in LA and struck lucky with the Penguins' "Earth angel," which went to the top of the r'n'b chart in 1954.

The Vee-Jay label was started by husband and wife Vivian and James Bracken (hence the name) in 1952. Vivian worked as a dj in Chicago and the couple owned a record shop in nearby Gary, Indiana. The interlocking nature of the music business in the 1950s meant that, as proprietors of a record shop, the Brackens came into contact with scouts, agents, managers and musicians. Success in one aspect of the business gave the Brackens confidence enough to diversify and they started the Vee-Jay company from capital earned from the store.

In the first ten years of operation, the label claimed several national and, occasionally, international bestsellers, including Betty Everett's "Shoop shoop song (It's in his kiss)" and Gene Chandler's "Duke of Earl" (released on a subsidiary label). Culling the talent of Chicago, the Brackens signed up all manner of musicians, including a white quartet, the Four Seasons, who had considerable success on both sides of the Atlantic. The Brackens' most inspired piece of opportunism was their release of the Beatles' first US single "She loves you," though the band's subsequent singles were handled by the Capitol corporation. The label appointed Ewart Abner as its president; he was later to join Motown as director of its management division.

An eye for talent and a knack at churning out hit records were, it seems, not enough to keep the business afloat and, in 1965, with its records (including

Little Richard's "I don't know what you've got") still in the charts, the Brackens' profligacy caught up with them. Vee-Jay was declared bankrupt, its profits squandered on lavish expenses and celebrations.

The Brackens' tragedy pales beside that of Sam Cooke, who died in 1964 at the age of 33. The mention of Cooke's name elicits appreciative acknowledgments from aficionados of both gospel and soul, but there was an entrepreneurial side to him. "Control was very important to Sam," one of his producers, Hugo Peretti told writer Gerri Hirshey. "He said I don't want to be Perry Como or Tony Bennett" (1994: 112). So determined was Cooke not to be compromised into blithely imitating white artists that he built a business infrastructure to support his career, at one stage starting his own record company.

Originally a gospel singer for a group called the Soul Stirrers, Cooke was signed to Specialty Records owned by Art Rupe, who founded the company in 1944. Rupe's LA-based operation produced many commercially successful records by black artists, including Lloyd Price's "Lawdy Miss Clawdy" and Little Richard's "Tutti frutti," which was released in 1955 and became an international seller.

Cooke's co-managers James W. Alexander and Robert "Bumps" Blackwell encouraged Cooke to record a ballad called "You send me," which was a departure from gospel and which Rupe felt had little chance of success. Accordingly, Rupe gave Cooke and Alexander the master tapes in settlement of a $15,000 debt. Alexander did a deal with Bob Keen, an aircraft manufacturer, to press and release the track on his tiny independent label, Keen Records. The record came out in 1957 and sold a million copies. With the royalties, Cooke and Alexander set up Kags Music publishing, one of the first publishing companies owned by African Americans.

This was an important move, as publishing was where the serious money lay. As we saw in Chapter four, Chuck Berry's dispute with Chess had its source in the lucrative area of publishing. A publishing organization controlled the incoming revenue from sales and then redistributed it to writers. Cooke and Alexander were litigious: they successfully sued and, in the process, ruined Keen for back royalty payments. Cooke was also disappointed with Blackwell's advice and split with him.

Cooke was mindful of the way several other black artists of the day were making saleable records, yet ending up with little to show for it. In particular, Little Richard's music was played, sold and copied, yet the artist continued to struggle and actually cited Rupe as one of the reasons for his leaving showbusiness. "He wanted to buy me body and soul – with my own money" (quoted in White, 1984: 94). Not that all of his business ventures were geared to music: Cooke went into several different areas, in one instance buying a brewery. In another, he and Alexander began two record label, SAR and Derby, which signed the likes of Bobby Womack, Billy Preston and Lou Rawls, all of whom went on to have successful careers. Malloy Music was the publishing arm of the operation. There was even an SAR Pictures. After Cooke's death, Alexander shut down SAR and gave all artists releases; Kags was left with 120 of Cooke's songs in its catalog.

Cooke's business efforts suggest that he was intent on insulating himself from the pressures typically experienced by black performers. So that when, in 1959, he was offered a deal with the RCA corporation, he felt confident that he would not be manipulated. If this was so, we must assume that Cooke was quite comfortable in transferring to the mainstream. "He was photographed in starched white shirts and cardigans and fitted with a repertoire suited for both record hops and supper clubs," writes Hirshey. "Whatever was thrown at him, from teen anthems like 'Only Sixteen' and 'Tammy' to pop standards like 'Summertime' and 'The Wayward Wind,' Sam obliged" (1994: 109). Cooke explained this strategy to his protégé Womack: "When I record I got to sound white to cross over." Yet, he also believed he could switch: "On the other side, I sound black to keep my base" (quoted by Murray, 1989: 84).

RCA had only one black artist on its books at the time of signing Cooke: Harry Belafonte. Previously, it had tried to promote Jesse Belvin as what *Waiting for the Sun* author Barney Hoskyns calls a "sepia Sinatra" but Belvin died in a car crash in 1960 (1996: 47). The record company was clearly intent on creating a new Nat King Cole, or Sammy Davis Jnr. And, were it not for his death in 1964, it is at least conceivable that Cooke would have settled into a relaxed supper-club-type entertainer. Only his occasional, truly exceptional works prevent this type of extrapolation: "Bring it on home to me" and "A change is gonna come," for example, exposed a side of Cooke almost obscured by much of the more sugary material he served up during his RCA period. Yet, for all the reverence he is afforded, one sees in the last years of Cooke's life, someone on the brink of bland-out. If this is a criticism, it was not regarded as such by Gordy: he plotted Marvin Gaye's career in a way that paralleled that of Cooke's; their deaths also evoke grim parallels.

The circumstances surrounding Cooke's death were indistinct enough to prompt suspicion. Cooke had already declared his intention to concentrate on the business rather than performance side and, as Hoskyns writes, his death "fuelled endless speculation that vested music interests had decided to cut this 'uppity nigger' down to size" (1996: 67).

Like Cooke and Ray Charles, James Brown sought what Peter Guralnick calls: "A measure of independence that was not just artistic but financial as well, enough economic clout to buy into the business" (1986: 67). We saw in the previous chapter how Brown outlasted his contemporaries and journeyed on into the 1980s. His career was given an unexpected new lease of life in 1985 with the movie *Rocky IV* in which he performed the song "Living in America." In 1994, he reflected that his life story was "the kind America can be proud of." Hirshey, interviewing Brown, reports: "None of it, he says, would have happened without the men who helped him learn the business: white men" (1994: 61).

The people often cited by Brown are Syd Nathan and Ralph Bass, of King Records, based in Cincinnatti. Like Leonard Chess, Sam Phillips, Art Rupe and many other owners of independent labels, Nathan made records by black artists and sold them to a mainly black market. Brown always had yearnings for more independence, but acknowledged that, in the 1950s, "you could get shot for even tryin' to learn." So, he stuck with Nathan, who gave him his first recording deal. As with most other artists, Brown had to modify his style. Nathan did not rate his keyboard playing and actually wrote it into Brown's contract that he could not play and sing on the same record.

Brown had a mind to stay independent of the major promoters and booking agents and was wary of his manager working with them: to avoid this, he set up a contract with his manager Jack Bart that involved him in decision-making. This meant that even if Brown was unable to dictate his own agenda, he had a mediating role in it. One of his innovations was to eschew promoters and booking agents when touring. Brown, for all his gratitude to Nathan, went head-to-head with him over his move to another label. Perhaps it was a case of the master teaching the pupil too well.

The Queen Booking Agency was started by Ruth Bowen, wife of Billy Bowen of the Ink Spots, a black vocal group which toured in the 1940s. She was the personal manager of club singer Dinah Washington when Washington was at the height of her powers in the mid-1950s. Urged along by Washington, Bowen took office space in the CBS building and ran a one-woman booking agency with Washington her only client. The agency became more expansive in the 1960s when Queen handled the likes of Aretha Franklin and the Motown acts. Like many other black people in the music business at the time, Bowen's fortunes were linked to those of Gordy.

Kenny Gamble was an exception. He, along with co-writer Leon Huff and producer Thom Bell, was responsible for a number of records made in Philadelphia's Sigma Sound Studios in the 1970s. "Their records featured beautifully intricate hooks, a sophisticated blend of R & B force and mainstream strings, and irresistible internal riffs that stood up under hundreds of listenings," is how Greil Marcus describes their sound (1976: 102). A strong rhythm section was their trademark: drums and strings dominated. It was sweet to the point of stickiness. In this sense, it was a sublime antidote to the sharper sounds of Atlantic/Stax, a liaison which was, as we saw, devastated by the death of Otis Redding in 1967. It was the year in which Gamble decided to go it alone, opening Gamble Records as an independent label.

Inspired, it seems, by the examples of Atlantic and the then emerging Motown, Gamble saw himself as the doyen of a new kind of black music, sophisticated, orchestral and ornamented with delicacies that had been missing from any previous genre to emerge from black culture. Conceptually, Gamble was ahead of the field, though supporters of Isaac Hayes might argue that some of his Stax work anticipated Gamble's formula – and it certainly became a formula, a winning one. But, in practical terms, Gamble Records struggled to sell its products beyond its local Philadelphia market.

The 1960s were not great years for Chess Records. After the label's pioneering efforts with blues and, later, r'n'b, its fortunes flagged: the inventiveness of Atlantic and Stax had effectively redefined black music. In 1968, the Chesses sensed an opportunity for a comeback. Gamble approached them with the idea of a link-up: he would make the music, they would sell it, both through their established distribution network and over the air waves. But Chess belonged to another era and it was ill-suited to the needs of Gamble's operation, so Gamble continued to search for a major player.

He found it in CBS, which was prepared to leave him and Huff with full artistic autonomy over their products plus (with Bell) their own publishing company, known as Mighty Three Music. Gamble Records was reborn as Philadelphia International Records, or just PIR, and the sound of Philadelphia was heard by a wider audience than ever before. At first mistaken for lavishly upholstered soul, PIR music actually had an identity of its own. The almost suffocating use of strings, layer on layer, overcompensated for any frailties in the singers' voices. The melodies were strong to the point of being overpowering. Ballads gripped, perhaps too tightly. Love songs were too sentimental. Everything was blown slightly out of proportion. And yet it worked. The lush sound of Philadelphia was heard around the world. The Three Degrees, a female vocal trio, earned a certain cachet from being publicized as Prince Charles' favorite group. Gamble and Huff in the early and mid-1970s could do no wrong. Soloists, like Teddy Pendergrass, bands, like Harold Melvin and the Bluenotes, and vocal groups, like the O'Jays, helped put Gamble and Huff at the fore of black music and establish Philadelphia as its center of gravity.

CBS quietly prospered from the liaison, selling millions of albums, rather than singles (album sales increased generally through the decade). PIR's specialty was long, rhythm-led dance tracks that went on for five or six minutes and were therefore too long for singles. The market generally had changed by the time of PIR's ascent. CBS, as a large corporation had done its homework: the African American market was there to be exploited, but so too was the much bigger and more prosperous white market. Independent outfits, like Atlantic, had revealed how it was possible to grow rich harvesting black talent and selling it to blacks and whites. But the scale of their efforts was small. They were not in the same league as CBS when it came to marketing and distribution. Research had revealed to CBS that it needed a division specifically for music produced by blacks for white consumption. PIR was perfect.

Gamble's career swerved a little in 1976 when he became involved in a payola scam and was fined $2,500. Unlike the payola of the 1950s, this affected only black-owned radio stations, which constituted about 1.6 percent of the US's total number of stations at the time. Earnings for black djs and producers tended to be lower than those in the rest of the sector. Spurred into action by the court case, Gamble and a number of African Americans in the music business formed the Black Music Association designed to protect the interests of blacks from a rapacious industry dominated by whites.

If Gamble's motivation in leading the Black Music Association was a fear that white corporations were flexing their muscles, his fear was borne out. PIR's best years were the 1970s: a plateau in the early 1980s presaged a decline and Gamble and Huff went back to their smaller scale operations as Gamble and Huff Records in 1988. Obviously, musical tastes change and the Philly sound that fitted the previous *Saturday Night Fever*'d decade was just not right for the 1980s. Yet, there were additional and perhaps more important factors that aided the decline. Acts that would, in previous years, have been developed and recorded by Gamble and Huff were being signed directly to CBS's Columbia and Epic labels, thus shortcircuiting PIR.

Interestingly, the first release of the later Gamble and Huff label was the most overtly policitical track ever recorded by either: "Run, Jesse, run," an exhortation to Jesse Jackson in 1984 to run for the Presidency.

George reckons that Gamble created a template for black music entrepreneurs: "No significant black-owned record company or white label with significant black acts had risen and stayed important without corporate assistance since

Philadelphia International established the pattern in 1971" (1988: 179). The racial hierarchy works, often surreptitiously in cultural areas, to ensure that, even in territories ostensibly under the control of blacks, final authority typically rests with whites. This also serves to invest value in the products of organizations owned by whites even if those products themselves bear the stamp of black people. Gamble's venture no less than any of the others we have encountered so far illustrates the durability of the racial hierarchy as a kind of ordering institution.

We noticed in Chapter four how Leonard and Phil Chess had discovered the commercial possibilities of recording blues music and selling it to the black population. By urging southern bluesmen, like Muddy Waters and Howlin' Wolf, to use electric instruments, they affected the content of blues. And, in creating a national distribution network, they affected the entire structure of the genre. In 1959, they struck a deal with a tiny independent record company called Anna Records, owned by Billy Davis and two sisters, Gwen and Anna Gordy, who were based in Detroit. Unlike many other deals between labels in which one company would effectively lease their records to another, this one was simply for distribution: Anna would make the records and release through the Chess outlets. This way, Anna kept control of their products.

The sisters came from a family possessed of an entrepreneurial spirit: their father had owned a grocery store, having moved north from Georgia; he organized a family co-operative association in which all members could pool their resources and draw when business needs arose. To access even small amounts from the co-op, the applicant would have to submit a virtual business plan and convince other members that the funds were for valid business purposes.

Many of Anna's records were written and produced by the sisters' brother Berry, then 31, who had written several commercially successful songs for Jackie Wilson but was scratching together only a barely decent weekly wage from his royalties. After spurning life on the Ford assembly line and floundering in construction and retail, Berry Gordy had tried his hand at writing music. Unable to read music, he hummed his songs and had them written up as sheet music for $25 each. His sisters ran a cigarette and photography concession at a nightclub and it was here Berry introduced himself to Al Greene, a Detroit-based manager, and presented him with his sheet music for possible use by Greene's artist Jackie Wilson, who had replaced Clyde McPhatter when he moved from Billy Ward and the Dominoes to the Drifters (who made records for the Atlantic label).

Wilson recorded Gordy's songs, including the virtual standard "Reet petite" which was released in 1957 and reached number 11 in the r'n'b national charts. Gordy later branched into production, renting small studios, then, after a dispute with Greene, split from Wilson and set up a production business with his wife. Shortly before the argument with Greene, Gordy had met William "Smokey" Robinson, with whom he formed a close – and, as it turned out, influential – friendship. Robinson sang for a band called the Matadors, though they later changed the name, at Gordy's behest, to the Miracles. Gordy began writing for and producing the Miracles.

There was enough in Gordy's track record to convince Chess that he would be an asset and that his connection with Anna Records was worth exploiting. The most successful product of the arrangement was a composition written by Gordy with Janie Bradford, a receptionist, in 1959. Although it was one of the very first tracks cut at Gordy's "Hitsville, USA" studios, "Money (that's what I want)" was coded as "Tamla 54027" to give the impression of an established operation. The name Tamla was adapted from Debbie Reynolds' number one hit record "Tammy," Gordy's reasoning being that millions of people were familiar with it and so would not forget the label's name; unfortunately, there was already a label called Tammy, so Gordy effected a minor change. The deal was that Gordy would sell the record to Anna Records, which would handle local sales then sell on to Chess for national sales. "Money" was subsequently recorded by many artists including the Beatles (in 1964) and earned the composers substantial royalties; but, its first release proved disappointing for Gordy and, as he puts it in his biography *To Be Loved*: "I was the furthest away from the money" (1994: 123).

Discontent drove him to set up a company designed to give him more leverage in marketing and distribution as well as production. Like his sisters, Gordy opted to start a record company with its own publishing division, Jobete Music, and an assortment of labels, each specializing in a particular style of music. Tamla, for example, was originally intended for solo artists, while Motown was for groups. Gordy had learned that, while many of the record-selling artists in the late 1950s were black, the industry was controlled by whites, just like every other area of society in fact. So, in 1960, he took on a major challenge: to write, produce, advertise, market and distribute a record nationally and control all facets of the operation.

The record was "Way over there" by the Miracles, and Gordy recruited the help of family, friends and practically anyone who would help in packing boxes, making calls and doing anything they could to push the records out. Gordy took out a paid advertisement in the music trade magazine *The Cash Box*, in which he described himself as "one of the young driving geniuses of the music business today" (July 23, 1960). Knowing the value of radio station plays, Gordy literally took copies of the record by hand to key djs. The record ultimately sold a respectable 60,000 copies; not the major success Gordy had hoped for, but a triumph logistically as he had demonstrated his fledgling company's ability to take a record through all phases of manufacture and sales independently.

A period of consolidation followed, with Gordy releasing a series of pot-boiler blues numbers that sold well in Michigan, but had no potential outside. Gordy himself had no taste for blues: his early retail venture, 3-D Records, was intended as a jazz outlet, but failed largely because blues dominated the African American market. But, Gordy was able to keep his cashflow active and create stability for his company. One of his philosophies was based on his experiences working on the Lincoln-Mercury assembly line, where he had watched cars start out as a frame pulled along on a conveyor belt until they emerged at the end of the line as complete cars ready for the road. He believed that, given the right internal organization, he could produce hit recording artists by comparable processes.

"I broke down my whole operation into three functions: *Create*, *Make* and *Sell*," he reflects on the early 1960s. "We were doing fine with the *Create* and *Make* phase but the *Sell* phase – placing records with distributors, getting airplay, marketing and advertising – was the area I needed to develop" (1994: 140). He was able to address both problems by befriending one person, Barney Ales, a local white distributor with good contacts in the radio stations, black and white.

The selling phase created problems for most independent companies, especially those owned by blacks. Say a record's sales reached 100,000 and climbing: the company needed to manufacture more copies to keep sales alive and this meant settling the bill for the first pressing of the record. Distributors were notoriously slow payers and probably would not pay on sales for a month or two, possibly three. Meanwhile, the record pressers demanded payment. The big corporations and even the established white-owned independents, like Chess, had the money to handle the shortfall. Ales appeared to offer a solution. Gordy offered him a job in charge of distribution with the kind of brief that allowed him to present himself as the owner of the company. If the distributors with whom Ales did business thought they were dealing with a white company, neither Ales nor Gordy were going to spoil the illusion. Ales was one of a succession of white personnel Gordy brought in to run the administration of his company.

Cashflow remained a problem and Gordy decided to confront it by sending out his budding stars on a package concert tour known as the Mototown Revue. Beginning in 1962, the tour comprised the four principal Tamla and Motown acts who had sold most records (the Miracles, Marv Johnson, Mary Wells and the Marvelettes) plus some as yet unknown artists (the Supremes, Martha Reeves and the Vandellas, Sammy Ward, and the Contours). The tour was promoted by black promoter Henry Wynne. Gate receipts minus promoter's fee were hastened back to Detroit to ease the pressure of debts and, in this way, the tour was a success. It was also successful in exposing the company's talent and effectively promoting records in new markets.

Two incidents rocked the tour. The tour bus was fired on, probably by racists, when in Birmingham, Alabama, scene of one of Martin Luther King's greatest confrontations with Eugene "Bull" Connor, the city's commissioner of police, earlier in the year. In 1955, Nat King Cole had been assaulted on stage when giving a concert in Birmingham. It was here that in 1957 a carload of drunken whites had dragged a black male off the streets, bundled him into the car, taken him to a barn and castrated him. Gordy was aware of the intensity of the racial conflict then raging in the southern states and, according to his auto-biography, contemplated calling off the concert. He was persuaded otherwise. Three weeks after the shooting, two members of the tour were injured in a road accident. One of them was carrying $12,000 in receipts. To Gordy's relief, this was recovered. For the show's New York date, a new "discovery" named Little Stevie Wonder was included in the line-up.

Despite the tour's commercial success, Gordy's company still struggled to balance the books. So stretched were his resources, he reformulated his original philosophy to "Create, Sell and *Collect*," the emphasis being on getting the money in faster than it was going out. Years later, he was to modify it further, changing the collect to "reinvest." In spite of his longing to keep his company a tightly knit family operation, Gordy recognized the need to appoint professionals to handle his finances. He began to add a tier of skilled practitioners, including accountants and attorneys, mostly whites. It was a move that introduced some tension to the organization, but one that paid off. In the years that followed, all manner of half-baked rumors and myths circulated about Gordy's purported links with the Teamsters Union and the Mafia. How could a black man rise to such prominence without being involved in some kind of seedy operation? Gordy's meticulous attention to detail in all finance-related matters enabled him to defend himself against attempts to undermine him.

If Gordy was able to fend off accusations of finanancial impropriety, he was never able to satisfy critics of some of his other practices. The first suspicion that he exploited his artists came in 1964 when Martha Reeves made it known that she was dissatisfied with arrangements at Motown. Unlike most of the others, Reeves had some experience with the music business prior to her association with Gordy. She had recorded with Chess in a group with the name of the Delphis, but without much success. Failing an audition with Gordy she took a job as secretary for Mickey Stevenson, Gordy's A & R man, hoping an opportunity might crop up. It did and she succeeded with a hit record in 1963. "(Love is like) A heat wave" was composed by the songwriting team of Holland, Dozier and Holland and recorded by Martha and the Vandellas, this being an arrangement of interchangeable backing singers rather than a permanent group. It was the first of a series of internationally acclaimed records, such as "Quicksand" and "Nowhere to run." So, Reeves knew a little about the music business and realized that hit records usually make money for the artist, even if they are at the end of the food chain. "I think I was the first person to ask where the money was going," she told Gerri Hirshey (1994: 153). Her request to examine the royalty acounts in 1964 was interpreted by Gordy as a challenge and, from that point, the search was on for a suitable replacement as the label's top female vocal group.

The next challenger was Mary Wells, unlike Reeves an *ingénue*, having signed with Gordy at the age of 17. In his history of black female superstars *Brown Sugar*, Donald Bogle cites Wells as the first black woman singer with anything resembling commercial longevity. Bogle writes that, prior to Wells, there "wasn't a center for the young black woman, no one to groom her or promote, to help her develop and branch out" (1980: 163). But, Gordy saw in Wells the perfect raw material for his assembly line. "I wanted a place where a kid off the street could walk in one door an unknown and come out another recording artist – a star," he writes, recalling his first meeting with Wells.

Wells got the full treatment. Aided by Ales' efforts to promote her with white radio stations and distributors, she had her first commercial success in 1960 and, by 1964, she was the first of Gordy's artists to make it into the British charts. "My guy" was to be her biggest success. Gordy, sensing his first genuinely international star, developed and promoted her with a vengeance, placing her on television shows, persuading magazines to run stories on her and hiring coaches to improve her stage persona. On a promotional trip to Britain, she met up with the Beatles, who sang her praises. This endorsement did her reputation no harm; in fact, it elevated it to a level none of her colleagues had reached.

Wells apparently felt that she could aspire to the kind of status enjoyed by the Beatles or, for that matter, many of the other white bands that were popular at the time. Her records outsold anybody's on the label. Offers from 20th Century Fox about a record and film contract inclined her toward believing she was not just a product of the Gordy assembly line. Gordy was later to insist that it cost him $300,000 in tuition and promotion.

In 1964, restless and approaching her twenty-first birthday, Wells stayed away from the studio; when he contacted her, Gordy was told to talk to her lawyer. Gordy's version of events is that he showed Wells' lawyer around the Motown building, first to the writers' and producers' rooms, then to the studios and finally to the administrative offices. This apparently convinced him that his client was making the wrong choice: she wanted to leave Gordy because "she could get a better deal from another company." The attorney was persuaded by Gordy that she could not. The attorney conveyed the news and was fired. Wells retained a second attorney, Herbert Eiges, who locked Gordy in a long legal case, which culminated in Gordy losing his most famous artist. Wells had three months of her contract with Motown to run, but she won the right to have it disaffirmed at the age of 21 and was free to sign with the 20th Century Fox corporation. She did so and continued to record for the next several years, releasing six moderately successful singles but without ever coming close to the success she had with Gordy.

Wells' experience was chastening for other members of the stable. Reeves was also obviously discontented with her situation, having peeked at the royalty accounts; but she continued to make hit records into the late 1960s by which time Wells had disappeared from public view. But, Reeves lost her position as the leader of the company's top female vocal group. Gordy's endeavors had shifted to a new group, which had done some studio backing work and released two singles on a small independent label as the Primettes. The group had been rejected by one of Gordy's producers at an earlier audition, but by 1961 they were signed and rechristened the Supremes.

Gordy's impact was immediate: he installed Diane Ross (*sic*), then 16, as lead singer. As the group was originally the idea of Florence Ballard who envisaged herself and her schoolfriend Mary Wilson taking turns at lead, with Barbara Martin and Ross backing, this did not go down well. For three years, the calculus looked flawed: only one single drifted briefly into the lower reaches of the charts. Then, Gordy added the missing component. He assigned his most successful compositional team, Holland, Dozier and Holland, to work up a number for the Supremes. "When the lovelight starts shining through his eyes" climbed into the top 30 in January 1964 and effectively began a new phase in Gordy's entrepreneurial career. His company was to move from being a significant but small independent to a corporation.

Unlike many of his predecessors, Gordy made no claim to authenticity: his music was not sold as if salvaged from a forgotten or neglected culture, such as gospel or blues – both of which were rooted in the black experience. Motown was an entirely new and unique artifice: it did not exist separately from Gordy's studios. Even the artists themselves seemed to have no life apart from Motown. The demise of Wells and subsequent artists who left Gordy added another meaning to this observation. Gordy was becoming the star-maker and, in Ross, he sensed the possibility of a star like no other.

Chapter seven

Back to
the Holy
Waters

S OMETIME IN HIS EARLY CAREER as a freelancing songwriter/ producer, Gordy promised his brother Robert that he would record one of his compositions. He did so and sold it to Carlton Records. It was called "Everyone was there" and Robert called himself Bob Kayli. Sales were impressive and it was decided to send the artist out on a promotional tour. No sooner was he on the road than sales tapered off. A problem with the visual aspects of the act? Gordy thought so, but Robert assured him the performances were fine. Gordy had the chance to see for himself when "Bob Kayli" appeared on a Saturday night television show. "The problem then became clear," says Gordy. "This white-sounding record did not go with his black face. Bob Kayli was history . . . When that happened I realized this was not just about good or bad records, this was about race" (1994: 95).

This may have been a formative moment in Gordy's business career, because all his efforts from that time seem to have been keyed to creating music that was, to use a cliché, color-blind. He even excluded his artists' pictures from early album covers; so a cartoon mailbox bizarrely appeared on a Marvelettes' cover. Robert Townsend's 1991 movie *The Five Heartbeats* which dramatized the career of a band not unlike the Temptations recalled this: black faces are excised from the Heartbeats' first album cover to maximize the chances of a crossover success. And, as if to cement the episode's place in folklore, the rap band De La Soul's 1993 track "Patti Dooke" is all about the same thing, ending with an observation about never seeing an Elvis Presley album cover adorned with black subjects.

For all his commercial success, some of his contemporaries think he failed in this one respect. As Steve Cropper, of Atlantic/Stax, once put it: "To me, Motown was white music" (quoted in Hirshey, 1994: 307). From a white musician so closely associated with black music, this is a harsh appraisal. Yet it could be construed as a compliment. Gordy's gift, as I suggested at the beginning of the previous chapter, was his understanding of the dominant culture. From 1964, he had the perfect opportunity to demonstrate this by producing music by black artists that sounded white enough to cross over into the mainstream. It did not work for Bob Kayli, but Gordy learned from the experience.

As Mary Wells left Motown amid acrimonious court wranglings, the Supremes earned their first major hit with "Where did our love go?" another Holland-Dozier-Holland number that went to number one. They followed up with an even bigger single: "Baby love" topped bestselling lists in Britain as well as the States. The Supremes were suddenly the jewel in Gordy's crown and, after Wells, he knew he could not rely on serendipity a second time. So, he locked them into an airtight contract, a four-year agreement that committed them to a minimum of three singles in the first year for a standard royalty return of 8 percent of receipts, that is 90 percent of the monies received by the record company from the wholesalers. The contract specified that the record company could actually record the Supremes even if some of the contracted parties were not present at the studio, giving Motown effective ownership of the name of the group.

Nelson George stresses another important element of Gordy's contracts with his acts which was to be a source of tension as the business grew (1988). Like most of the other independent labels we have covered so far, Motown utilized a cross-collateralization of accounts system, meaning that artists could be charged costs against their earnings regardless of how those costs were incurred. For example, if a recording session yielded nothing, then the cost of it could be balanced on another account. Artists would find unanticipated subtractions from their royalties.

Gordy himself took a direct interest in the negotiation of contracts. Virtually everything that went on under the Hitsville USA roof was under his control. "On a typical day, I'd go from one end of the spectrum to the other – songwriting to corporate finance – problem-solving, encouraging, motivating, teaching, challenging, complaining," he reflected (1994: 175). His company was created completely in his image. In the Supremes he saw the opportunity to produce a group of black singers who would not only sell records to whites but could integrate smoothly into white culture. But, they would need sculpting. This is where Gordy's production line concept kicked in. Central to this were his sisters Gwen and Anna, who headed up the company's artist development department. Gwen, a former model at Maxine Powell's Finishing School, helped select the female artists' costumes while Maxine Powell herself worked with them on all facets of their appearance and manners, including how to eat, how to apply makeup, how to walk, sit and so on. Years later, in 1977, Diana Ross acknowledged Powell as "the woman who taught me everything I know" (quoted in Ritz, 1991: 91).

The Supremes benefited from this and from the efforts of dancer Cholly Atkins, who worked with them and other Motown acts, on dance steps, entrances, exits and gestures. Harmonies and band arrangements were developed by Maurice King, who spent two hours every day working with the group. No effort was spared in refining the Supremes especially for the market Gordy envisaged. This was in contrast to his approach to Motown's house musicians, who were not credited by name on any Motown album prior to the 1970s, nor cited in popular publications and did not receive top rates for their services.

One of the most revealing aspects of the development department's remit was its speech training: King admitted to writer Gerri Hirshey that he considered Gordy's attention to this detail "a little cruel." Hirshey adds: "This was particularly painful for some kids from the projects, facing a tuxed white café crowd. They could sing beautifully, but theirs was not the type of English spoken at bridge clubs" (1994: 167). Gordy used to write Ross' lines for her, sometimes as late as five minutes before a show, and she practised so that she could deliver them perfectly.

The Supremes led Gordy's attempt to break into the British market, in the mid-1960s dominated by white bands that seemed to sprout daily from industrial centers like Liverpool, Birmingham and Manchester. It was a hard sell and the first tour of the Motown Revue (as its name was modified) in 1965 was only a so-so affair. But, "Baby love" had been monstrously successful and the sales figures of other Motown acts were respectable. There was also status from the Beatles' recording of three Motown/Jobete titles for their second album. Tamla-Motown, as the label was called in Britain, was making inroads into what was then the world's second largest record selling market.

Marvin Gaye reflected that Gordy appreciated the power of transistor radios, probably better than any other record chief. "Back then [in the 1960s] transistors were selling like hot cakes, and Motown songs were mixed to sound good on transistors and car radios," Gaye told his biographer David Ritz (1991: 98). "Diana's voice was the perfect instrument to cut through those sound waves."

Some measure of the mainstream success of the Supremes was the fact that they were featured not only in black magazines like *Ebony* and *Jet*, but in *Time* and *Look*. It was also noticeable that the Supremes were landing bookings in places like New York's Copacabana club, where the likes of Frank Sinatra and Perry Como regularly performed. This was perfect for Gordy. He also secured a booking on the networked television show *Hullabaloo* on which the Supremes eschewed original material from Motown and performed the standard "You're nobody 'til somebody loves you." It was an interesting and revealing selection, but perfectly consistent with Gordy's master plan, summarized by Gaye as "to win a mainstream middle-class audience, crooning the ballads he thought white music lovers wanted to hear" (quoted in Ritz, 1991: 107).

At some point, Gordy must have glimpsed in Diana Ross an artist capable of transcending the traditional categories reserved for African American females to become an artist regarded neither as a sex toy to be leered at by white males nor a housemaid at their beck and call. Certainly his efforts at redefining her role in the Supremes, then her role as an entertainer suggest someone with an "obsession," as Ritz suggests (1991: 212). Ross was no puppet: forceful, even pushy, she was a willing partner to Gordy's strategy. In this respect, she may have differed from many of the other Motown artists. We can gauge this by Gaye's comment about himself and his colleagues: "We were being molded into something we weren't." Ross, it would seem, had no compunction about conforming to white audience's expectations to begin with: the bigger project was to recast those expectations. Gordy had Ross performing with all the spontaneity of a synchronized swimmer in her early years; only later did he encourage her to project her own particular image.

By emphasizing Gordy's role in the project, we are able to highlight the industrial aspects of the star system without necessarily underrating Ross' ability. Ross was, according to Gaye, Gordy's "living breathing brainchild. He made millions off her and she made a few dollars off him" (quoted in Ritz, 1991: 165). There is no way of knowing whether Gordy without Ross could have become a prime mover of the black culture industry: his judgement was by no means flawless, as is indicated by some of his other projects, Tony Martin, Barbara McNair and Connie Haines, none of whom did much commercially. It is also quite possible that Gordy could have flexed his patrician muscles and worked hard at kneading any other young artist into a saleable commodity.

Before moving on to reveal how this was done for Ross, we need to take a detour and explore the historical context of black female entertainers, specifically those who have crossed into the mainstream and achieved recognition by whites. Once we have understood the limitations set on successful black women entertainers, we will better appreciate the scale of Gordy's achievement in steering free of them.

Black artists' access to mainstream culture has been, or perhaps *is* conditional. In recounting the history of the black culture industry, we have continually reinforced Jan Pieterse's argument about the unwritten permission granted black entertainers and, for that matter, sports performers who do not threaten the status quo and so conform to popular images of the "other." Variations on the entertaining sambo type and the fearsome brute nigger have been overwhelmingly popular. When we address black women, two further images predominate. As Pieterse describes them: "The black woman who is regarded as sexually available and equated with the prostitute – 'Brown sugar'; and the desexualized mammy of the Aunt Jemima type" (1992: 178).

Diana Ross was the first black woman to transfer successfully to the mainstream of entertainment without submitting to popular iconography. It is perhaps to Gordy's credit that he was able to fashion from an able and receptive singer a genuine star who diversified into films and continued to perform and make bestselling records for over three decades. This does not lessen Ross' own capacities: she was, by all accounts, confident in her youth, imitative (Smokey Robinson complained that she stole his stage movements) and shamelessly ambitious. Far from being lured into Gordy's marionette theater, she made herself available to his influences. Only by describing the tradition she broke can we grasp the magnitude of the task.

In the 1920s, blues singer Bessie Smith's ascent marked "the end of one tradition – the diva enclosed in the black community – and the beginning of another – the diva coming aboveground and openly affecting the dominant culture." So writes Donald Bogle in *Brown Sugar*, the definitive chronicle of black female "superstars." Smith surfaced in 1923 after she signed a recording contract with Columbia Records. Three other labels had rejected her. For ten years, she sold records, geared to the blues market, that is African Americans. While she had toured prior to the Columbia deal, her career changed up a gear in the mid-1920s and her concerts were sellouts, though she rarely played to white audiences. But, as blues went out of favor, so did she, and her contract with Columbia was not renewed. Her career was in decline at the time of her death in an auto accident in 1937.

Smith's earnings from records and concerts were considerable in the 1920s. She was known to pay for her many cars with cash and go on splurges, spending as much as $16,000 at a time on clothes. Bogle describes her as "a large woman, big-boned, massively-built, and very dark" (1980: 31). Her success, substantial as it was, came as a result of her popularity with blacks. Only in retrospect has the quality of her work been more widely appreciated.

After her, a succession of black women "started in the black community but eventually met with great success in the white world too." The first of these was Josephine Baker, who had left her St Louis home in 1919 at the age of 13 and made a living in travelling road shows. Being pale-skinned (her father was Spanish), she stood out as a member of chorus lines. She capitalized on this, dressing ostentatiously offstage and acquiring a reputation as a rising star. When Ethel Waters, the first black woman to succeed on Broadway, was unavailable for a European tour in 1925, Baker stood in.

Her impact was immediate: she appeared in *La Revue Nègre* dressed in nothing more than a pink boa. This was the first of several eye-catching numbers, including a skirt made of rubber bananas. Inhibition was a concept alien to Baker and she used her time in Paris to flout as many taboos as possible. Performing topless, using sexual imagery in her stage act, parading with a pet leopard; these would have been unimaginable in the States. In Europe, they helped elevate her to one of the most prominent artists, black or white, of the 1920s. Her periodic returns to the USA were never easy: audiences were wary of a black female whose mission seemed to be to break every rule. (Baker was one of a number of black entertainers, including the Nicholas Brothers, to find greater success in Europe than in the USA.)

The fragility of a black star essaying success in a white world was emphasized by the careers of two divas of the depression era. Ethel Waters' early career was studded with humiliation. Injured seriously in a car wreck, she was left to suffer by passers-by and refused hospital treatment. She also believed Baker had stolen her thunder – and her material. Her dealings with promoters, agents and colleagues were often affected by her perception that she was forever being underpaid. Perhaps she was; but, in the impoverished 1930s, she was the highest paid artist on Broadway, earning an estimated $2,500 a week. Her legal victory over MGM turned out to be Pyrrhic: she did not work for six years after.

Waters crossed several bridges during her career. Quite apart from becoming the highest paid black person, she appeared regularly on radio shows with the Jack Denny Orchestra; something no other black entertainer had done. Perhaps most importantly, her performances in stage shows suggested an ability for dramatic performance; her acting became progressively more serious. In 1939, she drew acclaim from New York's major theater critics for her work in *Mamba's Children*.

There was a symmetry, though far from a perfect one, between the careers of Billie Holiday, the troubled, tragic singer of the 1930s, and Ross, who was chosen to play her in the 1972 movie *Lady Sings the Blues*. It was Gordy in inspired form who wrapped the two celebrated careers together and Ross' creditable performance contributed to the film's commercial success. Gordy put the money together to fund the project.

The conventional assessment of Holiday's career is that she was loaded with more natural talent than she could handle. Her success with records (she began recording with Columbia in 1933 at the age of 18) and with bands, including those of Count Basie and Artie Shaw (who was, of course, white), was tempered by human failings and she had long periods of dependence on drugs and alcohol. Holiday was also affected by the particular problems she faced as a black woman achieving success in a white domain. She performed at clubs where she was not allowed to talk to the audience; stayed in hotels where she was told to use freight elevators rather than share with white guests.

Holiday was a glorious misfit: lauded by critics and sought after by audiences, she reached a public hardly approached by black artists and, as such, ventured into a world where she was welcome as a singer, but not as a human being. Her manifest disorientation was no doubt a product of this. Holiday did her best to hide her personal problems behind a glitzy façade, draping herself in expensive stoles, adorning herself with jewelry and rarely appearing in public without the signature gardenia in her hair.

We have seen how, up to the 1930s, there were more white performers in blackface than there were actual black performers. As movies developed into a dominant entertainment, there were also more blacked-up white actors than blacks in film. Mickey Rooney, Judy Garland (*Babes in Arms*), Betty Grable, June Haver (*The Dolly Sisters*) and Fred Astaire (*Swing Time*) are some of the better-known whites who played blacks. MGM, then the most powerful studio in the world, broke with tradition when it signed up Lena Horne and afforded her the kind of treatment usually reserved for white sex symbols. She was prepared and promoted as a glamorous artist. Baker had, of course, been virtually banished for projecting such an image twenty years earlier, but studio chiefs felt the world was now ready. Their decision was no doubt influenced by Horne's facial features: she had pale skin, straight hair and a narrow nose.

The NAACP took an active interest in MGM's initiative and monitored Horne's career, presumably wary of her being dumped into maid's and other subservient roles. She avoided these, but was never offered the kinds of roles available to whites, like Betty Grable or Rita Hayworth. As a result, she became almost typecast as the beautiful black vamp who could sing like a bird. Dissatisfied with this, she returned to the club circuit where she had been discovered, and interspersed this with the occasional film role. Television appearances became a feature of her *oeuvre* in the 1960s and 1970s. Her recording career is a study in sustained quality and she continued to produce albums into the 1990s as she approached her eightieth birthday.

In a sense, Horne traded on enigma. She was black, but had the kind of looks that made white audiences forget that; she rarely spoke to audiences or had personal contact with fans. This gave her an imperious presence on stage; even offstage, Horne was defiant. She was quite open about her determination not be pigeon-holed in the same way as other black performers. Her marriage to a white composer could almost have been designed to flout convention. Her friendship with Paul Robeson invited denunciation. All of this may have contributed to her success as a unique public figure, but also to her failure. In career terms, she made movies, tv shows and records of distinction. But, she never quite landed the great roles; they went to the likes of Ava Gardner and Hedy Lamarr.

Dorothy Dandridge, like Horne, tried to make the transition from singer to actor. Her first prominent screen role was as an African princess in *Tarzan's Peril*. Laden with heavy costume jewelry and animal skins, she came across as a new Josephine Baker, all exotic and untamed sexuality. Yet Dandridge aspired to serious roles. She got them to begin with: *Island in the Sun* was a singular triumph; she was the first black woman to be cast opposite a white actor in a major film. But, as Bogle points out: "The film industry failed to construct star vehicles, fearful that audiences would not pay to see a black leading lady" (1988: 377). And Dandridge was shunted into musicals such as *Carmen Jones* and *Porgy and Bess*. In these, her voice was too weak and had to be dubbed. Frustrated at her failure to find serious acting work, Dandridge turned to nightclub singing, though with no success. She was made to file for bankruptcy. In 1965, she overdosed on antidepressants and died aged 41.

In films like *Carmen Jones* and *Tamango*, Dandridge was quite deliberately cast as nymph and, although only four years younger than Horne, it seemed she was her natural successor. The "Black Venus" role with its allusions to primitive, exotic sexuality, had become a stock item in popular entertainment. For a while, Eartha Kitt seemed ideally suited. Her persona was more a caricature of the role than an enactment of it: hers was a contrived attempt to push the tormentor image to its limits. She shunned the press, made no secrets about her passionate desire for professional success at any cost and played up the exotic connections, wearing animal skin clothes. Like Horne and Dandridge, she also married a white man.

Ebony was so enraged by her unapproachable manner that it ran a feature "Why negroes do not like Eartha Kitt." She replied dismissively: "I do not carry my race around on my shoulders." Like Baker, on whom she overtly modelled herself, Kitt achieved a better reception in Europe than in the United States and, in common with all the women discussed in this section, her success was based on her appeal mainly to whites. If *Ebony* is to be believed, Kitt's success in the 1960s was based entirely on this. Her talent was in elaborating the jungle sex of Baker. Cue Grace Jones: in the 1980s, Jamaican-born Jones repeated the trick, stretching the dangerous wild seductress role toward satire, but with great success, especially in Europe where cultures were more disposed toward the adoration of primal black women (we find evidence of this in the poems of Baudelaire, Hugo's novels and Gleyre's paintings). Between Baker and Jones we find a continuing image of the black female: wild and beautiful, a sensual "other" to be drooled over. As if to emphasize the inflexibility of the type, it is worth glancing at the career of a woman who strayed from it.

There was a time when Diahann Carroll looked the perfect candidate for the title held by Dandridge. An ugly duckling turned hypnotically attractive swan, she had all the requirements: singing and acting talent, good looks and a naturalness that aligned her with the Black Venus types of the past. Yet, in the 1960s, Carroll set about remaking herself. Her ability went unquestioned; but her persona changed. Everything about her betrayed an artist earnestly seeking to break out of role: her accent, behavior, dress, demeanor all signified a woman on the way up. So bourgeois was she, that it was easy to forget she was even black at all. And therein lay her problem: her crossover was, to use Pieterse's term again, conditional. A television series, *Julia*, in which she played an educated nurse far removed from ghetto life, lasted only three seasons and Carroll's career went on hold. She re-emerged, her looks intact, in the television series *Dynasty* in the 1980s when she was turning 50. The role fitted her like a glove: classy, well-clad woman with intellect and guile to match her outward appearance.

Carroll's accomplishment was in changing the trajectory of her career. There seems little doubt that she would have been a better-known and better-paid superstar had she stuck with the original script and flaunted her sexuality. Her failure to do so cost her in one sense; but, it repaid her in another. As a case study, her career suggests the brittleness in the image of the untamed black sexpot. This has been one of the two hardy perennial roles allocated to black females, the other being that personified by Hattie McDaniel, who won an Oscar for her performance as Mammy in *Gone with the Wind* and rarely strayed from this caring and servile role. In fact, she made a career out of it before she died in 1952.

McDaniel was the archetypal mammy, a sort of female counterpart to sambo, except less foolish. Mammy was physically unattractive, though not repulsive, sexless, though maternal, uneducated, though intuitively wise and, above all, dependable. These qualities were comforting to several generations of whites, especially when augmented with an "I'se a comin'" accent and eyes that rolled like pool balls. It is no accident that the mammy type began featuring in popular fiction at about the time of emancipation and continues to the present. The Aunt Jemima character used to sell pancake mix remains a potent symbol of African American womanhood.

If McDaniel and her contemporary Louise Beavers, who was a model of stoicism and kindness, were the complete mammies, there were at least traces in divas like Smith, Holiday and Waters. None of them exuded sexuality. Bogle describes Smith as a "large woman, big-boned, massively built and very dark" and Holiday as a "well-decked matron"(1980: 31 and 69). Waters cut the image of a flapper in her early career, but later "relinquished her sexuality, becoming matronly far too early" (1980: 88). Bogle also favors the term "big-boned" to describe her. Aretha Franklin did not stray too far from this description. In 1968, at 26, she was the "Queen of Soul": the most successful female of what was a predominantly male genre. As soul's force receded, she selected her material more eclectically and augmented her stage presence with elaborate costumes, in the manner of earlier divas, so as to effect a transition to the Vegas-style club circuit.

These women did not pander to white fantasies of black domestication, of course; nor, for that matter, servility. Indeed, all commanded earnings sufficient to make them completely independent. Yet, there was something reassuring about their physical appearances: their attempts to glamorize themselves by dressing expensively and accessorizing with elegant items were never enough to change their fundamental image of staidness. These were women successful enough to avail themselves of the best money could buy, yet they could never rid themselves of one thing: they *looked* as if they could manage your house for you.

In her teenage years, Ross might just about have passed as a skivvy: slim to the point of being scrawny, she had the look of a mischievous goblin. Once on the Gordy production line, she acquired a womanly aura with a theatrical dash of vulnerability. Her clothes were dressy rather than elegant; her makeup stagey but not dramatic. With the Supremes, her movements were synchronized, never natural. There was precision in everything she did. Quite soon, Ross began to capitalize on her position as the focal point of the group. Mary Wilson complained to Gordy that: "She gets out there on the stage and acts like we're not even there." And Florence Ballard described her as a "show-off" (Gordy, 1994: 255). His reaction was a crucial factor in determining the construction of a new type of superstar that defied conventional types.

Perhaps sensing Ross was not quite strong enough to go solo, Gordy assured Wilson and Ballard that they were all equal parts of the group and were being paid as such. But the tension became more apparent on tour. Reports got back to Gordy that Ballard was drinking, putting on weight and showing up late for rehearsals and shows. This kind of indiscipline was antithetical to Gordy's approach. He fired her in July 1967 without disclosing details of the reasons; years later, he cited her alcoholism as the problem, although he also stated that Motown would have kept her on had ABC Records not signed her. Ballard's career, indeed her life, went into freefall and she died of a heart attack nine years later, aged 32. She had been living on welfare at the time of her death.

In his autobiography, Gordy gives Ballard's departure short shrift, though it was clearly a key development in his promotion of Ross. Ross, in her own auto-biography, barely mentions the episode, apart from the fact that Ballard's drinking had become an "embarrassment" and her leaving was "by mutual consent" (1993: 135–36). Ritz notes a long, unpublished interview given by Ballard in which she accuses Gordy of being "prejudiced" against her; he also notes Marvin Gaye's explanation of the split, which lays the blame more at the feet of Ballard than Gordy: "It was just a matter of temperament. Some people can deal with the business, some can't" (1991: 126). Mary Wilson's account shows how Ballard's growing independence jarred with Gordy. Ross, having Gordy's ear, became increasingly upset by Ballard's putting on weight and arguments between the two were frequent.

Ballard was no doubt resentful: the original group was, after all, her idea and the package with which she left Motown prevented her from ever describing herself professionally as an ex-Supreme. She received $15,000 over three years, later upped to $75,000 after legal action, according to George. Wilson writes of a "$160,000 settlement from Motown" (1987: 288). She would receive no further royalties from Supremes records. As part of the deal, she was not allowed to pursue further legal actions against Motown or its agents.

The prohibition against publicizing her former membership of the band made promoting her difficult and ABC dropped her. Things got worse in 1969 when her lawyer told her that all the Motown money was gone. She fired him and hired another to investigate the way he had handled her affairs. It was a long and costly case, but Ballard eventually won $50,000 from him. In 1971, Ballard filed an $8.7 million suit against Motown, alleging that Ross had "secretly, subversively, and maliciously plotted to oust her" (quoted in Wilson, 1987: 289). But the clause negotiated on her departure stopped her pressing this.

Ballard also revealed that, while she was in the Supremes, she had received only a $225 weekly allowance and had never seen accounts of the band's income. Wilson later confirmed that she had not seen accounts either: in 1971, she appointed independent accountants to investigate her financial affairs. Like Mary Wells before her and unlike Martha Reeves, who grinned and bore it, Ballard suffered after her departure from Motown. It speaks volumes about Gordy's mastery of public relations that none of the money-related gripes against him seemed to do much lasting damage; and even Ballard's adversity, which one might plausibly link to her Motown associations, did little to harm the company's image.

We can only guess at Mary Wilson's reaction to Ballard's dismissal in 1967. Even the founder member of the band was disposable. What did that make her? Any resolve she had to protest at Gordy's decision to rename the group Diana Ross and the Supremes must have drained away as she saw her childhood friend sacked amid much bitterness. She must also have noted the alacrity with which Gordy drafted in Cindy Birdsong as permanent replacement. Birdsong had been on standby for a number of months before Ballard's exit. A cynical interpretation of events might be that Gordy, realizing the time was right to make Ross prominent but not wishing to disband the most successful female group in the world, seized the moment to drop Ballard, a move which would disarm Wilson when he wanted to demote her. And the name change was, after all, a backward step for Wilson. With Ross foregrounded, the other members of the outfit were equally dispensable.

The new name was to last only two years anyway: in 1969, Ross ostensibly left the group, but effectively disbanded it. She had dominated the Supremes so comprehensively in the years leading to the split, that it was like an *Aliens* movie without Sigourney Weaver. Mary Wilson's second book *Supreme Faith* (co-written with Patricia Romanowski) is effectively a critique of Gordy: "Motown stopped promoting our records the way it had in the past" (1990: 53). She goes so far as to suggest that Motown "ruined" the Supremes when Gordy focused all his attentions on Ross (1990: 172).

The two years had not done too much for the Supremes, but they were essential to Ross' ascent. Gordy enthusiastically secured them work on television shows, all showcasing the now extrovert Ross, the others just making up the numbers. It became very clear that Gordy was singleminded. He also became involved in a relationship with Ross. The 1968 hit "Love child" had added poignancy. As far as records were concerned, the period produced only two number ones "I'm gonna make you love me" with the Temptations (co-written by Kenny Gamble) and "Someday we'll be together," this being the last number released before Ross went. The Supremes tried to replace the irreplaceable with Jean Terrell and continued to make hit records, though their path was one of gradual descent, while that of Ross was in the other direction.

Much of the Supremes' success in the 1960s was due to the quality of their material. The composers were Lamont Dozier who worked with two brothers Eddie and Brian Holland. Between 1964 and 1968, HDH, as the team was known, wrote 16 straight singles for the group, including ten number ones. Brian Holland and Lamont Dozier also produced the singles. Other members of the Motown stable profited from the team's output too. The Four Tops' best period, 1964–67, was based on HDH songs, and the team was responsible for most of Martha and the Vandellas' material. In terms of fecundity, HDH was up there with Lennon and McCartney.

In 1968, the Supremes peaked at number 28 in the national charts with an HDH song, "Forever came today." This was a relative "failure," the lowest ever chart position for an HDH/Supremes single. In fact, it was an old and rather stale recording, its release being forced on Gordy by the failure of his premier team to come up with any fresh material. The reason for this was that Holland, Dozier and Holland had gone on strike some months before, holding out for more money.

It seemed an extraordinary state of affairs: one of the most prolific song-writing teams in the world in industrial dispute with their employers, then one of the most prodigious popular music labels in the world. Gordy had clearly understood their value when he signed them to long-term writers' and producers' contracts in the early Motown days. Like many of his other decisions, this too was prescient: their worth to Motown in the critical 1963–68 phase was inestimable.

In his account, Gordy had acceded to a number of financial demands made by Eddie Holland, who negotiated on behalf of the team. But, Gordy refused him a personal, interest-free loan and this, Gordy believes, precipitated the strike. Next thing: Gordy heard that his songwriters were negotiating a deal with Capitol Records. Panicked by the thought of losing them, Gordy sued for breach of contract, claiming $4 million in compensation, though he really just wanted them back working for Motown. HDH countersued Motown for $22 million: their charges included cheating, conspiracy, fraud and deceit. As Gordy himself writes, they were "portraying themselves and all the Motown artists as exploited victims held prisoners by this Svengali monster" (1994: 268).

When Mary Wells defected from Motown in 1964 and slid quietly into oblivion, her action could have been interpreted as the action of a headstrong young woman to whom fame came too early. Then, Barrett Strong – who had recorded Gordy's first single on the Tamla label, "Money (That's what I want)" – left, to be followed by Brenda Holloway ("Every little bit hurts"), Kim Weston ("It takes two"), the Isley Brothers, the Miracles, the Temptations, Gladys Knight and the Pips, Jimmy Ruffin, Eddie Kendricks and the Four Tops. Later, Gordy was to own up to the reasons why his artists left: "Perhaps stubbornly, I would not always pay what it would take to get them to stay. That might have been a mistake" (1994: 354) Still, no artist was indispensable for Gordy: after all, they were products of his assembly line and there was always more raw material ready to be processed.

Harder to bear was the loss of people who staffed that assembly line. Maurice King and Harvey Fuqua, of the artist development department, were key personnel, as were songwriters Valerie Ashford and Nickolas Simpson. Their departures left Gordy with crucial roles to fill. Perhaps the most surprising exit was that of Mickey Stevenson, production supervisor and Motown stalwart who went to MGM after being refused stock in Motown. While the individual grievances were not serious in themselves, collectively they seemed to be bigger than the sum of the parts. Could it be that the first major African American player in the record industry, the purveyor of black culture to the world, the symbol of black capitalism, the very embodiment of all that's good about America could be coming up short with his artists?

Certainly, Holland *et al.* thought so and were prepared to try to prove it in court. It turned into a sprawling affair with accusations against Gordy revolving around his fast-and-loose approach to contracts. HDH were prepared to continue writing for Gordy when their contract expired in 1967, but demanded improved terms. They alleged Gordy wished them to continue writing and on better terms, but without a formal written contract. The case concluded quietly with an out-of-court settlement and the songwriters continued their career. As the case rumbled to a halt, Gordy was finalizing his plans to shift Motown from its native Detroit to Los Angeles.

Gordy's clairvoyant wisdom had alerted him to the change ahead. The Atlantic/Stax connection was uncoiling and black music was bifurcating. Messrs Gamble and Huff, whom we covered in the previous chapter, were practically outdoing Motown at what it did best: making black music for whites. The Philadelphia sound was sedative to the mind. Sly and the Family Stone's music was stimulating: tense, grim, it told of the parts of the black experience the record buying public did not want to know about. At least, not until the early 1970s, when the blaxploitation era ushered in all manner of new perspectives. The music that told of dope, dysfunctional families, police brutality and ghetto poverty was alien to Motown. (We will move to this development in the next chapter.)

Troubled by changing tastes and sniping among his employees and ex-employees, Gordy's attempt to restore stability to his kingdom was audacious. He made a film biography of Billie Holiday, featuring Diana Ross. Gordy had no experience in film production, but bankrolled the project anyway. Ross had only the most limited acting experience; physically she did not look at all like Holiday; her agitated stage style, all hand gestures and sideways glances, contrasted with that of Holiday, who kept a lid on everything. *Lady Sings the Blues* was released in 1972 and, despite mixed reviews, received five Academy Award nominations. Ross' unexpectedly competent performance took her within grasp of an Oscar, though she lost out to Liza Minnelli. Needless to say, this displeased Gordy, who had bought ads in all the trade papers to boost Ross' candidature.

Bogle writes about the image problem facing Ross and by implication Gordy after she had left the Supremes. "Ross herself was often thought of as the selfish, superficial, overly ambitious sister who had stepped on everyone else," he writes. She "knew intuitively that she would not be accepted as a goddess until she symbolically had gone back to the holy waters, been rebaptized and born again" (1980: 176).

Lady Sings the Blues must rank as the most self-aware movie of all time: it invited viewers to make the comparison between Ross and one of the great, haunted blacks divas of the past. Is this Diana Ross playing Billie Holiday, or is it Diana Ross touching the greatness that Holiday possessed but could never manage? It did not prompt audiences: it shook them. "You are watching [the] greatest black female singer of all time!" it proclaimed. Holiday or Ross?

Not yet ready to be a *grande dame*, but too dignified to slide toward the *grande amoureuse* roles that captured Baker, Dandridge and the others, Ross selected her parts carefully, sustaining a singing career with albums and concerts. Gordy not only produced but directed Ross' next major film, *Mahogany*, released in 1975 to scathing criticism. Again, Ross' acting was more than adequate, though it was pretty much a "Lady Sing the Blues II" type of job and, by now, audiences realized this was Ross *qua* Ross, as it were. In spite of awful reviews, the film made money for Gordy's film company called Motown Productions, which was set up essentially for Ross. During the making of the film, Ross' hitherto excellent relationship with Gordy took a turn when they argued and she walked off the set.

Worse was to come: Gordy's judgement in allowing Ross to play the lead in *The Wiz*, a version of *The Wizard of Oz* with an all-black cast, was for once flawed. After two roles entirely consistent with her own image as a sophisticate, Ross, 34 at the time of the film's release in 1978, tried to reprise the Judy Garland role of Dorothy, the naïve schoolgirl swept away to the land of Oz. Ross without her spider's leg eyelashes and coiffured locks looked bare and the movie flopped.

Ross shrugged off the embarrassment and pressed on with her singing career. The 1980 *Diana* was her bestselling album. When she left Gordy, it was not for quite the same reasons as the others. In her book *Secrets of a Sparrow*, Ross states: "I never felt ripped off" (1993: 204). It was Gordy's passion for control over all aspects of her career that she found "unbearable." Still, her agent gave Gordy the first option to match a $20 million offer made by the RCA corporation. Gordy declined and Ross left after twenty-one years. She was the only female artist from Motown whose career did not crumble after the halcyon 1960s. In fact, it veered in new directions: Ross, as if taking a leaf from Gordy's book, created a series of her own companies, Anaid Films, Ross Records, Ross Town, Ross Publishing and RTC Management.

The other ex-Supreme, Mary Wilson, found it tough going: she had dealt Gordy another damaging blow shortly before in 1977 when she sued her former employer, alleging he had taken financial advantage of her being a minor when she signed with Motown. All manner of irregularities were bandied around in the court case, Wilson at one point claiming she received only $200–300 per week while the Supremes were earning millions for the company. Wilson's settlement entitled her to half of the rights to the name "The Supremes." This was a small yet significant victory as it allowed Wilson to tour with a reconstituted set of "Supremes," though, of course, the unit was a spent force commercially and performed for only a fraction of the fees it commanded with Ross. But, Motown retained the rights to exploit the name and Wilson's case dragged on until 1990, when, short of money and with little prospect of a career comeback, she came to an agreement with Gordy and signed away the rights to the name forever.

At the time of Ross' departure, Motown's music division had enough artists to keep it competitive in the industry, though Gordy was made to relent on some of his first principles. Stevie Wonder, for instance, in 1976 closed a deal that would have been unthinkable ten or even five years before. In Gordy's own words, it was "unprecedented": worth $13 million with a 20 percent royalty rate, the reputedly 120-page contract contained a clause that, in the event of Gordy deciding to sell Motown, Wonder would have to approve the buyer. Not only that: Wonder could assume more creative control over his material than any other artist in the history of the company and certainly any black American musician in history. This was totally at odds with Gordy's philosophy and it bore sweet and sour fruit.

Wonder had already produced four virtuoso albums in the early 1970s: *Music of My Mind, Talking Book, Innervisions* and *Fulfillingness' First Finale*; and his first piece after the contract was of the same class, a double album called *Songs in the Key of Life*. Wonder was going through his most fertile and gifted period and, commercially, Motown reaped the rewards. But, the contract allowed Wonder freedom to record in his own time rather than turn out material to order and he took three years to complete his next project, another double album called *Journey Through the Secret Life of Plants*. It was a colossal commercial failure, selling about 100,000 copies compared to the several million anticipated. But it still reached number eight in the British charts.

In 1975, Gordy sued the Jackson 5 and CBS for breach of contract and was countersued by the band, members of which asked the now-familiar question, "Where did our money go?" Gordy was awarded a somewhat derisory $100,000, but, much more tellingly, lost a singer who would become the world's bestselling artist as well as arguably the most important male icon of the late twentieth century.

Meanwhile, it was an open secret that Marvin Gaye had been drifting away from Gordy for a number of years. His habitual use of drugs and his conflictual marriage to Gordy's sister Anna exacerbated his relations with Motown. Gordy mediated in the divorce settlement when he offered Gaye a package: record an album and absolve himself of responsibility. Gordy would appropriate all the royalties and pay off his sister. Gordy described it to him as a "win-win" deal. Gaye rejected it on the grounds that it might earn millions, in which case he would see nothing. Gordy, on the other hand, would get it all, settle with his sister and keep the rest.

In 1978, Gaye's debts were reported to be $7 million. Two years behind on the alimony payments of two previous wives and pursued by the Internal Revenue, Gaye was ordered by a court to make an album as a way of generating funds to pay off his debts. Anna was to receive $305,000 of the advance royalties and $295,000 from the album's earnings. Grudgingly, Gaye made *Here, My Dear*, released by Motown in 1978 and now recognized as his most personal, introspective work, a purgation of his feelings of the time. Its poor reviews precipitated Gaye's flight and he spent time alone in Hawaii, England and Belgium.

Motown went without a Gaye studio album for three years, then released what Gaye considered an incomplete, unsatisfactory mishmash *In Our Lifetime*. "Motown shafted me," he declared to Ritz (1991: 280). In the months leading to the album's release in 1981, Gaye had been approached by Larkin Arnold, the head of black music at CBS and the man responsible for the Jacksons, as they were renamed after moving from Motown. He had a reputation as a pragmatic African American who sought out the best and delivered for his corporation. In Gaye he saw a great but troubled artist in his mid-forties who could disintegrate entirely or remake himself. Touted as the "new Berry Gordy," Arnold offered to pay off Gaye's debts and buy the remainder of his contract with Motown.

Gaye's first album with CBS, *Midnight Love*, sold over two million copies and a single taken from it, "Sexual healing" a million and still counting (its sales were given fresh stimulus when it was used under a car commercial on British television in 1994).This must have been galling for Gordy. But, not so galling as when *Thriller*, also released in 1982, sold 35 million copies. He must have felt like Bobby Robinson, who let Gladys Knight and Otis Redding among other stars slip through his fingers. Gaye's revival was tragically short: on April 1, 1984 , his forty-fifth birthday, he was killed by his father.

His biggest stars gone, Gordy looked to the Commodores and specifically the band's lead singer, Lionel Richie, for his salvation; and, after a slow start, the band delivered a series of commercially successful records in the late 1970s.

In May 1983, Gordy, his ranks depleted, made a deal with MCA, which had up to that point shown no interest in black music. The decision had been forced on Gordy after an acute dose of the perennial problem of making people pay: distributors were scattered around the country and each paid Motown at different rates of slowness. Gordy had resisted throwing in his hand with one single network because of the loss of independence it implied. The upside was that, as he puts it, "we could now look to one company for one check – that we knew would be there on time" (1994: 383). Gordy had earlier contemplated a different solution to the financial problem. In 1983, he needed Wonder's signature on an agreement to sell the Jobete publishing company. Wonder, invoking the clause he included in his 1976 contract, refused. Gordy proposed the sale minus Wonder's music and the deal fell through. The MCA remedy was less drastic, but did not resolve the problem completely.

With MCA distributing, Motown got an immediate lift. Richie's first solo album, *Can't Slow Down*, sold more than 10 million. Momentum picked up with Motown Production's deals to make a series of television specials, though these were, in effect, costly promotional instruments. Record sales mattered most and the market was changing. Tastes aside, marketing had taken on a new form with the advent of videos and the prime vehicle for them, MTV. Jay Lasker, Motown's record company president, did not believe in videos, according to Gordy: "He was from the old school, didn't believe in spending a buck if he couldn't see two coming back in" (1994: 389). This was not a philosophy for the late 1980s when promotion was everything and records could be made or broken on the decision of an MTV exec.

Compounding Gordy's problems was a potential conflict of interest thrown up by the MCA deal: the larger corporation distributed its own products as well as Motown's. Lasker was having to fight with the bigger fish even over small things, such as positioning in record stores. MCA was prepared to resolve this by buying Motown. Gordy weighed up his options: go public; merge with another company; sell off his personal assets and plunge them into Motown; auction the rights to his master recording at Sotheby's. None seemed realistic. So, in 1986, he decided to sell Motown. As before, he needed Wonder's permission. This time, the position was so dire that Wonder agreed. The deal collapsed just before the end of the year.

Gordy fired Lasker, brought in Al Bell, who had worked at Stax, and promoted some of his younger staff. He cut salaries and downsized the company. But, the product did not move off the shelves and, by mid-1988, Gordy reopened talks with MCA. Virgin Records was also interested in acquiring Motown, but MCA in partnership with a financial investment group called Boston Ventures closed the deal worth $61 million. The package included the name Motown, the master tapes and the artists' contracts. Gordy retained Motown Productions, Stone Diamond Music Publishing and his powerhouse Jobete Music, then valued at $200 million. Gordy set up a new company, Gordy Productions, to house these remaining entities.

Gordy's departure coincided with the end of the composite consumer and the start of a market shattered into smaller pieces, each with its own values, tastes and preferences. In the 1990s, the rap genre, particularly gangsta rap, came to exemplify – rightly or wrongly – black culture. Motown struggled uneasily with the quiet revolution. In 1995, it tried to get to grips with the new markets by appointing Andre Harrell as its CEO. Harrell had headed the MCA-owned Uptown Records, a small, but successful label specializing in rap, swing-beat and the 1990s variants of soul. We will return to rap and Harrell in Chapters eleven and twelve.

The predictable cries of "sellout!" greeted Gordy's decision. Until 1988, Motown was the only African-American-owned music corporation to have eluded the major players. CBS, through its Columbia and Epic labels (to which Michael Jackson was assigned), WEA, PolyGram, RCA, MCA and Capitol-EMI had mopped up most of the other black music. Gordy had held on to his independence for almost three decades; he was the epitome of the black bourgeoisie, living proof that black people driven by ambition and talent could make it to the very top but, in the final mix, even he relented to white power. Five years after the sale, PolyGram bought Motown for $301 million, suggesting that Gordy may have undervalued his own company. His detractors had a field day: he had sold something worth much more than $61 million, they argued: this was one of the most important domains of black culture; it might still be occupied by blacks, but it was no longer owned by them.

Looked at in a different way, Gordy had kept his lucrative publishing interest, dumped a record company, whose music was perfect for the 1960s but anachronistic in the 1980s, and walked away with $61 million. The business sense of this could not be faulted. And, without wishing to underplay the enormity of Gordy's accomplishments, the sale, like all of his moves, was guided by baser imperatives than the preservation of cultural autonomy. We are tempted to ask: would a white entrepreneur have done any different?

One of Gordy's strategic moves was to integrate whites into his management team. This was not a move designed to appease his artists and staff who saw him as something more than a boss. By 1970, when Ross was on the cusp of her new career and the Jackson 5 were in their stride, four of Motown's eight vice-presidents were white. As he devoted more and more time to making Ross a fully fledged star, he appointed more executive officers to senior management positions at Motown, so that, by 1977, with Ross peaking, whites held four of the five positions of genuine power at Motown. Because people like Barney Ales, Harry Balk, Tom Noonan, George Schiffer and Ralph Seltzer had such control and Gordy preferred to concentrate on Ross, Motown in its heyday was a virtually white company, Michael Roshkind and Harold and Sidney Novack holding positions just beneath Ales and Co. As Mary Wilson later reflected: "I'm surprised that we artists never addressed these issues back in the late sixties and seventies . . . once we moved to L. A., Motown was white-run" (1990: 229). What's more, Gordy even dropped Ruth Bowen's Queen Booking agency (covered in the previous chapter) in favor of the larger William Morris organization for handling his major acts, such as the Supremes, Temptations and Stevie Wonder.

This is by no means unusual. In fact, it may be a generic phenomenon. Research of my own in the late 1980s revealed that many successful black business owners, once they have established their companies, promote or bring in white personnel to top administrative positions for a variety of reasons, all of them informed by the recognition that, to prosper, you need two things: to operate in a market that is, in numerical terms, dominated by whites; and to deal effectively with other companies, who will probably be owned by whites, some of whom may be racist enough not to want to do business with a black person (Cashmore, 1992). Everything in Gordy's behavior indicates that he was well aware of this. His whole enterprise might be seen as a testament to this awareness. The process of appointing whites to senior positions at the expense of well-qualified blacks is a case of "racism by proxy."

The timeliness of the decision to take Ross from the Supremes and issue her on a solo path, his acumen in underwriting her first movie with $2 million (when Paramount went cold on the project) and his refashioning an undernourished ghetto kid into a flamboyant, color-free diva strengthens the view that Gordy knew his market and had a plan for how to get into it. While his contemporaries at Atlantic and, to an extent, Chess annulled some of their artists' attempts to mimic white performers, Gordy in many cases reversed the process. Gaye is one of the clearest examples.

"Everyone wanted to sell to whites 'cause whites got the most money," Gaye told his biographer, adding that, at Motown, "Our attitude was – give us some" (Ritz, 1991: 73). Gaye's image was symmetrical with Gordy's. The singer was, as David Ritz describes him in his biography, a *Divided Soul*, a singer whose primary influences included Billie Holiday and Ray Charles, but who aspired to being another Frank Sinatra. He found an ally in Gordy. Passionate about success in white markets, Gordy booked him as often as possible on national television, being careful to present him as "wholesome" and, where possible, with big band accompaniment. Gaye, as Ritz observes, "did everything he could to win a mainstream middle-class audience, crooning the ballads he thought white music lovers wanted to hear" (1991: 107). He may not have felt comfortable doing it, but he went along with all Gordy's games, performing on the white dinner club circuit, dressed in tux and bowtie.

His big clashes at Motown were with producer Norman Whitfield, who was responsible for the Temptations' distinct sound. Whitfield was assigned to Gaye in 1968 and they came near to fighting. "He made me sing in keys much higher than I was used to. He had me reaching for notes that caused my throat veins to bulge," said Gaye (quoted in Ritz, 1991: 124). But Gordy knew what he was doing: the fruit of their conflict was Gaye's first number one record, "I heard it through the grapevine" and, later, the album *MPG* which signalled his arrival in the mainstream market. At the height of his success, Gaye confessed to feeling like "Berry's puppet," yet showed little resistance, at one point recording an advertising jingle aired on a Detroit radio station. (The Supremes took the prize for endorsements, allowing a loaf to be named after them, Supremes White Bread, and showing their armpits in a tv commercial for Arrid deodorant.)

In Gordy's relations with Gaye and, to a greater extent, Ross, we find processes intrinsic to the black culture industry writ small. Gordy, a black male guided by a vision of success in capitalist America, profiting from – and, according to many, exploiting – black entertainers, but not just by promoting them: by commodifying them in such a way as to make them assimilable by whites. Tailored exactly to the demands of a white market, Gordy's products were often well-paid and so willing accomplices to his deeds. Even Gaye, whose late career indulgences led him away from Gordy's influences, for all his protestations, was cheerfully obedient even if: "Sometimes I felt like the shuffle-and-jive niggers of old, steppin' and fetchin' for the white folk" (quoted in Ritz, 1991: 106).

Turning black artists into colorless entertainers (rather than the kinds of stereotypes discussed earlier) involves something akin to keyhole surgery. One can imagine Gordy standing over his patient, his fingers carefully inserting probes into the body, his eyes fixed on one of those monitors we are all used to seeing on *ER*. His hands are on one thing, his eyes another; yet they are co-ordinated. Gordy's predatory eyes were on the market while his hands were firmly on his artists. A precisian in all he did, Gordy would oversee every dance step, every hand movement, every note, in trying to calibrate his products to the needs of the mainstream market. And every move he made was affected by the pathos of inequality, the quality in western culture that excites the thought and feeling of a racial hierarchy. Gordy served up black culture for whites. He had few other options, were he to stay true to his visions of a black-owned corporation with power not just to reflect images, but to produce them. "Gordy's Motown plantation," as Murray calls it, did not turn out a succession of time-honored racist images (1989: 95). Ross, especially, was very much a one-off, though, of course, her mannered beginnings reflected Gordy's care as accurately as it reflected whites' expectations.

The criticism that Motown's stars were *fantoccini* may not be a criticism at all, but a commendation. Gordy, as I suggested before, understood whites. Famed gambler he may have been in many aspects of his life, but, on examination, he left very little to chance. What would a predominantly white market want of blacks? Not warrantable human beings, perhaps, but performing marionettes, all perfectly co-ordinated, moving fluently, even gymnastically in sync, the cadence of their motions keyed to the music. No evidence of the thought or imagination that contributes to spontaneous action: these were programmed performers. Wonderful to watch and listen to, but somehow inhuman. Few Motown stars developed their own personalities, certainly not in early years. It is at least possible that Gordy's insight into the white mind led him to dehumanize his artists, reducing them to components of a unit and only rarely releasing one to develop individuality. It is too crass to say that this was for the benefit of whites: Gordy was too artful to fall into the minstrelsy trap. He was playing a bigger game, giving a little to take a whole lot.

But, his game was a revelation: it showed the power of whites' images in affecting the ways or patterns in which blacks construct a culture that is, in a genuine sense, theirs. Gordy had grasped the importance of race early in his career; we noted this in this chapter's opening paragraphs. It could either beat him, or he could work around it: he could not beat *it*. His own failed business ventures and the minor but significant tradition of black entrepreneurs might easily have reminded him that the products of industries not managed or owned by whites were undervalued – another implication of the racial hierarchy, of course. To be an exception to this, he needed to work within parameters set by whites. He never really pushed hard against them: his success with Ross was more a congruence of time and subject than a tradition-shattering exercise. Then again, we might say that Motown itself and, for that matter, soul, the Philly sound and the blaxploitation era were congruences. But, let me conclude this chapter with a final comment about the man behind Motown.

Gordy could have paid his artists more; too many of them left and filed suit to dismiss the suggestion that he was tightfisted with them; as producer Clarence Paul, who worked closely with Gordy, put it: "Just about everybody got ripped off at Motown" (quoted in Ritz, 1991: 61). He could have been less of a martinet in his approach to running the business. He could have been less monistic about Ross and dispensed his attentions more equitably among his artists. He could have been less ruthless about artists who bore no great market value (compare the treatment of two awkward artists, Ballard who got squeezed and Wonder who got a $13 million contract). Gordy could have done all of these things and more; but would he have presided over an industry whose very name resonates like a thunderclap? These may look like failings; yet they may also be the reasons for his success where others had failed. If there is a fault in Gordy, it is not in endorsing a success ethic, but in showing that its pursuit requires a degree of assimilation many find abhorrent.

Chapter eight

Rejecting It,
Living Up
To It

SOMETIMES PARTICULAR EVENTS seem to contain a swirl of the conflictual social forces that surround them. Sometimes a crisis prompts one group to remind another that history has moved on. Sometimes an individual subject seems to embody a period. As America awoke after dozing in its postwar complacency, the 1960s exploded with demands for basic human rights. With those demands met, at least in a legal sense, the country approached the final two decades of the millennium in need of an idol who transcended the color divisions. The idol was able to do this, being an African American who was scarcely black and, ultimately, scarcely human.

America's tradition of keeping black and white entertainers on different levels of the racial hierarchy had been under threat for a while. In August 1968 the National Association of Television and Radio Announcers held its thirteenth annual convention in Miami, Florida. The organization known by its acronym Natra started life in 1955 as the National Association for Radio Announcers and comprised 400 black djs from small southern stations. In the 1960s the organization metamorphosed from a trades association to a more openly political assembly. The central power relation that engaged Natra was that of white ownership and black employment: whites owned radio stations and record companies and black people worked as djs and made records. The split over the means of production was as clean as that.

But, the social activities for which Natra meetings were famous still attracted paparazzi from all over the country. Motown and Stax usually threw the biggest press parties. Motown was enjoying good fortune with two solid-selling albums, the Supremes' *Love Child* and the Temptations' *Cloud Nine*. Stax and Atlantic, though rocked by Otis Redding's death, still had an armada of quality artists and was buoyant, as was virtually any other label that had black artists on its roster. It was a time when black music could do no wrong but in which black people were frequently wronged.

Natra's executive secretary, Del Shields, captured the spirit of the Miami convention when he addressed the gathered crowd: "We are not begging the record companies for anything, but they will have to make us part of it if they wish to stay in business" (quoted in Guralnick, 1986: 382). It was a curious allusion and one that owed much to the gathering momentum generated by the movement known as Black Power.

Foregrounded at this convention was Jerry Wexler, of Atlantic, who was scheduled to receive an award for his and Ahmet Ertegun's contributions since the 1950s. But, there was both negative as well as positive electricity in the air: an effigy of Wexler hanging publicly was evidence of this and Wexler was advised to flee for his own safety. Phil Walden, who was, as we saw in Chapter five, the manager of Redding and co-owner (with Wexler) of Capricorn Records, received death threats. Marshall Sehorn, a white New Orleans impresario was assaulted. And, in one memorable though apocryphal incident, a group of white record executives were forcibly removed from the convention, taken to a yacht moored in the Atlantic ocean and made to promise to give blacks a greater role in the running of their organization. The convention became a focal point for all the tensions that lay outside and, while the organizers disavowed any links with militant black movements, their influences were pervasive. Guralnick quotes Homer Banks, singer/songwriter with Stax, who summed up the source of the tension: "Blacks made the music, blacks made the audience, but the ownership was white" (1986: 384). About the same time, James Brown's "Say it loud, I'm black and I'm proud" made the bestselling lists. It was a lyric that valorized a quality demeaned or despised for much of America's history.

For a while in the 1960s, the United States seemed to be a society cracking apart. The streets of LA, Detroit and Newark were virtual battlegrounds where black people, frustrated by liberals' persistent calls for patience, issued notice of their intentions. For many, the gradual progress advocated by the civil rights movement was redundant. Progress toward what? they asked. The next step up the racial hierarchy, perhaps. Then, on August 11, 1965, a police officer's attempt to arrest a black youth in the Watts district of South Central Los Angeles catalyzed six days of destruction, in which blacks burnt and looted property, torched cars and hurled Molotov cocktails at the police. The National Guard was called in, but this only exacerbated matters and, for six days, the whole area was engulfed in a transforming urban drama that was to become a central symbol in the landscape of American race relations. The uprising spread to practically all major cities with black populations and, for two years, there were outbreaks all over North America, the last of these coming in July 1967 when a Detroit vice squad conducted raids on gambling clubs used by blacks. It seemed any incident involving police and blacks had the potential to spark disorder: in Detroit, at the end of one week, 43 people had been killed and arrests numbered over 7,000.

Many, incredulous at blacks' destruction of their own environments, saw only undirected, purposeless anger. But Douglas Glasgow, in his book *The Black Underclass*, was able to make some sense of the rioters' motives:

> Their rage was directed at white society's structure, its repressive institutions, and their symbols of exploitation in the ghetto: the chain stores, the oligopolies that control the distribution of goods; the lenders, those who hold the indebtedness of the ghetto bound; the absentee landlords; and the agents who control the underclass while safeguarding the rights of those who exploit it
>
> (1980: 106)

Glasgow cites "poverty, racial discrimination, long-term isolation from the broader society" as probable causes of the uprisings. We should include the sense of entrapment felt by African Americans in the inner cities after almost a decade of grasping at the hope offered by civil rights. Every successive generation of blacks had become beasts of burden, their task to carry everyone else's yearning and ambitions out of the ghetto. The generation galvanized by King and his movement at last ventured toward something more tangible than mere hope. Yet eight years after the Southern Christian Leadership Conference was formed and after bus boycotts, marches and a sustained campaign of black protest, King's utopian "I have a dream" had turned to "I have no time for dreamers."

The alternative posed by Huey P. Newton, Eldridge Cleaver and others was to generate black power by creating cultural, economic and educational institutions owned, governed and staffed by blacks for the benefit of blacks. It encouraged independence from whites in every possible way. This meant liberating consciousness from old colonial ideas, many of which, as we have seen, structured the entry of blacks into cultural spheres. Black people should *think* black and project this in their behavior. This is precisely why James Brown's number resonated: it proclaimed blackness as an ideal, rather than something to be ignored or concealed by cultural assimilation.

The term "black power" had actually been used by civil rights activist Stokely Carmichael at a 1966 meeting of the Student Nonviolent Coordinating Committee (SNCC) in Mississippi, though it took on added meaning when it became associated with the Black Panthers, an Oakland-based group founded in 1966 as a response to police violence against African Americans. At the time, it was not a cause that commended itself to the mass of Americans. Inspired by Bobby Seales and Huey P. Newton, the Panthers took advantage of local California law allowing them to carry guns. Tensions between group members and law enforcement authorities inevitably produced bloodshed. (In 1995, Mario van Peebles' movie *Panther* portrayed the groups in an heroic light, while promoting the theory that the FBI worked with the Mafia to flood ghettos with cheap heroin in order to neutralize the rising radical black movement.)

H. Rap Brown, on succeeding Carmichael as chair of the SNCC, summed up the Panther approach when he said: "America won't come around . . . so we're going to burn America down" (quoted in Sitkoff, 1981: 217). The words could have been set to music and come straight from an Atlantic/Stax track. Soul music was a virtual rallying cry for black power. For Brown, America was a place of licensed devilry; where the diabolical treatment of blacks had gone unchecked for the best part of 400 years. Civil rights campaigners were seeking only adjustments to the institutional order that had enslaved their ancestors and would continue to contain them.

While it was not recognized as such in its day, Martha and the Vandellas' "Dancing in the street," released by Motown in 1964 (co-written by Marvin Gaye), anticipated the restless, irresistible mood that was building when Martha Reeves told listeners to get ready for a "brand new beat," as if sensing the "long, hot summer," as it became known.

No nation has struggled more strenuously with the race issue. The United States' problem has been, in its own way, even greater than that of South Africa, which shamelessly pronounced apartheid as its constitutional policy. American culture recognizes no official barriers to progress, which is why it has been impaled on the horns of its own unique dilemma: how to keep up the pretense of the land of opportunity, while denying opportunity to a substantial minority because of its purported "race."

From the 1920s, blues was the musical expression of a larger human tragedy. The "separate but equal" doctrine ensured that America comprised two completely distinct societies, each with its own institutions, customs and culture. Blues was the music that issued from the lesser of those two societies. It gave disturbing particularity to the experience of being in America but never really part of it. In a way, its development as a genre reflected the exclusion: commercially exploited by patrician whites, blues records sold in the main to African Americans. It was also snubbed by many African Americans, who decried it as devil's music.

Plessy v. Ferguson (of 1896), the ruling that gave force to the idea that blacks and whites should exist separately, was not effectively challenged until the 1950s when the Supreme Court was asked to deliberate on whether segregated schooling actually harmed young black people educationally. On May 17, 1954, the conclusion to the *Brown v. Board of Education of Topeka* case arrived; it was that: "Separate educational facilities are inherently unequal." Lawyers were jubilant; the mass of the black population were more restrained: changes to the law would not necessarily spell changes in their material circumstances. Suspicions were confirmed. White backlash took various forms: from the burnings and lynchings that broke out in southern states, especially the virulently racist Mississippi, to the white flight – white parents fearful of having their children share facilities with blacks fled the cities.

At an intellectual level, the arguments against the *Brown* decision turned on an interpretation of a constitutional point rather than a neanderthal cry for a bygone age. In his article, "The other and the almost the same," Paul Berman makes the point: "Segregationists did not necessarily defend Jim Crow as such; they defended an individual's right to choose his own associates" (1994: 202).

Many southern black people moved north in the 1950s, Chicago being a booming urban center. As we saw, the Chess label, based in that city, was able to capitalize on many of the bluesmen who migrated. The Chicago blues was born in this period. Apart from the job opportunities it offered, Chicago's segregation was not nearly as fierce as that of the south; blacks could at least hold low-paying government jobs, for example. Fourteen-year-old Emmett Till, coming from Chicago, was not familiar with the southern folkways. Visiting relatives in Money, Mississippi, he managed to upset local whites and was brutally murdered for his sins. Photographs of Till's mutilated corpse which had been dragged from the Tallahatchie River, were published nationally. "It is difficult to measure just how profound an effect the public viewing of Till's body created," writes Juan Williams. "But without question it moved black America in a way the Supreme Court ruling of school desegregation could not match" (1987: 44).

It was a crucial, if gruesome landmark in the civil rights movement's history, especially as, at the trial of the two white males accused of the murder, an African American, Mose Wright, stood up when asked to identify the men who had abducted Till, and stretched out his arm to point. It was extremely rare, not to say dangerous, for a black person to testify against a white and, on this occasion, it carried symbolic importance. It captured the indignation and fury of many blacks for whom the legal abolition of discrimination meant little. This combination was vital to the civil rights movement. Triggered by a bus boycott in December 1955, the ethic behind civil rights quickly radiated across the south with more and more blacks and a substantial number of whites mobilizing behind King.

As we saw, King's philosophy worked up to a point. His successes in boycotts and demonstrations in Montgomery, Alabama, and Nashville were tempered by a reverse in Albany and Alabama. Less successful campaigns at the latter two prompted some factions of the movement to question King's resolutely nonviolent tactics. After Albany, King recognized what many entrepreneurs, like the Chess brothers and Ertegun and Abrahams, had already picked up: that the African American market has a power of its own. King said: "The Negro has enough buying power in Birmingham to make the difference between profit and loss in any business" (quoted in Williams, 1987: 183).

Birmingham was the scene of an extraordinarily violent confrontation in 1963, its drama heightened by the presence of television camera crews which were able to relay images to the nation. They were images of young children being blasted by water cannons and police dogs chasing protesters. Five hundred state troopers were called into action in what many suspected was an overreaction. It was another key event, coming as it did nine years after the *Brown* decision: it reminded the whole country how little the legislation had affected the lives of most black people. Here they were, still fighting for their legal rights and being treated in an almost subhuman way for their temerity. Black unemployment was over twice the rate of whites'. So, in the same year, when King chose to organize a march on the capital, he was able to garner the support of an estimated 250,000 people, as many as 60,000 of them white. It was the largest demonstration ever in North America and it culminated with King's mighty dream speech.

While King pursued his dream, Malcolm X offered a different strategy. As he once said in a barely concealed reference to King: "I think any black man who goes among so-called Negroes today who are being brutalized, spit upon in the worst fashion imaginable and teaches those Negroes to turn the other cheek , to suffer peacefully, or love their enemy is a traitor to the Negro." In 1965 he was assassinated, as was King three years later.

King's movement had sought to coax blacks out of their homes, sometimes, out of the ghettos and into the civil rights movement and his achievements were plain to see. Among the changes ushered in by the 1964 Civil Rights Act were an end to segregated facilities and the criminalization of racial discrimination. This was supplemented a year later by further legislation that guaranteed voting rights for blacks. King had accomplished this by a careful program of negotiation and nonviolent protest. Using Gandhi as his model, King trained his followers to tolerate extreme physical and verbal abuse without striking back. It was an approach that brought him into conflict with Malcolm X, in many ways King's *alter ego*, who was famously known to have regarded violence as one of the "means necessary" and a form of "intelligence" in certain conditions.

Issues on which King had based his movement began to seem less relevant. The right to vote and access to a decent education were ceding place to more basic concerns, such as access to jobs and housing. These were the issues that guided the more radical approach of black power, or black nationalism. Events from 1965 indicated that any coherence that the civil rights movement ever had was fractured and that many blacks thought change would come about only as a result of direct, violent action. For them, Sam Cooke's 1964 single "Change is gonna come" was only wishful thinking.

In his book *Martin Luther King, Jr.*, W. R. Miller describes his subject's most remarkable achievement as his success in making middle class blacks the "backbone" of his crusade. When King began to mobilize his organization in the south, one-fifth of the population in that region was black and, of these, at least one in three was above the poverty line. The import of this is that there was a sizeable proportion of African Americans who were beyond worrying about sheer survival and were ambitious enough to become the backbone of a mass movement for reform. King's association with a nascent black middle class was one of the secrets of his success in leading a movement of great scale and force, but it was also the reason why, even as early as 1960, when he was 31, "he seemed rather remote from the mind and mood that simmered across black college campuses," as Manning Marable put it in *Race, Rebellion and Reform* (1984).

During the period from 1960 when Marable reckons the nationalist movement began to rise and 1965 when rioting in Watts began, the civil rights movement picked up momentum through the support not only of middle class blacks, but of whites. King realized that the longevity of his movement depended on winning over whites and maintaining their allegiance. He was able to do this by appealing not only to their finer liberal spirits, but also to their pockets: black people, he reminded the nation, had disposable income too.

On May 19, 1968, three black poets and a conga player commemorated the birth of Malcolm X. After performing at Mount Morris (now Marcus Garvey) Park, in Harlem, they decided to stay together and record their poetry. Taking their name from a passage by South-African-born poet K. William Kgositsile, the Last Poets identified with the radical black nationalism that surrounded them and expressed this in their recordings, one of which was "Niggers are scared of revolution." By 1975, the Last Poets had released six invective-filled albums. In the same period, black singer-songwriters like Richie Havens and Gil Scott Heron aligned themselves with the nationalist movement, producing music that both embodied and ennobled nationalist sentiments. (The Last Poets reformed and toured in 1996, though by then their work seemed of only historical interest; Heron continued to write, record and appear in movies; in the 1990s Havens became a prolific singer of jingles for television commercials.)

It is difficult to imagine any aspect of American society that remained untouched by the social changes of the ten years after *Brown*; it is no exaggeration to say that the black presence was transfigured. With the world at the cusp of postcolonialism as African states gained their independence from Europe's former imperial powers, another form of independence was being fought for in the USA. The struggle against subjection in Africa offered a clear comparison with the civil rights struggle. In both situations, some form of accommodation had to be sought: how to incorporate groups which had been regarded as inferior for so long into a system based on the concept of racial hierarchy. The 1965 Voting Rights Act was the cornerstone of a political incorporation that ensured blacks held a stake in the system that many might otherwise have continued to oppose. Cultural incorporation was a different matter.

There is little doubt that swaths of the southern white population resisted what King had referred to as a self-evident truth: "that all men are created equal." But, in the ten-year long process, many white conceptions had been dislodged and a new generation of Wasps had grown. This was a time of reappraisal. Young people were becoming radicalized, prepared to drop their commitments to what President Lyndon B. Johnson was calling the Great Society, and hurling themselves behind causes that seemed linked, however tenuously, to American imperialism. Opposition to the Vietnam war sucked away some of the energy that had been vital to civil rights as young whites focused their efforts on ending US involvement in the Southeast Asian conflict. Blacks were either too concerned with their own struggles or, as Ronald Segal suggests in *The Black Diaspora*, keen to analyze the war in terms of a broader perspective: "For them, the war was a manifestation of an imperial white racism in the United States, and the developing preoccupation of young whites with opposing the war rather than confronting the racism behind it was evidence of the need for blacks to rely only on themselves" (1995: 258–59).

Relying on themselves was something blacks were well used to. In fact, they were actively encouraged to do so by President Richard M. Nixon, though, of course, he didn't have protest in mind when he applauded what he called "black capitalism." Still, the imperative that guides the one, guides the other. James Brown was known to have structured his ventures (documented in Chapter six) in terms of Nixon's recommendations for blacks. Brown became something of a yardstick for many black musicians who augmented their performing careers with business enterprises designed to enhance their autonomy. Jimi Hendrix, for example, opened his Electric Lady Studio in Greenwich Village; and the Artist ♀, once known as Prince, founded Paisley Park, which was a recording studio with many other facilities. But Brown's style was also an inspiration to countless would-be artists. In July 1968, Berry Gordy first saw a nine-year-old who auditioned with a respectable version of Brown's "I got the feelin'" with the moves to match. Gordy concluded: "His dazzling footwork would have certainly made the Godfather [Brown] proud" (1994: 280).

―――――――――――

Michael Jackson's first meeting with Gordy came one month before the Natra convention, in many ways a microcosm of wider conflicts. The morphology of popular black music had begun to change with the advent of bands that owed as much to white rock as to black soul. Despite the presence of Smokey Robinson on its organizing committee, the Monterey International Pop Festival, in June 1967, had showcased only one act that could pass as soul: Otis Redding backed by Booker T. and the MGs. The Jimi Hendrix Experience, which had emerged in Britain over the previous 12 months, planted an interesting signpost for black music. But, for the most part, the festival, which is often seen as the incubator for a generation of subversive rock, featured bands like the Mamas and the Papas, Jefferson Airplane and the Grateful Dead.

His musical abilities notwithstanding, Hendrix's unpopularity in the early 1960s seems to have been founded on the sort of performances that would later turn him into an iconoclastic rock star. His unkempt appearance and tendency to drift into abstract guitar riffs got him tossed out of an assortment of blues and rock'n'roll outfits. His period in Little Richard's band seems to have influenced his stage presence. Richard, in contrast to most black performers, was outrageously camp: his pompadour hairdo, pencil moustache and oversize suits gave him a wild, manic look and he lived up to it, screaming and vamping his way through the most theatrical of all rock'n'roll acts.

Hendrix was given more space in the context of a band led by John Hammond Jr which was gigging in Greenwich Village in 1966 when Chas Chandler was visiting from England. Chandler, having played bass for the white blues band the Animals, had sound connections in the music business, especially in London. He and his own former manager Mike Jeffery signed Hendrix to a management contract and paid for him to fly to England, where Chandler positioned him as the head of a trio. Hendrix's stage act was visually arresting, though his material was mostly taken from the Atlantic/Stax repertoire. Chandler, however, pushed Hendrix toward a much more abrasive sound, encouraging his virtuosity on guitar. As Richard used his piano, Hendrix was to use his guitar – as an intimate. Not only did he play it, he stretched it across his back, thrust it between his legs and bit its strings.

Chandler's choice of a first single was also quite interesting. Although Hendrix had been performing soul and writing his own compositions, Chandler dug out an old folk number, which had been recorded by a number of bands, including the Leaves and the Byrds. "Hey Joe" had been given a contemporary arrangement by Tim Rose. Neither Rose, nor the original composer, probably Billy Roberts (according to Hendrix's biographer, Murray), was credited on the single which stated "Trad. arr. J. Hendrix" meaning that Hendrix himself claimed the royalties. This move was no doubt motivated by the Animals' huge success, "House of the Rising Sun," also a traditional song for which the Animals claimed credit for a new arrangement.

Having recorded the track, Chandler then had to hawk it around several major record companies before closing a deal with London-based Polydor. A momentous appearance on British television boosted sales of the single. Hendrix cut across all popular images the British had of blacks; in contrast to the polished soul and Motown musicians who had toured before him, Hendrix looked almost dishevelled, his hair a frizzed, untamed mane, his clothes a colorful but unruly ensemble. And his furious handling of his guitar added to the wildness.

Chandler worked with Track Records for the next two singles, then signed a deal with Reprise Records, a subsidiary of Warner Brothers, for the band's US rights. By early 1968, Hendrix had sold over a million copies of his first album, *Are You Experienced?* and was on his way to becoming one of the world's premier rock acts. His stage appearances were outlandish affairs, Chandler having urged his charge to act up to the wild man image. Here and there, there was evidence that the image may not have been completely manufactured. The hush money paid to a woman who claimed Hendrix had beaten her up; the night spent in a police cell in Gothenberg, Sweden, after a hotel room scene; the fight with his white bassist, Noel Redding: these began to wear on Chandler, who sold his share of the managerial contract to Jeffery for $300,000. Despite having produced some tracks on Hendrix's third album, *Electric Ladyland*, Chandler's name was omitted and Hendrix claimed sole credit.

Commercially, the album was his most successful, as was the single taken from it "All along the watchtower." By June 1969, Hendrix headed reputedly the highest paid rock band in the world: he received $125,000 for a performance at the San Fernando Valley, then the highest sum ever paid a rock act for a single show. Hendrix regularly commanded between $50,000 and $100,000 per show. But his personal wealth did not rise proportionately. One reason was his extravagant use of studio time. Never one to stick to schedules, Hendrix was fond of spending days and nights on end at the expensive New York studio, the Record Plant. The cost of this became such a cause of concern to Jeffery that he suggested that Hendrix have his own studio. Finding the capital for what was to be Electric Lady proved a problem and Reprise had to kick in $250,000 to keep the project alive.

The second drain on Hendrix's potential income was the product of a contract he had signed some years before with an entrepreneur named Ed Chalpin. This was overlooked when Hendrix went with Chandler, but, of course, Chalpin became aware of the signature's value and took Hendrix to court. He was awarded 2 percent of the royalties from Hendrix's first three albums and a new album that Hendrix would make for his record company. It was a handsome return on a contract that was once practically worthless. Hendrix was resentful of Chalpin's good fortune.

At the height of his powers, Hendrix ditched his two white band members and linked up with Buddy Miles and Billy Cox, both African Americans, to form a trio and make an album, *Band of Gypsys*. The band did not last and a reconstituted Experience, with Cox and original member Mitch Mitchell, went on tour. Whatever positive part drugs had played in Hendrix's early career, their influence on his downfall outweighed. It is possible that the extremities of his performances were made possible by drugs; but several of his concerts were marred by his indulgence and, in 1970, Cox was hospitalized after having a drink spiked during a British tour. Waiting in London for Cox to recover, Hendrix, then 27, took sleeping pills and choked on his own vomit. Hendrix is an important figure for all sorts of reasons; but the only one that interests us in this book is his inadvertent impact on the black culture industry. Hendrix was an African American, discovered, managed and produced, at least in his early career, by whites; his two main band members were white; he played music associated with whites; his peers were mainly white; his fandom was overwhelmingly white; and he rarely uttered a word that might be construed as political; his "Star spangled banner" at Woodstock was his most dramatic instrumental statement. *Band of Gypsys* was dedicated to "all the soldiers fighting in Chicago and Detroit and, oh yes, all the soldiers fighting in Vietnam." David Henderson, in his *'Scuse Me While I Kiss the Sky*, recounts an incident in which "a black nationalist type" chastised Hendrix. "Hey, brother, you better come home," he said, to which Hendrix replied: "You gotta do what you gotta do and I gotta do what I got to do *now*" (1983: 287).

If, on September 18, 1970, he had been revived and had lived on, we would know him today, perhaps in the same way as we know Carlos Santana, another outstanding lead guitarist of the 1960s, or Ian Anderson, synonymous with Jethro Tull, which succeeded Hendrix as the highest grossing rock band in the 1970s. In other words, not very well. It is unlikely that he would have drifted into the middle of the road like Eric Clapton, to whose playing his was often compared. His death all but sanctified him in the same way as Jim Morrison, or Janis Joplin, both casualties of the same era. No other black artist has been afforded nearly the same reverence as Hendrix; his crossover was about as complete as it could be. The reasons for this are not hard to find.

In a sense, Hendrix was a retrograde, a throwback to the racist images of the early twentieth century when, as Frederickson describes the popular stereotype: "Negroes were literally wild beasts, with uncontrollable sexual passions and criminal natures stamped by heredity" (1987: 276). No one can be absolutely sure whether Hendrix's onstage performance was carefully thought-out theater, or untrammelled spontaneity; but, it certainly enhanced his bestial reputation, especially when set alongside stories of his private tantrums. His libido was another subject: known to favor white women, Hendrix was famed for his sexual appetite and the size of his penis was the subject of much debate. He lived up to the role historically reserved for threatening black males.

Yet, Hendrix was not threatening. Out of control, he might have been, but it was for no purpose save his own destruction. He never commented on the condition of blacks in America, nor for that matter, in Britain. While US cities lay in ashes, Hendrix was too preoccupied in a "Purple haze" to care. Even in 1968 when Martin Luther King was assassinated and the black population trembled in anticipation of what awaited them, Hendrix was silent. He was the perfect black superstud with not a political thought in his head. Even his demise accorded perfectly with expectations: a black man so bent on pursuing pleasures of the senses, he failed to notice how his binges were killing him.

Perhaps somewhere in his early conception, Chandler saw great value in an artistically brilliant yet apolitical black man with extraordinary virility and a wayward stage presence. If so, he was right. But what was Hendrix's value to the black culture industry? Simply put, he was the first black musician to gain access to a white worldwide audience playing rock music. The genre may have had deep roots in the blues, but its principal exponents were all white and the late 1960s/early 1970s were years when even labels like Atlantic were snapping up white bands, like Vanilla Fudge and Led Zeppelin. Hendrix was as odd as a white soul singer, though, of course, there were plenty of those too. As such, he was the precursor to black artists such as Vernon Reid, Lenny Kravitz and the Artist ♀. He also alerted entrepreneurs to the fact that existing categories were restrictive and unnecessary; blacks did not have to play soul or the Motown sound to make money. By the early 1970s, both were at best fading forces, anyway: hard rock was the thing.

Perhaps the band that best captured the temperament of the times was Sly and the Family Stone, the brainchild of Texan multi-instrumentalist, producer and dj Sylvester Stewart. The band worked the bars and clubs of the 1960s counter-cultural nucleus, San Francisco, honing its act to appeal to white audiences, but without necessarily trying to effect a crossover. As Greil Marcus writes: "Sly was less interested in crossing racial and musical lines than in tearing them up" (1976: 81).

In 1968, the single "Dance to the music" established the seven-piece band in both Britain and the USA. Conceptually, the track nodded a little to Arthur Conley's "Sweet soul music" and its delivery had a touch of the James Browns. But the dominant influence was white rock: lots of fuzzbox and wah-wahs, it gave its audiences no peace from changing leads, its singers swapping in a series of rhythmic to-and-fros. In this and subsequent records on the Epic label, Sly Stone, to use the band's shorter title, made an unnerving bid to produce a musical equivalent of the changes in black consciousness. The albums *Stand!* and the much tougher and untidier *Riot* echo the change from civil rights to black power. Of the latter, Marcus remarks: "It is not casual music and its demands are not casual; it tended to force black musicians to reject it or live up to it" (1976: 93).

Gordy was ready for the challenge. In the Jackson 5, he had the kind of raw material that could easily be dropped on to the production line for immediate processing. But better: the Jackson 5 were punchy enough to accommodate the rock impulses that were running through newer forms of black music. This funky sound was to become a mainstay of black popular music in the early 1970s and Motown's acquisition of the Jackson 5 positioned the label perfectly.

Unlike soul, funk was a musical form that could be defined in strictly technical musical terms: its syncopation was distinct and brass sections were emphasized. Parliament-Funkadelic, or P-Funk for short, led by George Clinton and Bootsie Collins (previously with James Brown's Famous Flames) expanded from a band to a complete theatrical troupe complete with costumes, almost challenging other funk outfits, like Earth, Wind and Fire and Kool and the Gang to match their extravagance. This was a self-conscious attempt by Clinton to dramatize his music in a way that met white expectations of blacks – as clownish performers. It also started a period of oneupmanship, in which many black ensembles became so preoccupied with performance that they neglected the substance of earlier funk.

Motown infused one of its leading acts with funk when it released the Temptations' "Cloud nine." The track, co-written and produced by Norman Whitfield, was a total departure for the band and included allusions to the kinds of drugs then being used and sung about (by Sly Stone among others). Its release began a sequence of what Murray (1989) calls "epic ghetto-realist singles" by the Temptations, most written by Whitfield and Barrett Strong, culminating in 1972 with "Papa was a rollin' stone," which had listeners "shivering," according to Marcus (1976: 94).

"Eventually, Motown co-opted Sly's sound even more perfectly by signing a young family vocal group named the Jackson 5," says Murray, suggesting further that "to emphasize their freshness and novelty, their new-age distinction from an older generation of soul stars, Motown's legendary grooming department kitted them out exactly like five miniature Jimi Hendrixes" (1989: 176). This probably exaggerates the extent to which Motown tried to mimic Sly and Hendrix, but the basic point is fair enough: the Jackson brothers were Motown's main response to the cultural changes of the late 1960s. And tame as they seem from today's vantage point, one of them caught the changing cultural currents and transmitted them through his music and his personae.

It is difficult to imagine a more perfect congruity of time and subject than the 1980s and Michael Jackson. From a James Brown mimic, Jackson bounded onward and outward, acquiring dimensions and qualities that made him the most relevant male icon of his time (Madonna being the female counterpart, of course). For much of his early career, Jackson was a child star who might easily have fizzled out amid the caprice of cultural tastes. Instead, he mutated into an enigma that fascinated the world.

Chapter nine

Infant Icon

THE JACKSON 5 were caught between conflicting demands. As a Gordy band, they would be taught to assimilate in such a way as to make them acceptable to a mainly white market. This meant that they could not be seen to endorse the black power ethic that pervaded not only America but vast portions of the world in the late 1960s. Yet, for a black band to appear utterly devoid of political awareness would have been suicidal. The very fact that they all wore Afro hairdos suggested a minimal identification with what was going on about them. But, when a Motown publicist was asked by a magazine journalist if their hairstyles "had something to do with Black Power," the question was met with a sharp riposte. "These are children, not adults," the publicist snapped. "Let's not get into that."

The incident is related by J. Randy Taraborrelli in his *Michael Jackson: The magic and the madness*, and the conclusion to it is interesting. "Michael – a media master at the age of thirteen – understood that his lack of social consciousness would not look good when the writer's story appeared. Before he left, he gave the writer a soul handshake and a big wink" (1991: 79). After that, Motown's press department insisted that anyone who wanted to interview the band had to agree not to ask any questions about politics or drugs.

At the time, the Jackson 5 was already on an upward-rising curve. Its early commercial success was unprecedented: each of the band's first four singles reached number one position on the *Billboard* pop chart. "Live" concerts were sellouts. Because of the band's age span (seven years separated the oldest from the youngest, Michael, who was born in 1958), it appealed to a wide spectrum of fans.

Ralph Seltzer had brought the band to Gordy's attention after a tip from his friend Bobby Taylor, who headed a band that had appeared on the same bill as the brothers. Joe, the father of the Jackson brothers, had already entered into a management agreement with a white lawyer named Richard Arons, but negotiated a release; though he retained control over his sons' activities to such an extent that it would ultimately damage the Motown connection. The brothers had already released two singles in 1968. They were little-known numbers called "Big boy" and "You've changed" on Steeltown Records, this being a small independent operation owned by Gordon Keith who signed the band to a limited deal.

At first, Gordy was concerned about how the band in general would mature. Very young acts do not typically have much commercial durability. Michael Jackson was but one of a team. His precocity was a factor, of course; but by no means the most important one. Gordy, mindful of the cultural changes afoot, decided the band should receive the full Motown treatment. One of the first moves he made was to assemble a writing team known as the Corporation for the band with the remit to recreate the feeling of Frankie Lymon and the Teenagers, a band from the 1950s, which specialized in happy, upbeat tunes, like "Why do fools fall in love?" Suzanne De Passe, then a creative assistant, was assigned a hands-on role in developing the band. Gordy launched them as Diana Ross' discoveries, even entitling the band's first album *Diana Ross Presents the Jackson 5*, released in December 1969. Its sales were encouraging (over 600,000), especially after a highly successful début single.

In using Ross, by 1969 an established star, as an endorser, Gordy guaranteed the band national exposure. He visualized the Jackson 5 quite differently to his other acts. The band was to be a fully marketable phenomenon. Gordy had watched the production of the Monkees, a manufactured white band comprising four actors brought together to feature in a comedy series. Yet, the public bought it: Monkees records sold on the back of the tv show. Gordy saw the Jackson 5 in the same light. Merchandise such as posters, T-shirts, lapel buttons were only a start. By 1971, Gordy had placed the band at the center of a cartoon series which aired on Saturday mornings and in which actors spoke the dialogue of characters supposed to be the band members. He also had the band appearing with Sammy Davis Jr, who was in the Motown fold at this point. Gordy had presumably learned important lessons in promoting Ross and he brought them to bear with the Jackson 5.

But, in 1971, his plans looked under threat. A white version of the Jackson 5, complete with cute youngster, had been plucked out of a Mormon community in Ogden, Utah. The Osmonds may not have been able to sing and dance quite as well as the Jackson brothers, but they were close and, more importantly, they were white. Oddly, the Osmonds were responsible for the start of Michael Jackson's solo career. They not only stole the Jackson 5's thunder, but they also foisted a wunderkind on the teen market. Donny Osmond had been singing with his brothers on a television series, *The Andy Williams Show*, since the early 1960s. He was 14 when the band sold over a million copies of "One bad apple," a number which had been turned down by Gordy as unsuitable for the Jackson 5. Although the band had been around for a number of years, its foregrounding of Donny, a toothy, wide-eyed and wholesome white boy, was a shock to Gordy. MGM, which had the Osmonds' recording contract, pushed Donny as a solo act, his first single "Sweet and innocent" being the first of a series of major successes. Within a month of its release, Gordy met the Jacksons' father, Joe, who also managed their affairs, and decided to issue a Michael Jackson single without the band, "Got to be there."

The success of the single encouraged further releases and Jackson's career was effectively folded inside that of his brothers: he appeared on stage with them and the Jackson 5 collectively made records, but the band became a culture for Jackson's solo career, allowing him to grow and mature as a performer without exposing him to the harsher elements that have undermined many young entertainers, like Drew Barrymore who was in dope and alcohol rehabilitation by the age of 13. By 1974, with Jackson approaching 16, the band appeared at Las Vegas, largely at the instigation of their father, who was ready to defy Gordy.

The Motown chief had plotted the course of Diana Ross carefully and his maneuvring of her into the Copacabana and Vegas with the Supremes in the mid-1960s was crucial to their ultimate success with the white middle class market. But he felt the time was not right for such a drastic move from the younger record-buying market to the dinner club set. In the event, the band used the opportunity to introduce other family members who were to have showbusiness careers, Janet, and LaToya, who became something of a Josephine Baker, leaving the USA to pursue a career in Paris.

Good reviews for the Vegas show satisfied Joe Jackson that his decision was right. But it was the first of several differences with Gordy. For instance, a planned film in which the brothers would play slaves was spiked by Gordy, who also cancelled a British tour after Jackson released details to the media in spite of Gordy's embargo. Gordy himself believed that, from 1973, after four years with Motown: "Their [the brothers'] father, Joe, went from being quietly behind the scenes to having many complaints and demands. It was everything from wanting a say in how they were produced, what songs they did or didn't do, to how they were being promoted and booked" (1994: 347).

Joe Jackson himself was known to be dissatisfied with all the areas mentioned by Gordy; he was particularly upset when Michael's fourth solo album, *Forever Michael*, made only 101 in the album charts, eight places lower than the 1973 *Music and Me* album which was considered a flop. Gordy appeared to believe the Motown formula was good for all and the brothers were allowed no room to write or produce their own work. Jackson "shrewdly realized that his sons would never make big money unless they owned the publishing rights to their own songs," according to Taraborrelli (1991: 143). Gordy's Jobete Publishing was, as we have seen, a crucial element of his empire and the Jackson 5's material was housed under this roof. Joe Jackson wanted his sons to write at least some of their own material and so draw some of the revenue that would otherwise flow into Jobete. This could be considerable; for instance, a million-selling single would typically generate 2.7 cents per copy sold for the band. This might be worth an extra 2 cents per copy more had the band also written the material.

In 1975, Joe Jackson told his sons that the situation with Gordy had become intolerable and that they were destined to leave Motown. Gordy first heard the news through Jermaine Jackson, who was by then his son-in-law, having married Gordy's daughter Hazel. Jermaine informed him that the rest of the band had signed with CBS, despite the fact that there was a year of the Motown contract to run. Unbeknown to Gordy, Joe Jackson and his business associate Arons, at this stage back in the picture, had been checking out options for some time before. They had met Ahmet Ertegun with a view to signing with Atlantic, but Ertegun was not interested. In Chapter six, we saw how CBS had enjoyed a successful artistic and commercial relationship with Kenny Gamble and Leon Huff, of Philadelphia International Records. CBS wanted a black music division and Gamble and Huff had relative autonomy to develop their own music. Their accessible Philly sound had helped them capture the important middle ground of the British and European markets.

Another one of CBS' subsidiary labels was known as Epic, run by Ron Alexenberg in the mid-1970s. Remember: in 1975, the Jackson 5 had been performing and recording for four years; Michael had detached himself temporarily for his own singles, but was not yet a star in his own right; record sales for both had sagged in the previous 12 months. There was every reason to suppose that the public had grown tired of the over-talented child star and his competent but unspectacular brothers. CBS took a chance when it offered a $750,000 advance and $350,000 guaranteed per album against royalties. But, it was the royalty rate that differed significantly from that received at Motown, which had paid out 3 percent on the wholesale price of each record sold. CBS offered 27 percent of the wholesale price for records released in the USA, according to Taraborrelli, who calculates that at Epic the band would make approximately 94.5 cents per album sold in the USA and 84 cents abroad compared to the 11 cents per album picked up at Motown in the States and Europe (1991: 152). There was also an escalator clause in the deal that stated that, after $500,000 in sales, the royalty rate increased to 30 percent or about $1.05 per unit. As Taraborrelli concludes: "In terms of income, this new deal was worth about five hundred times more than the one the group had at Motown" (1991: 152).

The move indicated that the conditions of cultural production were shifting in favor of the giant corporations, by this stage aware of the commercial potential of African American performers and eager to cultivate a mass rather than niche market. Gordy wanted to exploit the market himself, but Motown was no match for the major players. Gordy's gift for turning out commodities was proven. But, Ross apart, Motown's successes were record by record. CBS had the resources not only to produce, but to market, merchandise and produce in a continuing cycle; Jackson was to be developed as an artist.

Despite this, Jermaine refused to leave Motown and Michael had reservations; their father, however, had none. Although his sons could not record for CBS until the expiry of the Motown contract, he held a press conference to announce the split in an act of wilful defiance against Gordy, who had warned against it. Gordy's common contractual practice was to "own" the names of his bands. We noticed in previous chapters how he had kept "the Supremes" and "the Vandellas" as Motown properties, at least until it suited him. He argued convincingly that "the Jackson Five" was Motown's possession, as was the logo which read "Jackson 5ive." Gordy sued both CBS and the Jackson 5 for breach of contract.

The now-familiar tirade against Gordy's alleged sharp practices followed: the Jacksons countersued, claiming they were due additional royalty payments. Gordy raised the damages sought from $5 million to $20 million after an old picture featuring Jermaine was used to advertise a CBS television series called

The Jacksons. "In the end, we owed them nothing," reflects Gordy, "and we were paid a settlement of $100,000" (1994: 347). The Jackson 5 was the last act to receive the tried and tested Motown assembly line treatment. It was 1975 and Gordy's attentions were focused on Ross' film ventures.

The Jacksons was the first album the newly named band made for CBS. Its executive producers were Gamble and Huff, of PIR, which was also credited on the record label. The album, released in 1977, included "Blues away" written by Michael and "Style of life" written collectively by the brothers. Gamble and Huff also worked on the second CBS album *Goin' Places*. Neither was especially successful in a commercial sense, though they fared better than Jermaine's solo efforts with Motown. Joe Jackson entered into a business agreement with two white co-managers, who would replace Arons; they were Ron Weisner and Freddy DeMann. As we have seen in previous chapters, Gordy had loaded his senior executive with whites without feeling it necessary to explain his decisions. Jackson, as the manager and father of an African American band that did not seem to be progressing quite as he had hoped, presumably shared some of Gordy's concerns. To prevent black acts being ghettoized by a music industry dominated by whites, a few white negotiators pushing and shoving in the right places might be needed. It is still a common strategy, though never a popular one. But the results were evident in the band's next album, *Destiny*, which sold two million copies, making it the most commercially successful of the CBS records to date. The brothers took a greater share of the writing and producing of the work.

We mentioned Diana Ross' Motown-backed movie *The Wiz* in Chapter seven; to the annoyance of other family members, Michael appeared in the film, which, while not a success, had the effect of taking him outside the Jacksons context as an adult performer. Achieving success as a child prodigy was no guarantee of success as a 20-year-old artist. A solo single taken from the film was not successful, though making the single had the virtue of bringing Jackson into contact with its producer, Quincy Jones, with whom he was to have an extraordinarily fertile artistic relationship over the next several years.

Jones was a trumpeter and band leader, who in the early 1960s became a vice-president of Mercury Records; by the 1970s, he had finished performing and spent most of his time working on film soundtracks. His collaboration with Michael was opposed by Joe and the brothers: compared to the band's records, Michael's solo efforts were commercially indifferent. The consensus was that his energies could be more profitably spent on group projects. Jones' experience with the populist sound sought by the Jacksons was limited: his specialty was big band arrangements. Still, the project went ahead and the product was a more polished sound than ever before. Barney Hoskyns calls it "a triumph of studio-crafted miscegenation . . . the first real mass-audience black/white album" (1996: 301).

The sleeve for *Off the Wall* was carefully thought out to complement the move toward sophistication: it showed Jackson in white tuxedo. The inspiration probably came from white British artist Bryan Ferry's first solo album, which displayed him as Bogarde, *manqué*, straight out of *Casablanca*. Released in August 1979, the album was epiphanic: it effectively relaunched Michael Jackson as a newly-matured solo entertainer, selling six million copies (it still sells) and spawning four hit singles. (In the same year, Chic's "Le Freak" became the biggest selling single in Atlantic Record's history; the band, like Jackson, reinforced the image of the unrepentant middle class black sophisticate.)

Off the Wall's success convinced Jackson that the personal ambitions he had harbored were ready to be realized and, to this end, he retained the services of John Branca, a New York attorney with a background in corporate tax law and the music industry. This was a significant departure for Jackson, who had previously entrusted his father's lawyers and accountants with his affairs. Branca, under the terms of the arrangement was to have no interest in the Jacksons: his sole concern was with Michael. As such his first task was to renegotiate a separate record deal that gave his client a substantial 37 percent of wholesale on his records and an option to leave the band with impunity should he wish. It compared favorably even with Stevie Wonder's Motown contract which gave him a 20 percent royalty rate and a $13 million advance after four groundbreaking albums. Jackson's seemed an astonishingly good deal on the basis of one hit album, even if it did augur well; but, what did CBS have to lose? If future record sales dropped, the big royalty payments would have less effect; and, if this was the case, Michael would be disinclined to leave the security of the band which was a proven commodity.

By mid-1983 when the band's managerial contract was up for renewal, Michael's status was appreciably greater than that of his brothers. It was widely known that the singer entrusted most of his decisions to Branca; equally, he mistrusted his father's business partners, Ron Weisner and Freddy DeMann. Joe Jackson, in a sort of preemptive move, severed links with Weisner and DeMann, explaining to the media: "There was a time when I felt I needed white help in dealing with the corporate power structure at CBS . . . And I thought Weisner– DeMann would be able to help" (quoted in Taraborrelli, 1991: 301). The comments were potentially damaging to Michael and he issued a public statement to confirm that the sentiments were not his. He effectively fired his father as his manager and assigned more responsibility to Branca.

Around this time, the facial changes that were to become the stuff of myth began: two rhinoplasty operations followed an accident in which Michael broke his nose; the result was a narrower job in which the nostrils took on a pinched appearance. This plus the jeri perm that was fashionable in the early 1980s gave Michael a rather different look to the one he had on the *Off the Wall* cover.

Despite his commercial success, MTV was impervious to Jackson for a long while. The 24-hour, all-music cable tv station had started life in 1981, specializing in music videos and odd pieces of music-related news. Its success was based on a niche market: that of young, mainly white middle class people with disposable income to spend on records, tapes and, later, cds, as well as cars, clothes, beer, soda, hifi and any other consumer items that were advertised on air. MTV's income derived from cable subscriptions and advertisers who wished to target their markets precisely. Compared to other stations, whose programming was more diffuse, MTV could provide a demographically specific market for ad agencies wanting to reach young whites.

It is astonishing to think that as recently as 1983, MTV was featuring very few African American acts. Herbie Hancock's award-winning video "Rocket" was played only because it starred the limbs of mechnical mannequins, Hancock's face appearing only fleetingly in a box. Typically, a record company will send a tape of a particular track to MTV for the cable's consideration; a rejection can mean a struggle to market the track; an acceptance can secure high sales. Some artists have been "made" by MTV: the white band Duran Duran, for instance, was eagerly lapped up by MTV in the early 1980s and enjoyed great success as a result. But, CBS had Jackson's "Billie Jean" rejected and the suspicion arose that MTV was interested only in "safe" acts that appealed to white youths; and, for this reason, concluded that black artists were not good business. Considering the sales of Jackson's albums, the decision seems to have been guided by spurious logic. The album from which "Billie Jean" was taken went on to sell about 40 million copies around the world; which meant that Jackson grossed in the order of $50 million from album sales alone, plus royalties from the seven singles spun off the album, all top ten sellers. Jackson, remember, had negotiated an individual deal with CBS. The record company threatened MTV with a boycott by all its artists.

No one will ever know how far MTV's change of heart affected this. We can be fairly sure that MTV itself changed as a result of Jackson's video. Many more black acts began to appear and, in the late 1980s/early 1990s, *Yo! MTV Raps* became a staple series. Perhaps MTV, as a commercial medium, was grateful for the respite from the popular music of the late 1970s, much of it rude, elemental and exuberantly anarchistic. In short, not the type of music that would have advertisers breaking their necks in the hurry to part with money. The live-for-the-moment music blaring from London and New York courtesy of the Sex Pistols, Ramones *et al.* was not so much white as off-white. Jackson may have been black, but compared to punks, he was boynextdoorish; he would not cause parents to dive for the remote control.

A population that had found itself acquiescing in a racial hierarchy found its assumptions destabilized and its youth decentered. Jackson grew emblematic: an African American who asserted the continuing relevance of the American Dream amid a time of cultural change. Yes: the racial hierarchy was in need of revision. No: the structure of which it was part need not be destroyed. Maybe: whites should feel pangs of guilt for the wrongdoings of history. Certainly: that guilt was eased by the success of talented blacks – like Jackson.

"Billie Jean" was a commercially strong track, but the album of which it was part was a different phenomenon altogether: composed of the most incongruous elements, *Thriller*'s whole was much more than the sum of its parts. Its title track had little relation to softer ballads, like "Lady in my life" which in turn had nothing in common with "Beat it" which included the guitar of hard rocker Eddie van Halen. The only common thread uniting some of the tracks, such as "Don't stop 'til you get enough" and "Wanna be starting something" was that they were funky enough for dance clubs. By making such a heterogeneous collection, Jackson and Jones, who had actually crossed words over the production, conspired to supply something for all tastes. *Thriller* turned Jackson from a bestselling recording artist into *the* bestselling artist. Its sales were hitting 500,000 units per week and it became the top-selling album in history. Writing in 1994, Andersen estimated that Jackson's total take from sales exceeded $130 million.

The title track's spectacular looking video with an original story-within-story premise and special fx was, at $600,000, the most expensive made to date and contributed powerfully to the album's sales. Its first transmission was made into an extravagant tv event; it actually received a television première in December 1983 and went on to sell 48 million copies independently of the record.

Videos, of course, are marketing vehicles plain and simple; they are not conventionally evaluated on their dramatic resonance. Jackson broke this convention and had a covey of cultural theorists clamoring to "read" it. But, the real innovation was less visible. Because of the prohibitive cost of the video, someone, probably Branca, formulated a way of offsetting it through a second video, this one based on *The making of "Thriller"*. The production costs of this were relatively small: it was a documentary showing how the special fx were created and how the scenes were put together. The rights were sold to a video distribution company and MTV paid to première it, enabling Jackson and Co. to reclaim all the production costs plus a profit. This was a coup, especially considering MTV's policy of not paying artists or record companies to air videos. This in itself set Jackson apart from other artists: most acts would probably pay MTV for the exposure.

The path described by Jackson's career veered toward a new domain after this. Record sales apart, Jackson himself began to assume a mysterious, almost occult air: his stage presence was interesting, but the really fascinating bits of him were the ones that outsiders could not see. His solo stint as part of Motown's twenty-fifth anniversary celebrations in 1983 was Jackson's first "live" public appearance since the 1981 tour. The 50 million television viewers and attending fans witnessed a style exercise: they saw a highly polished choreographed performance and heard a note-perfect lip-synched sound; what they did not glimpse was spontaneous human substance; no winks, no asides, no improvisation and certainly no imperfections.

Because of his status, the media's glare became incessant. His friendship with Emmanuel Lewis, a child actor was the first documented evidence of his preference for young male companions and his cosmetic surgery seemed ever-more heroic. He also drew the ire of his church, the Jehovah's Witnesses, for the tenebrous "Thriller" video which had lycanthropic and necromantic themes (Jackson included a disclaimer on the video release). And his accident when filming a Pepsi tv commercial started a world media circus. For a former child star and an African American, Jackson was almost unique in that he had not disgraced himself by falling foul of drugs or the law, nor had he been involved in any sexually lurid affairs, though rumors of these were to mount in the years that followed. And, unlike Stevie Wonder, whose appeal was also large and diverse, Jackson made music that was innocent and bloodless. The type of scandals the media often use to cauterize black stars, whether in entertainment or sports, were not applicable. Jackson did not even drink: when Pepsi paid him an estimated $700,000 to endorse their product, it was public knowledge that he would not dare let anything so impure as cola pass his lips.

Like Greta Garbo and Howard Hughes, Jackson retreated from public view only to find his standing elevated as a result. Once a performer has reached a certain status, there is little he or she can do to deter interest. Keeping quiet never works: when figures disappear, there are always sightings; when they say nothing, the media make up quotes. Jackson, after *Thriller*, wanted the accolades, but not the glare. But, he was pushed by his father into one more tour with his brothers, by this time sliding rapidly into commercial oblivion. It took place in 1984 and was called "The Victory tour." This brought Jackson into contact with someone who became arguably the most influential sports promoter in history and most definitely the most powerful African American in the sports business, Don King.

If Jackson was too good to be true, the same could not be said of Don King. In 1995, he found himself in court accused of defrauding London insurers by concocting $350,000 expenses claims for two 1991 fights that were cancelled. It was one in a long line of alleged violations. In King's own words: "The Justice Department has charged me with every known crime and misdemeanor – kickbacks, racketeering, ticket scalping, skimming, fixing fights, preordaining them, vitiating officials and laundering money . . . But the missing link is the burden of factual proof" (quoted in Lidz, 1990: 96).

Once there was enough proof: in 1967, King was imprisoned in Marion Correctional Institution, Ohio, for manslaughter after killing a man in a fight on a Cleveland Street. After serving four years, King, who had been involved in numbers rackets as a youth, befriended three persons, who were to prove crucial to his rise: Don Elbaum was a smalltime boxing promoter who operated in Pennsylvania and Ohio; Lloyd Price was a rock'n'roll singer who recorded on Art Rupe's Specialty label (and sold one million copies of his own "Lawdy Miss Clawdy" before it was covered by Elvis Presley); Muhammad Ali was the premier boxer of the period and the symbolic leader of countless blacks in the USA and perhaps the world over.

Price had known King for many years and met him from prison. He also knew Ali, who had been beaten by Joe Frazier some months before. King persuaded Price to ask Ali to box an exhibition at a Cleveland hospital which was in danger of closing. The hospital had a mostly black staff and patients. Ali agreed and King sought the expertise of Elbaum in running boxing shows. At this stage, King knew little about booking referees, doctors, renting a ring, applying for licensing and so on.

Eight and a half thousand people watched Ali spar with four men. Price used his influence to bring Wilson Pickett, Marvin Gaye and others to the show and they performed a concert before the boxing began. The gross take was $81,000, an astonishing amount for an exhibition. Elbaum's recollection is: "Ali got ten thousand for expenses. I got paid one thousand instead of five thousand. The hospital got about fifteen hundred. And King pocketed the rest" (quoted in Newfield, 1995: 31).

Soon King had incorporated himself into a standing business partnership between Elbaum and Joseph Gennaro, who were cultivating a number of promising fighters, included soon-to-be contender Earnie Shavers. By 1974, Elbaum was out of the picture and Gennaro was suing King for a share of the profits from boxing ventures. This was settled with King paying $3,500. It was one of many boxing-related disputes to which King was a party, but it did not stop his progress. King

133

was perfectly poised on the space-time curve. The new consciousness that had inspired riots in the streets had counterparts in sport. The memorable black power salute by Tommie Smith and John Carlos at the Mexico summer Olympics in 1968 signalled a newly politicized black athlete.

Ali converted to the Nation of Islam, better known as the Black Muslims, and spoke acerbically about the "white devils" who controlled western society. As a black entrepreneur with an interest in boxing, King could present himself as the embodiment of what the Black Muslim strove for: black economic independence. Acting as an agent of a company called Video Techniques, King was able to convince Ali to let him promote one of his fights. Fortuitously for King, it was one of Ali's most momentous fights, when he regained the world heavyweight title at the age of 32, knocking out George Foreman in Zaire in 1974. "The Rumble in the Jungle," as the fight became known, was as much a showcase for King as it was for the protagonists. He presided over press conferences, gave interviews and made his presence felt at every opportunity. And King cut an unforgettable figure with his electric shock hairstyle.

King's next major venture was a $2 million boxing tournament televised by ABC Television. Allegations of kickbacks, fixing and mob connections surrounded the show, though King became adept at neutralizing them, often by arguing that every successful black person is immediately suspected of misdeeds. Berry Gordy would have probably agreed. But, unlike the stories about Gordy's involvement with the Mafia, the ones surrounding King had substance. Jack Newfield's book *Only in America: The life and crimes of Don King* charts the network of contacts King had with the underworld and his phenomenal resourcefulness in avoiding conviction. King emerged unscathed from an FBI operation code-named Crown Royal, which attempted to link him with organized crime. One of the investigators in this operation, Joseph Spinelli, recorded details of this for the magazine *Sports Illustrated* (1991). Even the old tax evasion standby would not stick to King.

King kept an interest in the heavyweight championship, either by promoting fights or managing champions. The World Boxing Council (WBC) was extraordinarily careful in its treatment of King, giving rise to rumors that its president, José Sulaiman, was unduly generous. For example, when Ali lost his title to Leon Spinks in 1978, the fight was promoted by rival Bob Arum, who held a contract giving him options on Spinks' first three title defenses. It worked greatly to King's advantage when the WBC stripped Spinks of the title and declared it vacant, allowing King to promote a title fight between fighters he effectively controlled. The decision broke up the world heavyweight title into two different versions and King was later to capitalize on this, promoting a $16 million HBO subscription television tournament to unify the title again.

Mike Tyson left his manager Bill Cayton to enter into a business relationship with King. Interestingly, Tyson refused to criticize King even after several other boxers, like Larry Holmes, Tim Witherspoon and Mike Dokes, had turned against him, claiming financial peculiarities. Coming from African American boxers, these were trenchant criticisms of King. Witherspoon complained robustly after defending his world heavyweight title against Frank Bruno in 1986. He agreed to fight for $550,000, but received only $90,094, while Bruno, the challenger, made

$900,000 (challengers typically earn 40 percent of the total purse). King received revenue from HBO, BBC, Miller Lite and the live gate, making him at least $2 million. Witherspoon's deductions included $275,000 to King's stepson, Carl King, who acted as the boxer's manager.

Unlike many of the other boxers who griped, Witherspoon pressed his claims against King and, in 1992, received a million-dollar settlement. His verdict on King reads like a misanthropic epigram: "Don's speciality is black-on-black crime. I'm black and he robbed me" (quoted in Newfield, 1995: 253).

King dismissed this and most of the other claims. But, as writer Mike Lupica asked: "Are they *all* lying? Holmes and Witherspoon and Tony Tubbs and Pinklon Thomas? Or is King a hypocrite, screaming about racism on one hand and preying on black fighters himself?" (1991: 54). Lupica did not answer the question, at least not publicly.

Certainly, King acted hypocritically in regard to South Africa, upbraiding boxers and promoters who went there in defiance of the Gleneagles Agreement to sever sporting links with a country which enforced apartheid up till 1990. Yet, Newfield points out that King had taken a million-dollar "under-the-table" payment from a South African promotion.

King's biggest promotion never materialized: Tyson's conviction and imprisonment for rape meant that a fight with Evander Holyfield (originally scheduled for November 8, 1991) fell through. It was expected to gross more than $100 million (£62 million), with the pay per view operation alone drawing $80 million, foreign sales $10 million and the promotional fee from Caesar's Palace $11 million.

Former heavyweight champion Larry Holmes once said of King: "He looks black, lives white and thinks green." He was thinking in terms of $30 million when he sat opposite Joe Jackson at the bargaining table in 1984. They planned a tour comprising 40 concerts which would net $24 million profit, 85 percent of this going to the Jacksons, 7.5 percent each to King and Joe Jackson. As most of King's experience was in sports, he linked up with Jay Coleman, another promoter, but a white boy who could, King reasoned, negotiate more easily with the likes of Pepsi-Cola, the corporation sponsoring the tour. The old black culture industry tactic of hiring whites as front men or intermediaries came into play once more. Coleman was given the job of squeezing $5 million out of Pepsi. In 1984, this was colossal money for sponsors to shell out on a concert tour, but King pulled it off.

His next step was to consult Irving Azoff, head of MCA Records, who advised on the more pragmatic aspects of concert tours for a reputed fee of $500,000. King was well-versed in how to stage a big fight promotion, but a tour of 40 dates needed additional expertise. Ironically, King later expressed puzzlement that Jackson had white men as his two key aides, Branca and Frank Dileo, whom he hired as his manager. The tour was, by all accounts, fraught with tension. Dileo had checked out King's background, including the various accusations, and Jackson grew suspicious. At one stage, Joe Jackson apparently tried to replace King with Frank Russo, a rock promoter. King was unfazed and apprised Jackson of the consequences of breaking a contract. Russo then filed suit and eventually settled out of court.

King's success in sports promotion has been based on his knack of judging demand to perfection. So, in 1995, when he promoted Mike Tyson's first fight after his prison sentence for rape, he charged $1,500 for a ringside seat at a contest *everybody* knew was a total mismatch. Tyson duly despatched Peter McNeeley in 89 seconds. It seemed poor value at over $16.85 per second; but no one, not even any of the 1.52 million households who had bought the pay per view package, demanded their money back. King would stretch the market as far as it would go, in this case to $96 million in gross receipts worldwide.

He brought the same approach to the Jacksons' tour, introducing a complex voucher system for ticket applications in which applicants would have to order in blocks of four at a cost of $120 and then wait until days before the concert before learning whether they had received an allocation. This made it an expensive concert by 1984 standards. But, extremely lucrative for the organizers. Christopher Andersen spells out the logic behind the plan in his *Michael Jackson: Unauthorized*:

> Assuming some twelve million fans shelled out for the forty-plus concert dates, that meant $1.5 *billion* in sales. But since only a little over one million tickets were available, the rest of the money – well over $1.3 billion – would have to be returned. That, however would take about two months – a period during which the Jacksons stood to collect well over $100 million in interest on that money.
>
> (1994: 154)

In addition, requests were made to have stadia rental fees and taxes waived together with a cut of concessions. Most rock tours make little, if any, profit: they are principally used to promote interest in records. The Jacksons' *Victory* was released to coincide with the tour. Boxing promotions, of course, do not work like that: merchandise and ancillaries generate decent revenue, but the real money comes from television or pay per view and the "live" gate. Andersen reckons that the overheads were so enormous – one million dollars a week to move the equipment alone – that the tour actually lost money, though the Jacksons agreed their fees up front and were paid in full (1994: 168).

Jackson gave his share of the tour revenue away; his brothers, by this time little more than MJ's backing singers, did not. Michael made it fairly well known that he did not get along with King, but the others were probably grateful to him for making them so much money. King went on to make a whole lot more money, though he steered away from music concerts, concentrating on boxing and television. His big promotions were shown on HBO before his split, after which he struck up a deal with Showtime. Under this arrangement he set up his own service, KingVision, which worked as a pay per view carrier. Say King promoted a fight for which there was a high demand, he would work with Showtime to make it available to cable tv subscribers in the States and satellite/cable subscribers in Britain, but at a price. Viewers would be asked to pay an additional amount on their monthly bill. King became very rich as a result of such operations, but he also spent a lot of time in court defending himself against all manner of allegations.

Despite his personal wealth, his extensive contacts and his obvious gift for promoting sports and entertainment, King either avoided or lacked the acumen for building a stable structure for his many enterprises. Don King Productions was ostensibly the master organization, but King harbored too many suspicions, sometimes bordering on paranoia, to delegate tasks on the scale needed for a largescale corporation. Because of this, he remained a maverick.

In one of his most reflective interviews, with Richard Regen, King suggested that he was the epitome of the American Dream: "But instead of getting plaudits and accolades, I get condemnation and vilifications." A predictable pattern for a successful African American entrepreneur? "Absolutely! As long as I stay black! And I don't see no change coming. I want to be black. You know the reason that I use 'nigger' is because it's consistent. It has longevity" (1990: 115).

One can imagine the tension between King and Jackson. "What Michael's to realize is that Michael's a nigger," he said in another interview.

> It doesn't matter how great he can sing and dance ... He's one of the megastars in the world, but he's still going to be a nigger megastar. He must accept that. Not only must he understand that, he's got to accept it and demonstrate that he wants to be a nigger. Why? To show that a nigger can do it.
>
> (quoted in Taraborrelli, 1991: 377)

Jackson may have been repulsed by these kind of remarks, but he must surely have recollected some of them after the "Victory" tour, when stories about him seemed to grow exponentially. In the fall of 1984, Jackson issued a press statement to deny the many allegations. He threatened legal action against perpetrators. Apart from stories of his cosmetic surgery and hormone treatment, his sexuality was a subject of speculation. What Jackson had missed was that, in issuing denials, he had ingenuously supplied new material to the purveyors of his oddities and paradoxes. Michael Jackson was the bestselling singer of all time. But, ask anybody to name something for which he is known and maybe eight out of ten will cite plastic surgery, albinotic skin color, sexual proclivity, sleeping chamber or weird pets.

Even allowing for King's questionable practices, one can understand his irritation with the media. Business deals are done in sport every day. When King approached Tyson, he elicited the following description from James Dalrymple, a journalist writing for the respected British *Sunday Times*: "Like some dark, crooning nemesis, he came to Tyson, when he was down and beaten and bewildered, took him in his arms and whispered to him that it was time finally to leave the white man's domain for good and join the brothers" (*Sunday Times Magazine*, September 18, 1994, p. 21).

King was talking of Mike Tyson, but he may well have had Jackson in mind and could have included himself when he said:

> The media always twist anything where black success is concerned. They always want to couple a black's success with a negative association – undesirable conditions, evilness, lewdness, depravity – anything demeaning

to black ambition, because it's always got to be put in some kind of subordinate capacity in order to justify the superiority of the racist point of view.

(quoted in Regen, 1990: 104)

Michael Jackson was a product of the 1980s. I use the noun "product" with care: our interest here is less in what he possessed, more in what he was believed to possess. What Jackson actually had, did or thought is of secondary importance. People attributed to him all manner of things and deeds. He was, according to popular lore, berserk with oddities and laden with natural gifts; he was clearly no ordinary performer, but a star nonpareil.

Few performers and certainly no black performer can ever have commanded a following like Jackson's. Even measured by sales, it was gargantuan. In one remarkable decade, Jackson sold 110 million records (over 75 million as a solo artist). *Bad*, his follow-up to *Thriller*, was considered a virtual failure, selling 20 million copies. The tour to promote it in 1987 was watched by a total of 4.5 million people. The video of his single "Black or white" was simultaneously shown to an estimated 500 million television viewers in 27 countries in 1991. These kinds of figures enabled Jackson to build a virtual one-man culture industry of his own. He may even have begun to believe this: disappointed at the sales of *Bad*, Jackson dispensed with the service of Dileo, under whose management he had amassed more than $150 million (Andersen's estimate, 1994: 221). Dileo received a $5 million severance payoff.

The six-album deal he signed with Sony, which took over CBS Records, was worth up to one billion dollars: according to some reports it included a $3 million "gift" from his record company, an $18 million advance and a royalty rate of 25 percent of the retail price of units sold, or more than twice the industry average (royalties, as we have seen, are usually paid on wholesale price). Significantly, it also made provision for Jackson to have a label of his own, Nation Records, financed by CBS, but with artistic autonomy for the performer and half the overall profits. Other related ventures, including films, would come under the umbrella of the Jackson Entertainment Complex. Sony advanced Jackson $60 million.

Jackson, for all his earnings capacity, had harbored entrepreneurial ideas at least since 1984, when he bought ATV Music Publishing for $47.5 million, after hearing that Paul McCartney earned over $40 million per year from record and song royalties. Quite why Jackson wanted to earn more than he already did, we will never know; but his first purchase was the catalog of Sly and the Family Stone, which included many of the numbers referred to in Chapter eight. But ATV was a much bigger proposition: it housed the Beatles' numbers between 1964 and 1971 plus thousands of others, including several Little Richard tracks, like "Tutti frutti" and "Long tall Sally." Although McCartney recorded with Jackson and offered friendly advice about the value of publishing, he was upset by Jackson's actions; effectively, he had to pay Jackson for performing his own songs. Even more galling for McCartney was the fact that, in 1995, Jackson sold the publishing rights to Sony for almost $95 million, giving Sony a 4,000-song trove valued at about $500 million.

The image of haunted man-child belied the cool business rationality. Even in November 1993, when besieged by journalists chasing stories on his alleged abuses of children and dependence on drugs, Jackson managed to take time out from his group therapy to close the biggest publishing deal in history. EMI guaranteed him $150 million over five years and paid $70 million on signature to administer the ATV Music catalog.

The kinds of stories that have retarded the careers of some artists seemed almost perversely to complement Jackson's. At least, until 1994. Rob Lowe's intimate home-made video delivered a kick to the corpse of his once promising career. Jackson's reputation seemed to gain new life from each new rumor. Did he really sleep in an oxygen chamber? Why did he want to buy the bones of the Elephant Man? Was he so obsessed with Diana Ross that he actually tried to look like her? Or was it Elizabeth Taylor? Did he seriously believe, as suggested in an *Ebony* interview, that he was a messenger from God? And how come he always seemed to be in the company of young boys? This last question was asked time and again and eventually turned into one scandal too many.

In August 1993, Jackson was accused of child molestation by a 13-year-old boy. Jackson agreed to talk about the charges on a "live" satellite hookup from his California ranch called Neverland in the following December. He complained that the police had subjected him to a humiliating inspection and taken photographs of his genitalia. In 1994, Jackson agreed to pay Jordy Chandler, then 14, an undisclosed sum, thought to be over $25 million, to stop a sex abuse lawsuit ever reaching court; his parents were also paid off in millions. Jackson was never put under oath for a civil deposition which could be used in a criminal trial. The deal was negotiated on Jackson's behalf by his lawyer, Johnnie Cochrane Jr, later to represent O. J. Simpson, and Larry Feldman who was retained by Chandler's parents. Part of the agreement reached was that the payment did not constitute an admission of guilt by Jackson.

The payoff was not the first in Jackson's career. Tarborrelli notes how Jackson took a 10-year-old Californian boy named Jimmy Safechuck on one leg of his "Bad" tour in 1988. Jackson gave the boy's parents a Rolls-Royce valued at $100,000, for no specified reason. Dileo advised Jackson that he should consider breaking off his friendship. Andersen recounts how Jackson made payments of up to one million dollars to the parents of children who stayed with him (1994: 188).

But the Chandler episode was headline news around the world for weeks. It centered on a friendship Jackson had formed with Chandler prior to the "Dangerous" tour of 1992–93. After the tour, Chandler accompanied Jackson to Monaco where he attended a music awards evening. Jackson paid for Chandler's family to travel too. Chandler was also known to spend time at Neverland. Jackson's sexual proclivities had been the subject of gossip for a number of years, but they turned into allegations of sexual abuse when Chandler's parents filed suit. Other suits followed, including one from Dave Schwartz, Chandler's stepfather, who claimed damages against Jackson for breaking up his marriage. And, according to Maureen Orth, in 1995, there was "another boy negotiating a settlement with Jackson" (1995: 50).

For a few years before, Jackson's idiosyncrasies had earned him the nickname "Wacko Jacko" and his bizarreries contributed to his iconic status no end. The lawsuit was the start of perhaps the most gigantic muckraking exercise in history. Neverland was staked out night and day by the world's media. The excesses of checkbook journalism were unashamedly laid bare and people with even the remotest knowledge of Jackson – like former employees – were persuaded to part with their once worthless, now priceless pieces of information. The tabloids were gaga with delight. Disclosures were still making headlines in 1995, a year after the settlement, by which time Jackson had made a double album *HIStory Past, Present and Future, Book 1* containing an answer to his critics in the tracks "Scream" – which is what he apparently felt like doing when all the fuss was going on about him – and "They don't care about us," which contained lines that might have been construed as antisemitic and for which Jackson apologized; they were changed in future versions. Chandler's father and his attorney were both Jewish.

Perhaps the Chandler affair dislodged Jackson from his position as the supreme idol of his day, his fads and foibles freaky but somehow suited to the times. Perhaps he was not so safe after all. Perhaps there was a side to his character that was more than just unusual; sinister even. There were telltale signs of damage limitation in some of his behavior. A surprise marriage to Lisa-Marie Presley, daughter of Elvis and devotee of Scientology. An interview, accompanied by wife, with Diane Sawyer watched by 60 million people on ABC News' *PrimeTime Live*. A "chat" with fans via the Internet, believed to be the first time a celebrity has turned to the information superhighway to communicate with followers. A whopping $30 million marketing campaign for *HIStory*. It was almost as if Jackson was trying to appear like an "ordinary" pop star. Certainly the sales of his double album were ordinary. There was surely some desperation in Epic Records' press release in fall 1995 stating that sales – then less than one million copies in the US – would save small black mom-and-pop record shops in various parts of the country.

By the mid-1990s, Jackson's status was in doubt. The public fascination with recluses escaped Jackson. After the charges, Jackson was forced out into the open and made to defend himself, whether he liked it or not. In the process, the qualities that were once integral to his appeal became implements of immolation. Was he weird-unusual, or weird-sicko?

Questions were important to Jackson's adult career; the more people asked, the more his mystery deepened. But, history never stands still: perhaps this is the last thing people will want to know about him. Whatever his future, Jackson, over a 12-year period, stood aloft as the star of his time, possibly the most interesting cultural icon of the late twentieth century (and I remain mindful of Madonna's presence in the same era). Why?

To understand Jackson the subject as opposed to Jackson the individual we need to recall the cultural context of which he was such a significant part. For all the Afro hairdos, the knowing winks and the brothers' handshakes, Jackson was not reflective of the mood of 1960s and early 1970s. On the contrary, he came to represent complete detachment from the mood: a young black male who looked like he had all the trappings of black power but lacked any substance, a complete innocent. He was a child and, as such, could be admired paternalistically: living proof that blacks had natural gifts uniquely their own. Even young Donny Osmond, his rival for a while, could never match him.

But, in manhood, Jackson was even more comforting: a black man with no axe to grind, who had risen to the top on merit. In a way, he was proof that the civil rights 1960s and the days of what was once called the American dilemma were things of the past. Not all black people, he seemed to suggest, were preoccupied with racism and the obstacles it strewed in their paths. Many were interested only in progress as people, not as members of a group which claimed special status. This was a time when the United States was witnessing the appearance of a warrantable black bourgeoisie, upper middle class people who prioritized their own careers and wished to enjoy what the system had to offer, rather than destroy that system. Calls for "black power" were a very distant cry for this group.

The election of Ronald Reagan in 1980 followed that of Margaret Thatcher in Britain in 1979 and heralded a protracted period of reactionary politics in which social problems were collapsed into personal deficiencies and remedies for them were the responsibility of people not agencies. Thatcher's oft-quoted repudiation of the concept of society would have had the blessing of Reagan, whose loathing of affirmative action was consistent with his damnation of all things liberal. Strange to think that the "L" word, as it was ridiculed, was a label slapped on anything that veered only slightly from Reagan's steadfast conservatism. It was a conservatism that had both energy and direction sufficient to deliver minority causes to the mercies of market forces.

Jesse Jackson's Push (People United to Save Humanity) organization had some success with its marketing oriented approach. Instead of appealing to fine ideals, Jackson would demand results of an organization and threaten a boycott of its products should those demands not be met. Covenants would be signed by corporations pledging to hire and promote x number of African Americans inside established timeframes. Whether the corporations did so out of fear of a market boycott or out of a commitment to equal opportunity was irrelevant to Jackson: his interest was in results. His most serious snub came when he steamed into Nike which pays many black athletes to endorse its sportswear. It decided to tough it out against Jackson, probably reasoning that its cachet among African Americans was strong enough to overcome any boycott.

The backlash against abortion was evidenced in the militant pro-life groups: abortion clinics were bombed. And each new offensive drew retaliation from pro-choicers. Feminist writers reflected on the changing sentiments: women in the 1960s and early 1970s had fought for the legal and, indeed, moral recognition of their fundamental equality with men, only to see much of it ebb away in the sea of conservative politics. The black females who were given the star treatment had a familiar exotic quality. Yet-to-be-born-again Donna Summer hyperventilated her way through a series of sensual numbers that established her as the Dorothy Dandridge of the 1970s. Summer's onstage performances were slithery fake foreplay with the singer cooing and sighing to the machine-like backing of Giorgio Moroder's music.

For all Summer's over-the-topness, she was upstaged by the Jamaican Grace Jones, whose attraction was rather like one of those flesh-eating plants that you edge toward, knowing that you might get snapped up at any moment. She frightened and seduced in equal measure. Jones, in the 1980s, was Eartha Kitt Goes Jungle Crazy: her studied primitiveness and conspicuous sexuality made her the perfect stereotype of the horny black woman.

Jackson could hardly be accused of conforming to a racial stereotype: no one could have dreamt up such an unlikely combination of quirks. Yet he was black. And this was important: he was unwittingly making a statement about America's ability to accommodate black progress; about the possibilities awaiting black people with talent and determination enough to make it to the top; about the absence of the American dilemma. The days of conflict were a thing of the past. Jackson, as a child, may have affected an Afro hairstyle, but, in the 1980s, he was a black man who could almost make you forget the fact that he was black. You could almost forget he was a man.

In his book with bell hooks, *Breaking Bread*, Cornel West defines a "race-transcending prophet" as "someone who never forgets about the significance of race but refuses to be confined to race" (1991: 49). Jackson was almost the exact opposite: he did forget about the significance of race and was, at the same time, confined by it. Throughout the 1980s, Jackson's appearance became ever more bizarre: the cosmetic surgery seemed less to improve his facial features, more to remove any trace of African ancestry. In an interview with Oprah Winfrey in February 1993, Jackson said that he suffered from a skin disorder vitiligo that causes discoloration, but few accepted that Jackson himself had not treated his skin with some bleaching product. We need not impute motives, for no one will probably know whether Jackson actually did want to rid himself of his blackness. One thing is for sure: he gave that impression. And that made him perfect for the times. A black man so successful that he could have almost anything in the world; and the one thing he appeared to want more than most was to be white. In one stroke, he convinced America that it was truly the land of opportunity, while emphasizing that whiteness was still the most valued commodity in that land. But, to repeat Don King's reminder to Jackson: he was a megastar, a nigger megastar.

Megastardom can be a dangerous thing: it can flatter its incumbent with delusions of infallibility. Had Jackson heeded King's warning, he would have realized that his status was granted by a culture dominated by white people, by white values. As such, his acceptance was destined to be a conditional one. Here was a black boy, a cornucopia of natural talent, who developed and even expanded those talents in manhood. His dancing could mesmerize people, his singing could enchant them. He did not talk politics and his comments about the condition of black people were so fluffy as to be meaningless. Andersen believes that the public played a role in "infantilizing" Jackson: "We were happy as long as he played Peter Pan and never grew up" (1994: 356).

At a time when America was almost embarrassed by its never-ending racial problems, it was comforting to know that blacks, however humble their origins, could soar to the top. Even more comforting to know that, however high they soared, they still wanted to be white. Gordy was not around long enough to reap the benefits of this. How he would have longed for a male artist with an equivalent marketability to Diana Ross. CBS may have wished for warmth as well as technical ingenuity, more spontaneity than calculation, real life movement over stop-motion animation; but the corporation could not complain that Jackson was formulaic in his output or mechanical in his behavior. In any case, Jackson the commodity was perfect for a computer-literate, video-wise and, latterly, net-educated generation. Flesh and blood were irrelevant, especially, it seems, flesh.

Sexually, Jackson was puzzling, but not threatening: the only time he fraternized with white women was when he sought the counsel of older ones, like Elizabeth Taylor, or the companionship of escorts, like Brooke Shields, to celebrity functions. As an asexual figure, he remained innocuous. The dread that might have been engendered by a virile young man who could command the fantasies of countless young women of every ethnic background did not apply Jackson. He was a symbolic eunuch when it came to women. Of course, this sweetness-and-light conception suddenly went grainy as a darker image emerged. His public humiliation may well have functioned as the equivalent of a lynching.

Whatever his fate, no one can deny that, in cultural terms, Jackson remains a compelling subject: an icon, the supreme product of the black culture industry, a creator of a different and sometimes bewildering image of black people. He reflects not only changes in the circumstances of the African American population, but changes in the circumstances of white America. Jackson was objectified, perhaps even refied, into an extraordinary being, an "other" for whom there were no established reference points in whites' conceptions. Looked at one way, Jackson is a total enigma. Looked at another, he becomes one of the most illuminating figures to stand on America's postwar landscape.

Chapter ten

Your Name
Is ⚦

Y OU USED TO BE Prince Roger Nelson, later you became just Prince, then, on your thirty-fifth birthday in 1993, you changed into a peculiar runic hieroglyph, seemingly made up of male and female gender symbols. No one knew how it was supposed to be pronounced, so, people now refer to you as the artist formerly known as (afka) Prince. It is 1995 and you are frustrated: you have made it known to the world that, like James Brown in his heyday, you wish to release about four albums per year. But your record company will not let you; to do so would defy every known principle of marketing. The music industry has learned that the best way to exploit the market is by using a three-year product cycle long enough to convert a big-selling album into a blockbuster. You are less interested in maximizing revenues, more in making records: you want your music heard.

Early in 1994, your "boutique" label, Paisley Park, a subsidiary of Warners jointly owned by you and the multinational parent company, was wound up. Behind all the talk about a mutually agreed decision lay a history of mutual resentments. During its eight-year existence, Paisley Park had put out dozens of albums, most by your protégés or heroes and, in spite of the media attention and a steady flow of million-plus sellers from you, none of the ancillary releases made much impact.

You grumbled about the lack of promotional support for the label. Warners began to question your judgement. Not about your ability to write and record commercial music: but about spotting talent and developing it into saleable commodity. Warners' view was that you were a superstar on par with Michael Jackson and Madonna, so why try to be a talent scout? As a consequence, the corporate giant lost interest in your endeavors. Evidence of this came at the end of 1993 when Paisley Park issued albums by the gospel veteran Mavis Staple and former P-Funk chief George Clinton, both of whom you admire greatly. Staples' record was not even released outside the United States and Clinton's work did nothing of note commercially.

Then, with your commercial acumen severely in doubt, you approached Warners with a view to releasing a single called "The most beautiful girl in the world." You knew as well as Warners that the days of profit-making singles had long gone: the cardinal purpose of singles is to work as trailers for an album. If people buy and like the single, they might be tempted into buying the album from which it has been taken. Trouble is: your next album was not scheduled for release for four months, so Warners were wary about the prohibitively high promotional costs for a single which might not yield much of a return. On the other hand, you reason, it might. After all, compared to the $60 million that is needed these days to produce and promote a typical film, the cost of getting an album into the charts averages only $2 million.

A resolution was sought and found in NPG, which stood for New Power Generation, a label which was the successor to Paisley Park but in which Warners had no financial stake and no obligation to promote. You went it alone: distributing the single through an international network of independents (including Bellmark Records and, in Britain, a two-man company called Grapevine). Smugly, you sat back and watched the sales figures rise to the point where the overheads were met and the release went into profit. It made you realize that perhaps you could do without Warners after all. So, you get busy and crank out more and more material. Then, in 1996, you announce your intention to split with Warners. "Irreconcilable differences," you say are the cause.

Nobody apart from you knows for sure, but it is reckoned that you have recorded between 300 and 500 tracks that are just lying around waiting to be released. Warners, guided by the logic of the market, will not let them out. You plead your case for the creativity of the artist; Warner Music replies with standard-issue arguments about the requirements of commerce. In your eyes your position is analogous to servitude. So much so that you take to having a word drawn with a marker pen on your cheek. It describes how you understand your relationship to your record company: SLAVE. Yours is a struggle within a wider struggle.

The origins of this conflict lie in 1977 when Nelson, by then performing under his Christian name, signed a recording contract with Warner Bros (WB). There had been a three-cornered pitch for Prince, CBS and A & M Records also expressing interest in the singer from Minneapolis who was represented by his friend Owen Husney and a lawyer Gary Levison, who operated as American Artists Inc. Husney had struck a deal with Nelson two years before and persuaded him, first, to drop the Roger Nelson bit of his name, and second, to lie about his age. He was then 16, but Husney's idea was to project him as a new Stevie Wonder, a man-child multi-instrumentalist, who wrote, produced and performed his own material. Prince was paid an allowance of $50 per week and, in return, Husney underwrote the cost of his equipment, promotional material (the press kits cost an extravagant $100 each) and studio time for recording demos.

Husney and Levison were joined by an LA music attorney, Lee Phillips, when they started to negotiate for Prince. Two labels, RSO and ABC, rejected him and, of the remaining three, WB agreed most readily to his demands, the most testing of which was that he be allowed to produce his own first album. As a completely unknown quantity, Warners were reluctant to grant Prince such artistic autonomy, but Husney knew Russ Thyret, a vice-president, and secured a provisional understanding, whereby Prince would produce, albeit in the presence of more experienced producers who could oversee the operation. WB wanted one of the producers to be Maurice White, of Earth, Wind and Fire, though they eventually opted for Tony Vicari, who was known for his work with Santana.

A second component of the contract called for a three-album condition rather than the more usual year-by-year, or one to two album arrangement which afforded record companies more flexibility. Three albums meant that the label was locked into a medium-term commitment. Thus started a delicate alliance. In time, irreconcilable tempers were to expose a tension germane to the black culture industry: creative autonomy vs. the injunction to commodify.

The contract was said to be more than six figures, so even at a low of one million dollars, it was an astonishing amount for the services of an unproven artist, especially one who insisted on such control over his own product. From Warners' point of view, it was a gamble they probably thought they had to take. Jimi Hendrix was unprecedented: a black performer capable of crossing genres and succeeding in the lucrative world of rock – as opposed to the ailing soul tradition to which the vast majority of blacks were consigned. CBS had shown its confidence in black artists' profitability when they signed the Jackson brothers and left Berry Gordy with the crumbs. Warners had no magic powerful enough to contend with the Jacksons, in particular Michael, then two years off releasing his *Off the Wall*. In Prince, WB saw someone capable of the giving Hendrix's improbable heirs a run for their money.

There was abundant evidence of Sly and the Family Stone's style in Prince's first album *For You*, released in 1978, though Prince himself resisted comparisons between his guitar playing and that of Hendrix. He was later to acknowledge a different inspiration: "Hendrix plays different guitar than I do. If they [audiences] really listened to my stuff, they'd hear more of a Santana influence than Hendrix" (quoted in Rosen, 1995: no page numbers). The album sold moderately, about 350,000 copies, but made only number 92 on the *Billboard* pop charts. Prince had spent almost double his entire advance on making the album.

Warners began to see some return on their investment in 1979 when Prince's single "I wanna be your lover" reached number 11 in the national charts and presaged a commercially successful second album, released two months later. *Prince*, like its predecessor, featured extensive use of synthesizers, though the electric guitar solos guaranteed that comparisons with Hendrix persisted. The vocals were a different thing entirely: Hendrix's voice was a study in slurred, near-demented machismo; Prince's had a shrill, brittle quality that could match Michael Jackson's falsetto; he also multitracked it to produce cascades of sound. The effeminate voice complemented the androgynous character Prince portrayed on stage. For a tour in 1980, Prince wore zebra striped bikini briefs, leg-warmers and stilettos. He simulated fellatio and various other sexual acts; these were to become features of his increasingly explicit stage shows, which later incorporated double beds and guitars which squirted white liquid from their necks.

By the time of the tour, Prince had left his management team and signed with Perry Jones and Don Taylor, though this arrangement was soon supplanted by another managerial team comprising Bob Cavallo and Joe Ruffalo. Cavallo and Ruffalo were recommended by WB-appointed agent Steven Fargnoli, who was to occupy a central role in Prince's career development. Prince supported Rick James, a one-time member of the little-known Motown band, the Mynah Birds, whose largest claim to fame was to come years later when MC Hammer (before he dropped the "MC") used his "Superfreak" as the basis for his multi-million-selling "U can't touch this."

Both James and Prince were black artists striving to appeal to a white market, though the audiences on the tour were "predominantly black," according to Per Nilsen in *Prince: A documentary* (1993: 18).

The theatrical sex gave Prince a certain notoriety, on which he capitalized in his third album *Dirty Mind*, to date his most carnal. Among its themes were oral sex ("Head"), incest ("Sister") and spontaneous sex, anywhere, anytime ("Dirty mind"). This was Prince's first album to make an impression abroad, especially in Britain, and, to promote it , Prince travelled to England in 1981. His first concert in London bombed so badly that the rest of the tour was cancelled. But, in the States, touring helped build his reputation. Still, the comparisons with Hendrix flowed. A black performer with overt sexuality who played rock music was a rare phenomenon; but at just over five feet tall and with a high-pitched voice he was unique.

The hyperproductivity that was to cause friction in later years, was evidenced in 1981. Morris Day and the Time was a band virtually sponsored by Prince. Day was a personal friend and collaborated with Prince on a number of projects, one of which was an album called *The Time*. The producer credited on the album sleeve was "Jamie Starr"; no writing credits were given. The suspicion was that Prince had written, produced, played several instruments and possibly sung on the album, but, for contractual reasons, remained anonymous. The trick was repeated a year later when the second Time album was released. The band looked little more than a vehicle for Prince's unrecorded material. Another band named Vanity 6 served a similar function. Over the following years, Prince was to assume *noms de plume* such as "Joey Coco," "Christopher Tracy," "Alexander Nevermind" and sometimes generic names like Madhouse or Paisley Park.

Prince was made forcibly aware of the difficulties for a black artist trying to reach a white rock-oriented audience when he was booked to play on a Rolling Stones tour. His first appearance lasted only 20 minutes before he was pelted and booed off. His second was even shorter. But, a year later almost to the day, the double album *1999* was released and it was this that brought him mainstream recognition. By the end of 1983, US record stores had moved a million copies and sales continued upwards for the next several years, reaching five million worldwide. It was smalltime compared to Jackson's *Thriller* of course. MTV, which, as we have seen, relaxed its strictures on black performers to accommodate Jackson, included the single "1999" on its playlist in late 1982. The single was followed by "Little red Corvette," which gained significant airplay on the cable music channel.

In Europe, the ignominy of Prince's 1981 gigs was forgotten as *1999* sold ferociously, allowing Prince to push ahead with an autobiographical film project costing about $7 million. *Purple Rain* echoed the title of one of Hendrix's most famous tracks, "Purple haze," though Prince's style was now less derivative. The single "Purple rain" was released to coincide with the movie and became Prince's biggest seller. Combining the movie and soundtrack in this way demonstrated the symbiosis of different media. Consumers buying the record or cd would be tempted to see the movie, which grossed $70 million, and moviegoers would be exposed to the music. Bands as diverse as U2, Talking Heads and Pink Floyd have worked the same oracle.

Steven Rosen, in *The Artist Formerly Known as Prince*, writes: "It cannot be over-emphasized that *Purple Rain* made the man an international commodity" (1995: no page numbers). Selling over ten million copies in the US and a further five million copies internationally, the album earned Prince a glut of awards and enough capital to be able to build his own $10 million studio in Minneapolis known as Paisley Park. This opened in 1981. He also used his leverage to promote several of his protégés, including Sheila E. and the Family, an outfit which originally recorded "Nothing compares 2 U," which was later covered by Sinead O'Connor. A second film *Under the Cherry Moon* began production. In contrast to the generally favorable reviews of *Purple Rain*, the media response to this was almost wholly negative. Undeterred, Prince started work on another film, *Sign "☮" the Times*, a straightforward concert film that would be released in 1987.

Yet the music poured out of the Paisley Park studios. Bands and artists with names like Camille and Madhouse were scarcely disguised Prince projects, sometimes created for the benefit of one album only. Scottish singer Sheena Easton's career was kickstarted when she recorded one of Prince's compositions, "Sugar walls." The Bangles also benefited from "Manic Monday," an internationally successful single written by Prince under the pseudonym "Christopher." While much of the Paisley Park output sold poorly, Prince's solo work continued to succeed and, as writer and publisher of his own material, he earned the kind of money necessary to support the studio. His *Lovesexy* album of this period (start-to-finish recording time: seven weeks) was quickly followed by his soundtrack to the first of the *Batman* movie series, released in 1989. And, with the movie still playing, Prince had already completed his twelfth album *Graffiti Bridge*. Remarkably, another album codenamed *The Black Album* was made but never legally released after a last minute intervention from the artist, who never revealed his reasons for spiking it. This most coveted of bootlegs was eventually circulated in a solid black sleeve with just the catalog number on its spine. This rather puzzling series of events presaged a deterioration in relations between Prince and Warners.

Prince proved to be one of the world's most prodigious makers of music; yet, for Warners, he was totally unaware of what to do with it. Releasing it just as soon as it was completed went against every known rule of marketing. Sales of *Batman* had topped five million and might have benefited from a new lease of life when the video came out. Releasing *Graffiti Bridge* so soon after was simply not commercially expedient. This was one headache for Warners. But the hyper-activity created others.

Artists, such as Paula Abdul, Chaka Khan, Stevie Nicks and Joe Cocker, at various times recorded Prince numbers. His extraordinarily fertile period at Paisley Park left a surfeit of unreleased material, some of it leaked out in the form of bootlegs. There is surely no other artist in history, whose work has been so copiously distributed through illicit channels. The collection of 1983–86 outtakes known as "The Crown (sometimes New or Royal) Jewels" may be one of the best-selling bootlegs of all time, containing an hour of unreleased studio recordings. Of course, neither the artists, the label, nor the publishers saw a penny.

Workaholism in the music industry exacts a price, not always on the artist. The perils of bombarding a market with material were brought home with the 1988 *Lovesexy* album: which was Prince's weakest-selling album since *Controversy*, from 1981: selling just over a million copies in the USA, it fared better in Europe, but still disappointed Warner Brothers after *Purple Rain*. Nor were Prince's concerts automatic successes: a 38-date tour in 1988 lost money, for example. The lull in popularity prompted a change in management and legal teams in early 1989. Albert Magnoli, who directed the *Purple Rain* movie, was appointed manager and John Branca, who listed Michael Jackson as one of his clients, became Prince's lawyer. Branca, it will be recalled from Chapter nine, helped negotiate Jackson's contract with CBS in the early 1980s.

The changes gave further substance to the belief that the Paisley Park project was an expensive indulgence. Many artists with plummeting fortunes found refuge at Paisley Park. Prince was an open admirer of George Clinton. When he approached Prince, he owed $150,000. Prince bailed him out with an advance against royalties, though his records probably never sold enough to come near that amount.

In contrast, the *Batman* album turned out to be huge: six million units sold worldwide, once again underscoring the value of dovetailing films and music. The album was not even a soundtrack, but, as the cover stated: "9 songs inspired by the motion picture." But, any expectations that the trick would be repeated with *Graffiti Bridge* were shattered shortly after a first cut of the $10 million movie, which was made mostly at Paisley Park, was rejected by Warners following negative reactions to test screenings. WB then appointed an editor to take charge of the final cut.

Barely pausing for breath after completing the soundtrack, Prince took off on a tour of Europe, which saw him sell out venues in England and Holland, yet only half-fill stadia in Germany and Spain. From Warners' point of view, the tour had only marginal value as it was not tied into the release of a new film. The *Graffiti Bridge* soundtrack came out midway through the tour, but the movie, for which Prince received writing and directing credits, needed reshooting. When it finally did open in November 1990, the movie became an instant turkey, grossing $2.25 million and attracting few positive reviews. It was effectively a patchquilt of loosely stitched videos, rather like Jackson's $27 million *Moonwalker*, which also lost money.

Paisley Park's troubles continued and Prince installed Jill Willis and Gilbert Davison as executive vice-president and president respectively. He also removed

Arnold Stiefel and Randy Phillips who had taken over his management from Magnoli, whose tenure had lasted only a year. Prince opted for self-management, assisted by Willis and Davison. Cavallo, Ruffalo and Fargnoli, who were replaced in 1989, sued Prince for $600,000 in 1991, claiming that he had overruled many of their financial and marketing decisions from 1985 onwards. In particular, he released records in quick succession so that they sold "in competition with one another" (quoted in Nilsen, 1993: 124). At the same time, Prince filed a lawsuit against his former lawyers for negotiating an unfavorable settlement with Fargnoli *et al.* who were granted "payments in perpetuity" for work created by Prince during the ten years they were his managers. The lawsuit was settled.

There then followed a marketing masterstroke that went wrong. Prince busied himself at Paisley Park with a troupe of musicians and dancers he called the New Power Generation. In May 1991, an acetate extended play containing four tracks was prepared for distribution to radio stations. With interest in this EP building, Prince, in one of his apparently providential interpositions, pulled it and instead announced that one of the featured tracks, "Gett off" would be released as a strictly limited edition 12-inch single: 1,500 one-sided copies went on sale in June and quickly sold out. Fans clamored for what was a valuable collector's item, only to find that seven weeks later, "Gett off" was on general release in a variety of formats and mixes – 7 inch, 12 inch, cassette, "Purple pump mix," "Thrust mix," etc. The single did not even crack the top 20 in the US, though it reached number four in the smaller British market.

Relations between Prince and Warners were deteriorating. Already the fifth highest paid entertainer in the world, according to *Forbes*, the prodigious artist was less interested in record sales, more in releasing the material produced at Paisley Park. In September, redemption came in the form of "Cream," a single that reached number one, Prince's fifth US number one after "When doves cry," "Let's go crazy," "Kiss" and "Batdance." The marketing approach was similar to that followed with the disappointing "Gett off": a single release, then a maxi format disc that played for 38 minutes and included seven tracks, and two mixes of "Cream." The credits went to Prince and the New Power Generation.

The tension between Prince and Warners had tightened to the point where the record company wanted a firm commitment to a carefully planned sequence of albums. It was prepared to pay for it in the kind of figures previously only dreamt of by Michael Jackson and Madonna. Unlike the contracts of these two, the Prince–Warners agreement was announced only in the broadest terms. Reports of its value to Prince varied, though most settled on $100 million. It was a shocking deal, considering the run-ins of the past. The deal also allowed for the expansion of Prince's own label, Paisley Park, and the launch of a new label that would specialize in "cutting-edge street music." And more: Prince was made a Warner's vice-president, with his own office. Central to the negotiations must have been the assumption that Prince would remain an active recording artist. His sales had totalled 30 million since the first contract.

More evidence of his worth came when he persuaded Spike Lee, then thickly embroiled in budgetary crisis over his movie *Malcolm X*, to direct the video to accompany "Money don't matter 2 night." Lee had emerged as the leading African American film director, as we will see in the next chapter.

Late in 1992, Prince released an album bearing the figure that was later to be his name. The record was known as the *Symbol* album and included the track "My name is Prince" as well as "The sacrifice of Victor." The significance of the latter lay in the fact that many fans believed that the enigmatic symbol, when broken into its component parts and rearranged, spelled out the name "Victor." Months after the album's release the artist announced that, contrary, to the track on the album, his name was *not* Prince; nor was it Victor. In fact, it was just a symbol. Some theorized that he had experienced a conversion. Others thought it signalled a change in musical direction. A graphic novel entitled *Prince: Alter ego* tells a story in which he was wrestling with an oppositional aspect of his personality named Gemini (McDuffie, 1991).

By the time of the release of the single "The most beautiful girl in the world," it had become a little clearer: the name change had probably been intended to embarrass Warners. After all, it would tax the most ingenious marketing minds to promote an artist without a proper name; and "Artist formerly known as Prince" did not exactly roll off the tongue. The irony is that the Artist ♀ story attracted publicity around the world and no doubt generated sales of the single and *The Beautiful Experience* collection which featured several different mixes of the same track. From Warners' perspective, even bestselling singles can only show a profit if they act effectively as trailers for albums. With the next the Artist ♀ album four months away – and this song not even on it – WB was not prepared to mobilize its vast and costly promotional machine on behalf of what seemed to be a rather doubtful single. Instead, the record company allowed him to release it on his own label, NPG. Distributed through an international network of independents, the single's sales must have convinced the Artist ♀ that he could succeed with or without a corporation behind him.

In 1992: "Warner Bros. announced the dissolution of Paisley Park, while former Prince announced his retirement from music," writes Simon Glickman (1995: 187). The artist began to describe himself as "a man without a contract" and daubed in capitals SLAVE across his face. He rarely gave interviews and, when he did, often relieved reporters of their pens before they started the questions. Around the same time, the Artist ♀ merchandising acquired a new outlet when a London counterpart to the Minneapolis store that sold Princely products was opened. In February 1996, he announced through *Jet* magazine that he had ended his recording contract with Warners, citing "irreconcilable differences" and "the unstable and ever-changing management structure within Warner Bros. Records" as the reasons for his departure (February 5, 1996, p. 36). He stated that he had given the label official notice of his desire to end his two-decade-long relationship; as we noted previously, the first contract was signed in 1978 when the *For You* album was released. Between then and the 1996 announcement, the artist had sold 33.5 million records. He promised delivery of three more albums for Warners, then a new album with a working title of *Emancipation*.

Joining forces with Spike Lee in the same year, he wrote the soundtrack for the movie *Girl 6*, one of Lee's least commercially successful ventures.

Critics of the Artist ♀ accused him of immaturity, crudity, showy pretense and an exaggerated sense of his own preciousness. We do not have to agree with any of this to accept that his music alone was not unique, though some of it was spiced with original dashes – like taking out a bass line on "When doves cry" or dividing the harmonic structure of "Anna Stesia" into a binary pattern. His gentle voice was plain, his style eclectic and his physical appearance short, spare and wiry. The sexual component of his act was brutally overt, giving the act an almost comic charm. He dressed in clothes that would have drawn gasps of despair at a fashion show: the adjective "gaudy" scarcely does justice to the Artist ♀ taste. Yet, this diminutive fellow, lacking in innovation, grace, subtlety, wit and irony, became an irresistible, if unlikely, icon of the 1980s and a culture industry in his own right. Why?

My brief answer is that the Artist ♀ was a transgressive embodiment of ambiguity. Looking as if he had been assembled by an inept jigsaw manufacturer, the Artist ♀ threw into question the two categories of "male" and "female" and became, as a result, a hybrid – something made of incongruent parts. As a black male, he both reaffirmed the myth of black sexual potency and undermined it. His lyrics, stage act and constant allusions all pointed to a small but perfectly formed stud; yet there were signs of emasculation. The high-pitched voice, the surrounding cordon of beefy security guards, the elaborately coiffured hair – sometimes worn up – and, most obviously, the clothes were signifiers of something other than a regular member of the male phallocracy.

Showbusiness frequently encourages cross-dressing. Quite apart from the many movies that have used it as a central theme and the countless drag acts, stage performers from Freddie Mercury to Andy Bell, of Erasure, have blurred the lines of male and female dress with their flamboyant outfits. Liberace teased audiences about whether they should love or punish him for his effete manner and effeminate clothes. As a black male dressing in skintight, glitzy outfits made of fabrics such as satin and lace, the Artist ♀ was a model of sexual ambiguity. Was he a transvestite? Gay? Straight? Bi? The questions were more important than the answers. This was not the "essential" black male laden with sexual prowess; but one whose sexual prowess was visibly uncertain. To this layer of uncertainty, the Artist ♀ added another: was he even black? Generous use of eyeshadow and foundation cream gave him a curious countenance, that of a very pale African American (though without the blanched look of Michael Jackson). Was he trying to "pass" as white? Or was he effecting another definition of blackness? Kobena Mercer, in his *Welcome to the Jungle*, believes the Artist ♀ was "operating at the interface of cultural boundaries defined by 'race'" (1994: 36).

The effect of this could have been dislocating and might easily have banished the artist to ranks of obscurity, or gay subcultures – as happened to disco star Sylvester in the 1970s. But, as Anne McClintock points out in her book *Imperial Leather*:

The disruption of social norms is not always subversive, especially in postmodernist commodity cultures where formal fluidity, fragmentation and marketing through difference are central elements. Indeed, privileged groups can, on occasion, display their privilege precisely by the extravagant display of their *right to ambiguity*.

(1995: 68)

This is an interesting term and one which might be applied to the Artist ♀.

The image portrayed in early phases of his career was one of the horny leather-jacketed motorcyclist flanked by equally horny women. After a couple of movies and several million-selling records, he probably did own the "right to ambiguity" and, of course, exercised it to great effect. It could have been a mis-judgement; audiences could have stopped admiring him and grown restive over the developing gender-defiance in his image. In the event, it elevated him to a new status. We have already noted how the acceptance of black performers by a predominantly white market is contingent on their status. African American males frequently have to undergo a symbolic emasculation to affirm their lack of sexual threat. In Chapter five, the term "symbolic eunuch" described the talented black male performer who was somehow neutered, whether by blindness, as in the case of Stevie Wonder, or by a childlike demeanor that conjured up images of Uncle Tom.

Mercer writes of Michael Jackson: "His work is located entirely in the Afro-American tradition of popular music, and thus must be seen in the context of imagery of black man and black male sexuality." We may substitute the Artist ♀ for Jackson when Mercer suggests: "Jackson not only questions dominant stereo-types of black masculinity, but also gracefully steps outside the existing range of 'types' of black men" (1994: 50).

The Artist ♀ did not so much question them as confound them. His attempts to conceal, deny, defy, evade and remain unnamed were perfectly suited to a culture which welcomed black males but hesitated to grant them manhood. The androgenic star offered himself and was treated as if more manikin than man. Prurient but manageable. Sexuality was central to his persona, but he possessed the quality without presenting danger. There was a patina of homoeroticism, yet he was not a drag queen in the mode of Ru Paul, a black male rarely seen publicly out of costume. He had the build of a cabin boy and the money of a tycoon. He was self-obsessed, isolated, yet bold enough to create the most flamboyant stage productions.

Even his music resisted categorization in the column usually reserved for blacks. In this sense, his cultural progenitor was not Hendrix but Little Richard, who flounced about on stage in extravagantly florid outfits, a maddening reminder to white crackers of the day that not all black males were heterosexual bucks. But, in the case of Richard, like the Artist ♀, who knew *what* he was? This "Imp of the perverse," as Barney Hoskyns (following Poe, of course) has called him, teased and entranced his way to iconic status by raiding the past for images, then reassembling them in ways that brought confusion. Perhaps a similar sort of confusion to that experienced by audiences watching minstrels performing the cakewalk: was the parody that of blacks imitating whites, or of blacks imitating whites imitating blacks?

Chapter eleven

Brothers
and
Others

"I'M BRINGING THEM TODAY'S BLACK CULTURE," Russell Simmons told *Black Enterprise* writer Christopher Vaughn. "And I'm putting it out there for anyone and everyone who wants to buy it" (1992: 66). Simmons' assumption was that black culture was a serious business: something that should be made available to all who could afford to purchase it. In this sense, he was no different from the other black culture industrialists we have encountered in this book. Simmons differed only in his *acknowledgment* that he wanted to get rich by commodifying culture.

The origins of Simmons' empire are in the hiphop culture of New York's squalid black neighborhoods; though, by 1994, he presided over the most multifarious black culture industry, which included *inter alia* record labels, management agencies, designer label fashion houses and film/television production companies. Famed for his constant on-the-move cell telephone conversations and his Adidas shoes (which were an advertisement rather than a fashion statement), Simmons took a black culture redolent of the crime that comes from poverty and stylized it.

The rap music from which Simmons prospered was street poetry that used the language of "niggas," "bitches," "hos" (whores), slinging dope and icing cops; it frequently applauded sadism and machismo and celebrated the hopeless currency of ghetto life: gang feuds, drug deals, police oppression, black-on-black killings, sexual violence and antisemitism. Rap music's slogans of despair were raw and contemporary: it brought a bracing political and artistic radicalism, drawing from other genres with contempt rather than respect. The same music that became a shorthand for the violent implosion of black life was the source of Simmons' extravagant wealth.

When Simmons sold half his company to PolyGram for $33 million, he showed how it was possible to criticize crass commercialism and the white institutions that sponsor it, while profiting handsomely from both. Simmons' story is an object lesson in making poverty work for you. But first: an examination of the culture that was launched by that poverty.

The ingredients were the same, but the product was different. In the 1970s, a new type of music swept through the predominantly black neighborhoods of New York and New Jersey. Carried mainly by djs rather than musicians, it consisted of abstracting, or "sampling," pieces of previously recorded tracks, playing them repeatedly, sometimes backwards, often with another track playing simultaneously, and voicing over them.

It was a cheap form of entertainment well suited to the times. The heady days of civil rights had come to an end: Martin Luther King's assassination in 1968 symbolized the vulnerability of African Americans. His strategy had been one of survival and gradual integration into mainstream society. Yet, ten years after his death, the black world had subdivided psychically as well as physically. Some took advantage of affirmative action and equal opportunity programs, moving up toward a new middle class and out of the ghettos; "the talented tenth," as they became known. They left behind a large residue struggling even harder to stay above the poverty line. Fortysomething percent did not manage it and the rate of black unemployment stayed consistently double that of whites. The educational equalization promised by the *Brown* decision was undermined by the busing controversy that was a feature of the period. President Richard Nixon enjoined African Americans to create an enterprise culture that would yield what he called "black capitalism." Many tried.

One was Sylvia Robinson, owner of a troubled independent record label, All Platinum. In 1979, she attended a show at the Harlem World disco on 116th Street, New York, across from the mosque founded by Malcolm X. Robinson noticed the crowd react favorably to a dj who played tracks and voiced over them in a rhyming couplet style known as rap. Her interest piqued, she returned to her New Jersey studios and recorded a track with a bunch of session musicians and part-time band members. In the style of the dj, she used a track – in this case, Chic's "Good times" – to lie under a series of spoken rhymes and entitled the track "Rapper's delight." (The source track was one of a string of late 1970s successes by Chic, a band which seemed to signify the upwardly-mobile aspirations of the post-civil-rights black bourgeoisie.) "Rapper's delight" became a historically important track, selling well enough to make the mainstream pop charts. Prior to this, the only documented rap music was circulated on clandestine audio tapes recorded by bootleggers at parties or clubs, or tapes made by artists themselves, who sold their products on the street.

Djs would "toast" across the music in the manner of Jamaican djs: as the music played, the djs would speak or dub over their own rhymes or doggerel. Many accounts credit a Jamaican-born dj named Kool Herc with pioneering the approach in the late 1960s. Several US djs adopted and refined the technique, which, by the 1970s, had become known as rapping. Radio djs in the New

York/New Jersey area, particularly Gary Byrd, had used conversation, or rap, over prerecorded music in their shows, though it was the travelling djs who originated "scratching," which meant manipulating a stylus on a record to produce new sounds. Used together, the techniques made possible a unique and inexpensive approach to music: equipment needs were small compared to those of a full band.

Robinson, who ran the record business with her husband, was a recording artist herself: she performed as Little Sylvia and made records for the independent label, Savoy, in the 1950s. Her biggest success was with a single, "Love is strange" which she made with Mickey Baker. In 1968, her recording career over, she moved into business with the Blue Morocco club in New York's Bronx district before opening up All Platinum.

Folklore has it that Robinson's children alerted her to the potential of the monologue music form and she recorded a number of inexpensively produced forerunners to "Rapper's delight" before she struck rich with the Sugar Hill Gang's hit. At its peak, the single sold 60,000 per day and eventually logged up two million in sales. A major success for Robinson in its day, it was nothing compared to sales of "The message." Grandmaster Flash and the Furious Five had released an album on the Sugar Hill label in 1981. *The Adventures of Grandmaster Flash on the Wheels of Steel* was a chaos of incongruent, sampled tracks which were a collective *tour de force*.

In the following year, the combination of Flash's dextrous control of two turntables and the rapping commentary of Melle Mel, made "The message" one of the most original tracks of its time. It was a long, spoken rather than sung statement on life in the ghetto as seen through the eyes of a black youth. The lyrics were very different from those of the earlier Sugar Hill hit which was a lighthearted affair with scat-like "hiphop-de-hibby-dibby" lines punctuating a song about "boyfriends."

"The message" was an overlong ultimatum: "Don't push me," warned the ghetto dweller, who was, on his own admission, close to the edge. The track told of houses infested with roaches and rats and baseball-bat wielding junkies. It was a mean, dark side to the hiphop culture and one which made other versions of rap seem pallid by comparison. Music could radicalize the black experience, turning it into an invective against the police and an injunction to challenge its authority; criminal acts could be made political ones. This strain of rap was to be changed into a defiantly combative but perfectly commodifiable force.

In 1979, the year of "Rapper's delight," Russell Simmons, then aged 21, closed a deal that locked an artist he managed into a recording contract with Mercury Records, which distributed through the PolyGram network. This was a crucial moment for Simmons: it made him the first black entrepreneur specializing in what was then strictly ghetto music to secure a foothold in the mass market. The music Simmons purveyed was all about the experience of life in places like Harlem and Brooklyn. Simmons himself came from Hollis, which is a middle class district of Queens, New York. His father taught black history and his mother worked for the Parks Department. Simmons studied sociology at New York's City College (CCNY) and it was here he came into contact with Curtis Walker, who was a party promoter working under the stage name Kurtis Blow. Walker and his outfit, "Rush, The Force," were itinerant contractors who would rent out their sound equipment and play records at events.

Simmons was less interested in performing than he was in promoting and marketing the then new music form. He began working with Walker, promoting him in small venues – which he would rent out at about $500 per night – but all the time trying to interest record executives in the potential. By 1978, Walker had developed a local following sufficient for him to hire a permanent dj. Simmons' younger brother, Joseph, took to the turntables, while Walker concentrated on the rap.

Simmons saw the deal with Mercury as the start of a rap boom. "Christmas rappin'" was the first rap single to be distributed by a major label. It was followed in 1980 by "The breaks" which sold more copies, but was hardly the breakthrough Simmons had hoped for. He had to wait until 1983 for this: Rick Rubin, a white New York University student, was brought in. Rubin had been working independently of Simmons, renting studio time, making records and selling to record companies. He coined the name Def Jam. He and Simmons each invested $2,500 to launch Def Jam Records, which would produce its own records. The tiny label's first release was L. L. Cool J's "I need a beat" and, while its total sale of 120,000 copies would have meant nothing to a major corporation, it was wondrous for Def Jam. The label was to become the capstone of Simmons' Rush Management, eventually accounting for 60 percent of its annual revenue.

Run DMC were Joseph Simmons and Darrel McDaniels, managed by Simmons through his Rush Management. By the time of their major international success, "Walk this way," rap and the hiphop culture of which it was part were known. Not only had Grandmaster Flash and the Furious Five gained acclaim in the USA and Europe, but Herbie Hancock had enjoyed an international hit in 1983 with "Rockit," which introduced scratching to a world audience and, in that same year, a movie *Flashdance* had featured breakdancing, an acrobatic style of dancing perfectly suited to rap music. Hiphop described the music, the dance and the inventive graffiti that plastered New York's subways. "Walk this way" was re-recorded, rather than sampled, from an original by white rock band Aerosmith, prompting some to suggest a break with the subculture that gave rise to rap, others to suggest it had reached a new level of maturity in fraternizing with other genres.

By 1985, Def Jam's presence in the black culture market had caught the eye of CBS records. Sales of 500,000 units per year with no institutional support were impressive. CBS Records made a $600,000 label deal with the company that included marketing and promotion. The contract involved no compromise over creative control: Simmons and Rubin selected the acts, made the records and commissioned the artwork. CBS pressed the records, distributed them and sold them. Within two years, Def Jam had produced albums by the Beastie Boys and L. L. Cool J which together sold seven million copies. The Beastie Boys, whose *License to Ill* sold four million, were three whites from middle class backgrounds who had a string of hits on Def Jam, then defected to LA and Capitol Records. Their reason for leaving echoed that of many other artists in the black culture industry: despite sales, they did not receive what they considered their dues. S. H. Fernando, in his book *The New Beats*, quotes Mike D. of the band: "Russell is a lot of fun to hang out with and brilliant marketing guy, but when it comes to scruples, there's not that many that he has" (1995: 169).

During the late 1980s, when the CBS/Def Jam contract came up for renegotiation, Simmons and Rubin disagreed on the direction their record company should take and the partnership came to an acrimonious end, Rubin leaving to start his own record company, Def American Records. Simmons explained: "I was a manager and I wanted to break and establish acts. I knew I couldn't do it on my own. I needed a big company with marketing and promotional muscle like CBS to do that and to fully develop the artists' potential" (quoted in Vaughn, 1992: 68).

Def Jam accounted for 70 percent of sales in CBS's black music division. Simmons continued to negotiate with the corporation, by then part of Sony Incorporated, and in 1990 the two parties set up a joint venture agreement that became the new standard for rap music contracts. In what was a typical record label deal, the major label/distributor takes the profit, and then pays the independent label a royalty. The most distinguishing detail of the Rush Associated Labels (RAL)/Def Jam deal with Sony was that Def Jam enjoyed full profit participation. In addition to splitting the profits, the Def Jam/Sony joint venture gave Def Jam $3 million annually for operating costs.

CBS's Epic Records had flirted with rap as early as 1983 when it struck up a distribution deal with an independent label called Tuff City. The label was run by Aaron Fuchs a smallscale entrepreneur who specialized in the then relatively new and untested music form. Epic was disappointed with the results: "One for the treble," a single by Davy DMS, sold 80,000 copies. Simmons' setup obviously showed more potential. Simmons himself had nailed his colors to the mast. He wanted to become the most important person in black entertainment; he wanted the value of the company to double in five years (this was achieved in two); and he wanted his artists to move into film and television, while he continued to have control over them.

Among his ventures was "Def Comedy Jam," a television show he produced and sold to the Home Box Office (HBO) subscription channel. The show featured African American acts doing gags about black life, police racism and so on. This spun off several profitable national tours of standup comics. He also experimented with rap concert movies, incorporating his own name into film titles: "Russell Simmons presents" in the same way as other movies had used "David Lynch presents" or "Martin Scorsese presents" to get access to wider markets. By 1992, Rush Communications, the parent company of all Simmons' enterprises, included seven record labels, artist management companies, a radio production company and a film and television division. His designer label produced clothes and his model agency produced models who wore them.

Lacking knowledge in many of these spheres, Simmons recruited a black Harvard- and Yale-educated member of a New York law firm and made him vice-president of business affairs. David Harleston was to use his business, legal and organizational skills to create a genuine corporate structure for what was, after all, a culture industry specializing in the sounds, the humor and the perspectives of the ghetto. With a staff of more than 40 and $15 million in annual revenue, Harleston was given responsibility for drawing up artists' contracts, negotiating music licence deals, drawing up marketing plans, balancing budgets; in other words, he ran the company. Harleston had worked for Sony/CBS when it negotiated the earlier contract with Simmons.

This may have been precipitated by a couple of missed opportunities for Simmons. One of these was the loss of Will Smith, whom he once managed, but who left Rush and later went on to stardom as *The Fresh Prince of Bel Air*. The other Simmons still gripes about: he read the script of film director John Singleton's *Boyz N the Hood*, spotted its potential, wanted to produce it and approached Sony/Columbia. The movie did eventually get made and was a commercial success for Columbia, which had earlier turned down Spike Lee's *Do the Right Thing*. But Simmons had no part in it. "I got jipped," is his version of events (Lorez, 1995: 28). Christopher Vaughn of *Black Enterprise* magazine has a slightly different interpretation: "Columbia Studios then-president Frank Price was loath to set up a film deal with a man who came to meetings dressed like a messenger and whose conversation was filled with the rawest of obscenities" (1992: 71).

"It's about time there was a black man who doesn't have to give up his blackness in order to play with the white guys," Simmons told *New York* magazine writer Stephen Dubner (1992: 71). This was put to the test in 1994. The headline in the November 26 *Billboard* read: POLYGRAM BUYS HALF OF RAL/DEF JAM RECORDS . . . FOR $33 MIL. Simmons signed a five-year contract with PolyGram, part of the Philips group, which at the time accounted for 14.37 percent of the total US music market and was the second leading company behind Warners, which controlled 22.65 percent. It was not an altogether unexpected move. PolyGram wanted to strengthen its portfolio of black music, whose commercial viability had by then been tried and tested; the company had, in 1993, bought Motown Records for $301 million.

Rush and Def Jam had emerged as tasty game for the big predators with a roster that included big-selling artists such as Public Enemy, Warren G., Nice 'N' Smooth and Terminator X. RAL/Def Jam's previous year's sales figures hit $65 million, mostly in the domestic market, though it had made a worldwide licensing deal with PolyGram in summer 1994 that would boost its presence in Europe and elsewhere. This deal had confirmed Simmons' willingness to work with big – and, we might add, white-controlled – corporations. He became a mediator between street rappers and multinational corporations. Many black entrepreneurs followed suit.

Under the arrangement, Def Jam was to remain "creatively autonomous." Records were to account for nearly 60 percent of Rush Communication's sales, though Simmons wanted to use the corporate scaffold to build a multi-entertainments conglomerate. His movie *Russell Simmons Presents the Show* gave valuable exposure to his own acts. The arrangement also allowed him to produce films, like *The Funeral*, directed by Abel Ferrera, and the Eddie Murphy remake of *The Nutty Professor*.

Christopher Vaughn has argued that, unlike Berry Gordy, who "sweetened black musicians for mainstream consumption," "Rush makes the mainstream swallow its artists and their messages black – with no sugar and no apologies" (1992: 66). Although there is little question about Simmons' ability to address a mainstream market, he has resisted suggestions that he deliberately courted a white audience for his music, movies or any other commodity. Responding to a question about his line of clothes, priced toward the Calvin Klein end of the range, he answered with reference to black consumers: "They're the only people who buy up other than the rich. They buy into the American dream. They buy success. They buy Hilfiger. They'll pay whatever for a shirt. They'll pay for the name, the cut, the logo, the marketing" (quoted in Lorez, 1995: 29). His successful exploitation of this market underscores his point about the purchasing propensities of blacks.

"Berry Gordy sold black entertainment to white people. The difference between me and him is that I sell black entertainment to people who are into black culture," he insisted to Jim Shelley, of the British *Guardian Weekend*, adding: "Some of them just happen to be white" (1996: 39).

Spurning Motown as a model for development, Simmons saw the media giant Time Warner as his blueprint. This is probably a reflection of the 1990s rather than an indictment of Gordy. At the start of the decade, *New York Times* journalist Stephen Holden declaimed that popular music had become "an adjunct to television, whose stream of commercial images projects a culture in which everything is for sale" (August 5, 1990, section 2:1). The writer saw this as a cause for concern. But it was the key to Simmons' success.

This was based on the observation of two rules. One, owning only one element of an increasingly multilayered media complex leaves one at the mercy of whoever owns more of the others; the record industry lives in a symbiotic relationship with film, video, television and, increasingly, the Internet. Two, it is possible to sell cds through films, clothes through recording artists, videos through tv and so on. His vision was and is to have control over interlocking media, each complementing the rest and each generating revenue from different areas of the market.

He seems to have learned these rules early in his business career, possibly when he approached sports goods manufacturer Adidas to sponsor a Run DMC concert tour. Rush's vice-president of operations Lyor Cohen, who had joined the organization in 1985, invited Adidas representatives to a gig at which the band, wearing Adidas shoes, asked the crowd to throw their shoes in the air. The cloud of Adidas footwear that ensued clinched the deal. (The band also released a track entitled "My Adidas.") Further evidence, though of a quite different kind, arrived in the form of Spike Lee's movie *Do the Right Thing* which featured Simmons' band Public Enemy on its soundtrack. "Fight the power" blared at the start of the film, which narrowly missed out on the Cannes Golden Palm award, and became a commercial success worldwide. It highlighted the synergy emerging from movies and movie soundtracks.

Soon after the release of the film, Public Enemy became Simmons' top performer, its albums outselling all others in the organization. The band is to date the most fierce representative of an aggressive, nationalistic form of rap and was ideally suited to Lee's groundbreaking film.

In *Do the Right Thing*, a young African American male is seen drifting through the streets of Bedford-Stuyvesant with a ghettoblaster perched on his shoulder. Radio Raheem, as he is called, wears knuckleduster rings that read LOVE on one hand, HATE on the other. Throughout the movie, he wanders in and out, the same track issuing from the speakers. Public Enemy's "Fight the power" is the film's leitmotif.

The band did not appear in the movie, but the music became synonymous with it. The invocation of the title was not so much an expression of rage as a reminder that black America had fallen asleep since the politicized days of Malcolm X. The band's first album *Yo! Bum Rush the Show*, released on Def Jam in 1987, signalled the hopes and terrors of African Americans. The band's leader Carlton Ridenhour, better known as Chuck D, was an acolyte of Malcolm and of the Nation of Islam (NoI) movement, whose philosophy was evident in some of the album's tracks. Many of the titles could have been taken straight from the graffiti-sprayed walls of Bed-Stuy. "911 is a joke" exposed the police as ineffectual and uninterested in blacks' protection. The central NoI concept of black economic self-sufficiency was dealt with in "Shut 'em down" which urged blacks to boycott white companies that profited from black consumers.

Public Enemy made its points like someone jabbing an index finger in your forehead. Its music was perfectly suited to Lee's equally portentous movie, which foreshadowed an urban doomsday in which police kill the aforementioned Radio Raheem amid the sweltering heat of mid-summer. This was art for entertainment and for propaganda. It was to the late 1980s what Melvin van Peebles' seminal film *Sweet Sweetback's Baadasssss Song* was to politicized blacks in 1971: a literal and metaphorical vignette of black life. Lee, in this and subsequent work, held a mirror to blacks, showing their internal quarrels, their petty jealousies and, perhaps most significantly, their hypocrisy. Lee visualized a world in which there is little to choose between victims and oppressors in terms of their prejudices. *Do the Right Thing* had little use for the type of realism in which every black person was either a dope pusher/user/clocker/all-of-the-above. His Brooklyn had a chilling restlessness that seemed to have leapt straight from the streets on to the screen.

After his first two movies, *She's Gotta Have It* in 1986 and *School Daze* in 1988, had stirred critics with their playful dissections of African American life, Lee tricked many into thinking that he had sacrificed principles at the altar of Hollywood. But, *Do the Right Thing* was as much a "boyz 'n' the drugs"-type movie as *Moby Dick* was a mere sea adventure.

In the year of the film's release, 1989, one of Public Enemy's members, Richard Griffin, or "Professor Griff," gave an interview to the *Washington Times* (May 9) in which he gave his views on history. This was history as interpreted by Drew Ali, Wallace Fard, Elijah Muhammad and, the most recent successor to these past leaders of the NoI, Louis Farrakhan. Griff, as a devotee, accepted the NoI orthodoxy that Jews were responsible "for the majority of wickedness that goes on across the globe." Farrakhan's views on how he believed Jews had disempowered blacks became widely known after a well-publicized conversation with Jesse Jackson during Jackson's 1984 Presidential nomination campaign: New York was referred to as "Hymietown." Farrakhan also alleged that the Aids pandemic was the result of whites' attempts to annihilate the population of Central Africa. The antisemitic dimension to NoI philosophy served to alienate many blacks, though not the estimated 800,000 followers who joined his "Million Man March" on Washington in 1995.

The anti-Jewish statements introduced a tension in Public Enemy. Chuck D's politics seemed much nearer to the Stokely Carmichael position: racism in North America is "pervasive and permeates society on both the individual and institutional level, covertly and overtly," as Carmichael and Charles Hamilton put it in their 1967 book *Black Power*. In this book, black people were encouraged to identify the sources of their poverty and exploitation in the institutions controlled by whites and not just in prejudiced individuals. The solution was to organize on the basis of collectivities and, as the title of the Public Enemy track suggests, fight the power. As if to underline the affinities with the earlier black power movement, Public Enemy concerts incorporated guards in military garb carrying Uzi replicas; these were known as the Security of the First World. The PE logo found on countless pieces of merchandise featured a rifle sight.

Interestingly, Rubin was much more enthusiastic about Public Enemy than Simmons, who initially dismissed the band, according to Fernando (1995: 168). And it was possibly Rubin, the white partner, who first saw the mileage in promoting an emblem of a different world: a world populated by black people who saw their redemption only in a radical re-routing of history. "Public Enemy became the white idea of Black neighborhoods," writes Michael Bernard-Donals in his article "Jazz, rock'n'roll, rap and politics" (1994). Bernard-Donals, while referring to the band, may easily have stretched his idea to include Lee's film, which eventually gained a wide, international box office. Marshalling the support of David Samuels, a writer for *New Republic* (November 11, 1991: 24–29) who located Public Enemy's success in allowing whites to become "guilty eavesdroppers on the putative private conversations of the inner city," Bernard-Donals argues that Public Enemy "consciously rejected white icons and authority and set up an alternative ethic" (1994: 131). *Do the Right Thing* realized this on screen.

Two white icons in particular came under scrutiny in "Fight the power": Elvis Presley and John Wayne, both of whom were disparaged. The remarks are audible on the mix that appeared on the *Fear of a Black Planet* album, but a different version was cut for radio. Eager to use the number to cross-promote the movie, Lee linked up with band member Flavor Flav to produce a third mix of the track, this time a 12-inch single featuring a conversational prelude with Lee and Flav discussing a variety of issues such as African American artists who spurn the label "black singers" and white artists who aspire to be black.

Lee's first abortive liaison with rap music ended when Sugar Hill Records snubbed his self-financed video to accompany the international hit by Grandmaster Flash and the Furious Five, "White lines." He opted for jazz as a score for his first full-length feature, *She's Gotta Have It*, which he financed with some assistance from New York State Council and sold to Island Films for $475,000. It went on to gross over $5 million, playing in the main at movie theaters in urban black areas, to begin with and then to a wider audience. In the years preceding 1986, there had been few films aimed at the African American market. The blaxploitation era started in 1971 by Melvin van Peebles' *Sweet Sweetback's Baadasssss Song* had ended and only occasional films, such as *A Soldier's Story* and *The Color Purple*, both directed by whites, tackled black themes and used black casts. Lee, as a black director, was later to criticize Steven Spielberg for his direction of Alice Walker's *The Color Purple*.

The commercial promise showed by Lee's first film persuaded Island to sign him to a two-picture deal, but the corporation pulled out during the making of *School Daze* and Columbia Pictures stepped up and was rewarded with a $15 million return in 1988. Lee's next proposed movie aroused more interest. Tony Chapelle recounts how: "The brass at Paramount [Pictures] gave Lee $6.5 million for the project but asked him to abandon its bleak ending" (1991: 62). The denouement involved a violent conflict in which blacks torch an Italian-owned pizzeria and a white police officer kills Radio Raheem. "Another studio, Universal, gladly accepted it any way he wanted it to end," writes Chapelle. *Do the Right Thing* became not only his most commercial film to date, grossing $25 million, but also the work that established him as the world's best known cultural critic. Much was made of the fact that, during the making of the movie, Lee hired the Nation of Islam's security arm, known as the Fruit of Islam. In the film itself, Lee's own character refers deferentially to Minister Farrakhan in a way that could almost be a commercial for the NoI. Lee himself had no reservations about doing official commercials: he joined Michael Jordan to advertise Air Jordan shoes for Nike, an organization that was in dispute with Jesse Jackson's People United to Save Humanity (Push) organization for its avoidance of equal opportunity policies. Lee also appeared in television commercials for Apple Macintosh and made commercials for Levi 501 jeans.

In his next film *Mo' Better Blues*, Lee commented on one of the central issues of the black culture industry: that of Jewish ownership, or control. Jewish impresarios are depicted as hawkish exploiters of poor black jazz musicians. There was little nuance in Lee's characterizations. As Alex Patterson writes in his biography *Spike Lee*: "Spike's portrayal of shekel-grubbing shysters who live only to chisel black artists out of what is rightfully theirs is like something out of a Klan comic book" (1992: 156). Or, we might add in the light of the above, from a NoI publication.

When the NoI's most famous son Malcolm X became the subject of a film project, Lee crowed so loud that Warner Brothers removed their original director, Norman Jewison, and installed Lee at the helm. Lee's own company, Forty Acres and a Mule, was named after the Emancipation deal offered to ex-slaves who were encouraged to become self-sufficient. Lee's intention was to become precisely that: he set about selling merchandise related to the movie with a vengeance. For a while, in 1992, it was almost impossible to get through a day without seeing at least one person wearing apparel bearing the "X" logo. Lee's commercial acumen was also evidenced in his penchant for writing books on "the making of . . ." his movies, and in his opening of a store called "Spike's Joint" which sold merchandise related to his own movies.

During the film's production, Lee was embarrassed by the Completion Bond Company's exercising its right to take over control. This was occasioned when the film went over its original $33.5 million budget found by Warner

Brothers. The corporation put up $18 million plus $8.5 million from the sale of foreign rights with the balance supplied by the completion guaranteed investment firm. This effectively meant that, while Lee had virtual autonomy during most of the film-making, the final stages, including postproduction, were liable to intervention. Lee strenuously tried to resist this, at one point passing the hat round the likes of the Artist ♀, Bill Cosby, Janet Jackson, Magic Johnson, Michael Jordan, Oprah Winfrey and Tracy Chapman to refinance the project.

The eventual movie, *Malcolm X*, was over three hours long, an immediate impediment to box office success as it limited the number of performances per day. While its reviews vacillated between rave and rank, the immense publicity it generated was equal to any other film of 1992. According to the often obscure methods of accounting used by major studios, the film lost over $30 million. Shortly after the film's release, Lee declared that he would concentrate on other aspects of his culture industry, Forty Acres and a Mule, emphasizing that he welcomed the day when black entrepreneurs could control the production, distribution and marketing of their own product. "Until then, I'm gonna stick with the Hollywood system, 'cause there's nothing like it in the world" (quoted in Patterson, 1992: 225).

In a sense, he had little choice, having signed a seven-movie deal with Universal. The final two projects, *Clockers* and *Girl 6*, were also commercial disappointments, the latter becoming a full-blown débâcle, making a paltry $4 million in its first five weeks of release in 1996; about the same as a modest film of the same period, *Mulholland Falls*, made in its first week. The knives came out. One was plunged into the heart of Lee's next mooted project, a biopic on baseball giant Jackie Robinson. Ted Turner's movie company had been negotiating with Lee, but the film was cancelled, Turner claiming the $35 million budget was too steep; mainstream directors typically operate with $60 million budgets in the late 1990s.

Los Angeles' first club to specialize in rap was the Radio, which opened in 1982 and brought over djs from New York to create the sound that was, by then, attracting national publicity. The club's success convinced Greg Mack, the programming head of Radio KDAY, that there was a west coast audience waiting to be lured. His station rose to the sixth most listened-to in LA on the back of a steady diet of album tracks and long mixes of often obscure material. Mack soon diversified, promoting tours of acts from New York. This was not an expensive venture as most performers with a record contract were paid for by their label. In the style of the independent record entrepreneurs of the 1950s, Mack opened a retail store and augmented this with his own label, Mackdaddy Records. Macola was his distribution arm. It was an parsimonious setup: he could make the music, promote it on his radio station, sell it through his stores and charge for promoting it "live." It came to grief in 1991, when the station was bought by realtor Fred Sands for $7.2 million. Sands had no interest in rap and converted KDAY into a business news station. But, it had created a strong interest in rap: LA was alive with young rappers, whose plangent grudge against the police came to characterize a distinct west coast style of rap.

In 1986, a 16-year-old O'Shea Jackson, known as Ice Cube, wrote a number called "Boyz N the hood," which was like a crackling gunpowder trail leading to a final explosive encounter between residents of the ghetto and the LAPD. It was a bleak, menacing number, quite unlike early hiphop, intended to unsettle listeners. The rap was recorded under the collective title of NWA (Niggaz Wit' Attitude), which featured Cube and his colleagues, Dr Dre, Eazy-E, MC Yella and Arabian Prince. The recording was a DIY affair, the band mustering $1,000 for production costs and distributing through Macola on their own Ruthless Records label.

David Cross, in his *It's Not About a Salary*, writes of the conversion of a "cottage industry into a multi-million dollar business" through the hardnosed dealings of Eazy-E (Eric Wright), who refused to deal with major corporations because of the delay in releasing records. As Berry Gordy and several other record company owners before him realized, the time lag between production and release was critical to the survival of a label. Cashflow was paramount in Eazy's mind. Only when he was satisfied that this would not dry up, did he sign a distribution deal with Priority; in the first year alone of this contract, Ruthless Records sold eight million units. The most successful album of the period was NWA's *Straight Outta Compton*, which featured the notorious track "Fuck tha police." "NWA placed themselves on the hiphop map with authenticity, capturing the aggression and anger of the streets of south central in their intonation and timbre," writes Cross, being careful to remind his readers that, despite the moralizing, "NWA were primarily interested in selling records" (1993: 36). Two million copies of their album were sold.

NWA's infamy, rather than just fame, gave Ice Cube the exposure he needed to launch a solo career, so that, when he left in 1989, he was already an established writer/producer. He went on to start his own label and management company, Street Knowledge Productions. On his 1990 album, *AmeriKKKa's Most Wanted*, Cube deliberately set out to personify the black criminalized population. He pushed the rap genre by integrating various perspectives from law enforcement officers, judges and so on; he also meshed in archival material, news announcements, sirens, gunfire. The album starts with the character described in the title being led to the electric chair. Gangsta rap may not have had very auspicious beginnings, but it went on to assume virtual hegemony of the genre in the 1990s when the genre itself transferred to the mainstream.

If an event symbolized the transfer – and one can think of quite a few, including MTV's capitulation and the 1988 release of Dennis Hopper's LA gangland movie *Colors* – it is the NWA followup album, *Niggaz4Life* which, in 1991, entered the *Billboard* pop chart at number two unassisted by a trailer single or a video. On their previous album, NWA had thanked for their patronage "gangsters, dope dealers, killers, hustlers, thugs, hoodlums, winos, bums" and a variety of other bona fide members of the underclass. But these were hardly the people with enough disposable income to buy albums. As the Eazy-E's's Jewish manager, Jerry Heller observed, the band "captured middle-class white America" (quoted in Fernando, 1995: 99).

Boyz N the Hood was turned into a movie by African American director John Singleton, who secured $6 million from Tri-Star shortly after graduating from USC film school. Recall how Russell Simmons failed in his attempts to gain an interest in the project, which went on to become a commercial success. Ice Cube was handed a role in the movie not unlike the role he had played in everyday life: ghetto resident; his lines could have been self-scripted. Singleton powered on to bigger budget movies, like *Poetic Justice* and *Higher Learning*, without garnering the critical acclaim he did for *Boyz*. Cube went on to a bigger roles in movies like *Trespass* and consolidated his position as one of the most consistently successful rap artists.

The low-budget underground record productions that had been so prized in the 1980s became things of the past as big money began to roll into the ghettos. Cube's departure was precipitated by a dispute over earnings and, in 1992, another NWA member, Andre "Dr Dre" Young, insisted on being released in order to start his own Death Row record label with entrepreneur Marion "Suge" Knight. Ruthless president, Eazy-E (Eric Wright), later reported that he let the artist go only after Knight and two men "came calling with baseball bats and pipes," according to *Newsweek*'s Jeff Giles and Allison Samuels (1994: 62). He filed a $13.5 million racketeering suit against Dre and Sony Music, which had released Dre's commercially successful début single "Deep cover" (from the Bill Duke directed movie of the same name). In the midst of these complications, Interscope Records, an outfit run by Jimmy Iovine and Ted Field and backed by Warner Brothers, paid Ruthless an undisclosed sum for the rights to release Dre's album, *The Chronic*, which went on to sell over two million units in the US. Death Row Records' relationship with Interscope proved fruitful: in 1993, the rap label grossed more than $60 million. Within a few years, Interscope was to become involved in a high-profile conflict over the conduct of its artists. In gangsta rap, art did not so much follow life as blur the distinction between the two.

Nothing guarantees a product's success more than a ban. In gangsta rap's case, radio stations have done the job admirably. Churches, mainstream African American organizations, women's groups, two US Presidents and a battery of other right-minded people and groups condemned it during its ascendancy. They only assisted it. Ice-T's "Cop killer" was one of the first gangsta numbers to stir upright consciences. As its title suggests, it was about a young man intending to shoot a police officer. His relish is evident as he discharges his sawn-off shotgun. In common with other gangsta tracks, it mythologized its eponymous hero. In 1992, Warner Brothers Records recalled copies of the cd after death threats, protests from police associations and denunciations from the White House. Later, Ice-T left Warners after a disagreement over the artwork of his album *Home Invasion*. It was the beginning of an extremely vexed relationship between Time Warner and rap music and its repercussions were felt elsewhere. A & M Records removed "Bullet" from an album by Intelligent Hoodlum. MCA disavowed themselves of the band FU2.

We have seen in previous chapters how WB, the single most profitable record company in the world and biggest earning division in the Time Warner conglomerate, took an active interest in black culture and was instrumental in elevating the Artist ♀ to iconic status. The relationship with the Artist ♀ proved troublesome, though this seemed minor when set against the gangsta rap brouhaha. Already embarrassed by "Cop killer" and a couple of other rap artists,

Kool G. Rap and Paris (both of whom were made to change albums), Warners were given cause to reflect on the wisdom of an earlier deal started in 1990 when Time Warner helped found Interscope Records, a small but potential-loaded label, which, as we have seen, distributed Death Row Records' output. An initially small investment in return for a 25 percent stake was the extent of Warner's interest.

Doug Morris, the head of Warner's US music division, was undeterred by the "Cop killer" contretemps and pressed ahead. In April 1995, sensing the growing enthusiasm for gangsta rap among the young cd-buying public, he raised the stake in Interscope to 50 percent at a cost of $100 million, valuing the whole company at $400 million. Warners, of course, knew the label purveyed the incendiary type of rap; they also realized that gangsta rap was more than just a nihilistic commentary on the wasteland of the ghetto. Its practitioners were too close to detach themselves. The closeness became a problem in 1993, when one of Interscope's Death Row Records artists, Calvin Broadus, was cruising in West Los Angeles with his bodyguard and another homeboy.

Once in the Palms district, the posse came across a dope dealer named Philip Woldermariam, a member of the By Yerself Hustlers gang; Broadus was a member of the rival Long Beach Insane Crips. A dispute over gang turf broke out and Woldermariam fled, only to be shot dead. The three claimed to be acting in self-defense, but they were charged with murder. If getting charged for murder can be a career move, Broadus showed how. Shortly after the charge was made, he released an album under his stage name Snoop Doggy Dogg. The album *Doggystyle* sold 803,000 copies within a week of its release and became the first début work in pop history to go instantly to number one in the US charts. It went on to sell four million copies, generating $40 million, despite being banned by, among others, Radio KACE in Los Angeles and New York's WBLS. The artist toured Britain while on a $1 million bail bond.

The combination of a homicide charge and a current release also proved successful for another Warner Brothers artist, Tupac Shakur aka 2Pac, who was arrested in 1993 for shooting two off-duty police officers in Atlanta (he claimed they shot first). Shakur, whose mother was a member of the Black Panthers, found his notoriety worked wonders for record sales. He was released only to be arrested in New York a few weeks later, this time charged with participating in a sexual assault. He was sentenced to 18 months to four and a half years but was out on bail after eight months in time to see his *All Eyes on Me* album for Death Row Records rack up sales. Shakur's albums, *2pacalypse Now* and *4 My Niggas* earned a total of $12 million in sales. The band De Lench Mob's first album had netted $6 million at time of the arrest of its member Terry Gray (T-Bone) on suspicion of murder in 1994. Def Jam's English-born Ricky Walters was convicted of attempted murder two years after the 1988 release of his first album *The Further Adventures of Slick Rick* which sold 1.2 million copies. While out on three weeks' bail, he cut two albums.

Time Warner's chair and chief executive, Gerald Levin, was so shaken by an onslaught led by former Republican education secretary Bill Bennett and leading black liberal C. DeLores Tucker, that he apparently agreed to commission Quincy Jones to produce an inoffensive rap album whose profits would go toward inner city projects. But the criticism continued.

A Rico suit landed on Time Warner's desk; this stands for the Racketeer Influenced and Corrupt Organizations law, which was passed principally to counter the Mafia. While Interscope formed only a part of the media giant's music division and gangsta rap only a part of Interscope's output, it was claimed that Levin and Warner Music president Michael Fuchs conspired to separate Death Row records from Interscope, which distributed its product. The byzantine plan, according to Interscope, was designed to distance Warners' Interscope investment from rappers like Snoop Doggy Dogg; it purportedly involved an offer worth $80 million to Death Row to enable the label to set up its own distribution network and thereby sever any connection with Warners. Intriguingly, DeLores Tucker, chair of the National Political Congress of Black Women and owner of ten shares of Time Warner stock, was also included in Death Row's Rico suit, the suggestion being that she had promised to stop her campaign against Time Warner if it dissociated itself from Death Row.

Warners argued the suit had "no merit," but the criticisms were being hurled like mud at a wall and, presumably fearful that some might stick, Warners, in a concession, sold its share of the company for an undisclosed sum thought to be about $120 million. This was in September 1995 – only six months after it had upped its interest. Warner Music Group agreed to distribute Interscope records for six months, but refused to release an album by the band Tha Dogg Pound. Warners' publishing wing, Warner-Chappell, retained a share of the rights of Death Row songs and continued to profit from the same lyrics that had embarrassed the parent company. In the midst of the controversy, Warner-Chappell renewed Death Row's existing publishing deal and gave the company a $4 million advance. "Owning the publishing was about Time Warner making money, not about what we put in front of our children," declared Michael Fuchs (quoted in Hirschberg, 1996: 30).

There were significant personnel departures in the run-up to the sale: executives, Doug Morris and Danny Goldberg, both supporters of rap, resigned within months of each other. In retreating from rap, Warners also turned its back on an area of the market that was yielding approximately $700 million per year at that point. MTV's top-rated program was *Yo! MTV Raps*, which started in 1989 and built a demographic profile out of white, suburban males aged 16–24 (which advertisers loved, of course). Virtually any movie that used the black ghetto topos incorporated rap into its soundtrack. And, as if to endorse the mainstreaming of the music, white rap artists, like House of Pain and Vanilla Ice, were multiplying. Death Row signed a deal with Priority Records to distribute Tha Dogg Pound's *Dogg Food* which went straight to number one in the US.

Warners not only risked damaging its position as industry leader (it held 22.65 percent of the music market in 1995), but laid itself bare to accusations of being regressive. The Artist ♀, as we saw in Chapter ten, took to daubing SLAVE across his face to try to inconvenience Warners. Back in 1977, EMI (Thorn-EMI) was labelled reactionary after dropping the Sex Pistols, one of the most egregious bands in postwar popular culture.

The parallels with EMI and the Pistols are far from exact: the predominantly white punk movement from which the band emerged was so resistively anarchic and almost accidentally rebellious that no prejudice could remain unscathed. Rap openly displayed enough age-old reactionary sentiments to make the Grand Imperial Wizard seem like a liberal. The music began as innocent rhapsodies about boys and girls, but changed to angry and often malevolent diatribes often against women. Early evidence of this came in Ice-T's 1986 track "Six in the morning," in which a "bitch" gets beaten up. Ice Cube's "Gangsta fairytale" contains a story of Jack and Jill in which the former contracts a venereal disease from the latter. The misogyny stuck: women were depicted fellating men on, for example, Tha Dogg Pound's "Let's play house," on the *Dogg Food* album, or Snoop Doggy Dogg's "Ain't no fun," on *Doggystyle*, which had a sleeve showing a generously-bosomed African American female depicted with an exaggerated rear end complete with tail trailing out of a kennel. As we have seen in previous chapters, the image of the oversexed, undercivilized black woman had been a serviceable one; even more serviceable, perhaps, when projected by black men.

Rap, to be sure, was not an art form that left its dominant ideas at the studio cloakroom: often, it took them to the streets. In her *Black Noise*, Tricia Rose gives an account of how she was part of Sisters Speak, a group of black women writers and rappers formed to discuss Dr Dre's public beating of Dee Barnes, a female rapper and tv show host. On Rose's account, Dre was so angered by the discussion, he found the host in an LA nightclub, punched her to the floor and kicked her in the ribs, while his bodyguards kept onlookers at bay:

> He held Dee "responsible" for a Fox television producer's decision to edit the materials in a way that mocked NWA, because it was clear that, although beating up a young black woman might give him a bad reputation, beating up a white man in the entertainment business might spell disaster for his career.
>
> (Rose, 1994: 179)

The "considered" response to rap's abuse of women was to explain how black males were engaged in a search for the causes of their obvious disempowerment. State authority figures, as epitomized by the police, were targeted, as were black women. Houston Baker, in his *Black Studies, Rap and the Academy*, suggests that the defense for the crudely sexist 2 Live Crew might rest on the "But, officer, the cars in front of me were speeding too!" plea (1993: 72). Cornel West writes effusively about the rappers' role in "the repoliticizing of the black working poor and underclass" in his book *Keeping Faith*, yet parenthesizes "(despite their virulent sexism)" (1993: 289).

In the mid-1990s, many female rap artists recoiled against this. In her 1994 single "Unity," Queen Latifah asked: "Who you callin' a bitch?" Roxanne Shanté proclaimed "Brothers ain't shit." Others used names in parody of their male counterparts: Hoes with Attitude was one example. Bytches with Problems was another, though their track "Two minute brother," in deriding a less than spectacular lover, affirmed rap's homeboy patriarchal values, those that celebrated the kind of man who could provide for his woman (or, more usually, women) both materially and sexually, and ridiculed others as "fruity" or "punks." As Rose observes: "This sort of homophobia affirms oppressive standards of heterosexual masculinity" (1994: 151).

One can appreciate that rap was a genre to try a critic's conscience. Did he or she treat it as so offensive and deprecating of women and minority groups that it deserved only silent contempt? Or analyze it as a genuinely subversive and authentic reflection of black underclass life – albeit one that endorsed the rights to free speech, bear arms and make money through capitalist gain? The latter held sway, but only after several million sales and an upsurge of condemnations from groups on all points of the political spectrum. For all the apologia, rap was sexist, homophobic, antisemitic and about as politically incorrect as it is possible to be. It was also a resolutely black culture: the successes of occasional white artists who forayed into rap were isolated and shortlived. Yet, by the mid-1990s, it was positioned slap in the middle of the market. As Bernard-Donals wrote in 1994: "Rap – though marketed as something belonging to the 'other' – has become mainstream" (1994: 132).

We have already touched on Bernard-Donals' analysis: rap exposed to white consumers what we might call a subaltern consciousness: an expression of the way underprivileged blacks looked at the world. The vision was intended to unsettle and, in this, it achieved its aim, at least with the major corporations which stood to profit most from rap. But whose blood was curdled by the stories of ghetto shootings, hard drugs and women who were treated like dogs? If these were true characterizations of black life, they suited whites' images almost perfectly: they confirmed the quality of "otherness" we have registered in previous chapters. Rap music may have reified this otherness; yet, in doing so, it stabilized an aged duality between "us" and "them," self and other. Rap may sound like liberal whites' worst nightmare: stories of violent, misogynist black men willing to resist the forces of law and order even if it means their own physical annihilation. But, it was also a dream. And the commercial success tells us more about the larger reality in which rap was *received* than about the people who produced it.

Think of the representation of black males in rap: aggressive and minatory; exactly the qualities imputed to brute niggers in colonial days. Now, blacks were bent on revenge. Ice-T actually described his "Cop killer" as a "revenge fantasy" (in Fernando, 1995: 142). They also regarded black women in a way that complemented early white stereotypes. Women were erotic, licentious creatures good primarily for sexual gratification. The prejudices, phobias and seeming unawareness of a common humanity all served to confirm the conception of an other which was different – irredeemably so.

Despite Russell Simmons' insistence that he was exploiting a hitherto neglected aspect of the market in black consumers, the real market base of rap was white. You do not sell four million copies of a cd, as Snoop Doggy Dogg did, without appealing to a wider market than African American youth. Samuels argues that, even from the mid-1980s: "White demand indeed began to determine the direction of the genre, but what it wanted was music more defiantly black." He believes: "The result was Public Enemy, produced and marketed by Rubin" (1991: 26).

Whites might have, as Samuels and Bernard-Donals both suggest, consumed rap with a near-voyeuristic pleasure, perhaps coming to terms with their own sense of guilt. But gangsta rap's eventual extension into the mainstream, and its refinement as a legitimate genre, added something else to the attraction. This was, to use Jan Pieterse's redolent phrase, "cannibalism by connoisseurs." Rap petrified images that corresponded with those once conveyed by colonial observers of nonwestern peoples. The cut-outs that had once been functional in justifying oppression and captivity were dusted off and brought back into service, this time by blacks themselves. As Errol Henderson points out, in his article "Black nationalism and rap music": " Much of the nihilistic imaging, in reality, is promoted, if not created, by White industry executives as well as by miseducated Blacks masquerading as chroniclers of the 'Black experience'" (1996: 332).

Is there satisfaction to be derived from feeling guilty? One of the contentions of this book is that the acceptance and integration of black culture is a reflection of two things. One, the persistence of racism. Two, attempts to resolve its coexistence with the equality of opportunity that marks the post-civil-rights period. Aspects of culture, such as those created by Lee and rap music, have political messages that remind whites how they are the inheritors of a ghastly, oppressive tradition. Analyzing Public Enemy, but with a resonance that makes his observation applicable to the whole rap genre, Samuels writes of "a highly charged theater of race in which white listeners became guilty eaves-droppers on the putative private conversation of the inner city" (1991: 26).

In Barbet Schroeder's 1995 remake of *Kiss of Death*, the scowling villain Little Junior, played by Nicholas Cage, preparing to beat an enemy to death, dons protective clothing to keep the blood off his white tracksuit. The scene offers a way of understanding the secret power of guiltsploitation – the exploitation of white guilt for profit. Imagine that, every so often, whites clothe themselves in waterproof coveralls and venture into the ghettos, whereupon they confront blacks, still angry at whites' historical sins. The blacks then symbolically exact their revenge by urinating over the well-protected whites. Cowering under the cataracts, whites observe studiously, admiring the arc, the jet, even the smell of the urine. Once returned safely to their own neighborhoods, they shed their wax clothes, shower and discuss the experience. "You know, the next time we go down there, we'll have to find this guy Ice Cube; I hear his piss is especially forceful." So goes a fable of the nineties.

Rap transformed racism into fashion: something that blacks wore to impress and whites liked to glare at without actually doing anything; both virtually countenanced it, at the same time keeping their distance from one another. What started as a radically different and, in many ways, dangerous music was appropriated, domesticated and ultimately rendered harmless.

Chapter twelve

America's
Paradox

IS THERE SUCH A THING AS GENUINE BLACK CULTURE?
The black culture industry has an interest in promoting the idea that there is.
Its products are created by blacks in concert with whites and consumed, in the
main, by whites. The industry that started with the rough recording of blues
players now recycles itself into cassettes, laserdiscs and cd-roms; it begets baseball caps and other apparel, it becomes a movie, a novelization and, perhaps soon,
a theme park ride – Disneyworld's "Hood" where visitors can sample life as it is
in LA's South Central.

Meanwhile, many Afrocentrists posit Africa as the site of the origins of a
distinct and unique culture that has mutated, but continues to animate the street
life of first world metropolises: an expression of a distinct and still-vital spirit, a
set of values that embodies an essential Africanness. "Black culture is the product
of an ongoing struggle between the extremes of defiance and assimilation, of
resistance and complacency," writes Ada Gay Griffin in *Black Popular Culture*,
adding that: "Those aspects of our culture and history that come most often to
our attention, usually because they have been popularized by or expropriated
by the dominant society, tend to line up along the side of assimilation and, as a
consequence, are available as vehicles for our oppression" (1992: 231).

On this view, much of what passes for black culture today would be
dismissed as assimilated and potentially oppressive. Real black culture, presumably, lies somewhere in an alternative space: "Black films, Black videos, and Black
media are those productions directed by Black artists on subjects and forms that
reference the Black experience and imagination." This somewhat preachy
approach suffers when we realize that, in the 1990s, the black culture industry has
actually been run by by black artists and producers, who have had more control
over their product than ever. Are they the genuine article, or have they been
coopted and assimilated by the "dominant society"?

The kind of argument advanced by Griffin is a perfect complement to those who profit from the black culture. Idealizing it sells it. Exactly who does profit? It is easy to be a cynic and answer: whites. In fact, since 1990, an even greater number of African Americans have maneuvered their way into the kind of positions historically reserved for whites. Berry Gordy was an exception in his day; but in the early 1990s dozens of black entrepreneurs listed themselves as company directors and sat on boards where they could wield power over their products.

By the mid-1990s, the music industry was carved up between six big corporations. Biggest was Warner, which claimed 22.65 percent of an industry worth about $11–12 billion per year; it formed part of Time Warner, the world's largest media company after the mega-merger with Turner Broadcasting in 1996. Its nearest rivals were PolyGram and Sony, which held 14.37 and 13.19 shares respectively. The other three were BMG (owned by Bertelsmann) with 12.12 percent, MCA (owned by Seagram, the Canadian liquor company) with 10.42 percent, and EMI (de-merged from Thorn-EMI, of Britain, in 1996) with 8.64 percent. The remainder was splintered among independents. In a typical year, Warners would expect to generate earnings before interest, tax, depreciation and amortization of around $800 million on $4.1 billion worth of sales through its various labels, including Atlantic, Elektra and Warner Bros. Thanks to its Island Records, A & M and Motown, PolyGram – 75 percent owned by Philips of Holland – was able to close the gap.

Bestselling artists were the corporations' principal assets. For example, up to 1996 Madonna sold some 180 million cassettes, cds and music videos, generating $1.5 billion for Warner Bros, which secured her services for $60 million. More than 30 million copies of Janet Jackson's three albums had been bought up to 1996, enabling Virgin Records, owned by EMI, to pay out $80 million for her next four albums, while brother Michael had to limp by with his $60 million from Sony. Yet, in the 1990s, the shape of the market altered in such a way as to make it impossible for corporations simply to bank on their safe stars. They needed to diffuse; and the manner in which they did this created a new tier of the black culture industry.

David Samuels recounts how, in the summer of 1991, Soundscan, a computerized system for tracking music sales, changed *Billboard* magazine's method of counting record sales in the USA. Soundscan accumulated its data from the barcodes scanned at chain store cash registers in malls across the country. Previously, the magazine had relied on a more haphazard and less accurate method, logging the sales of big city stores and from the subjective accounts of radio programmers. The change to a much more complete and accurate collection system yielded enlightening results. "So it was that America awoke on June 22, 1991, to find that its favorite record was not *Out of Time*, by aging college-boy rockers REM, but *Niggaz4life*, a musical celebration of gang rape and other violence by NWA." observes Samuels (1991: 24). (This did not stop Warner Brothers paying REM $80 million in a five-album deal in 1996.)

It was bracing news and one of its effects was to alert the major corporations to the need to stay closer than they had to rapidly changing tastes. Most of the big six had already set up divisions or semi-independent units specializing in music by black artists. In Chapter six, we noted how CBS had seized an early initiative in the 1970s, when it commissioned research, which revealed the potential of having a roster of black artists; acting on this, CBS set up its black music division under LeBaron Taylor and signed up the Philadelphia International pair, Leon Huff and Kenny Gamble. In this way, CBS kept an edge in a market that was to become increasingly influenced by black music.

The other option available to the corporations was predatory: to wait until a smaller independent outfit threatened to become a force, then buy it. As we saw earlier, every label of note specializing in black music, whether owned by blacks or whites, has eventually been bought by white-controlled organizations. This was workable, if expensive. The black music division was a leaner and more controlled way of keeping abreast of changing trends, though, as the Soundscan system revealed, far from guaranteed. A suspicion grew that, with the rise of rap and associated forms of street music – garage, house, jungle, newjack and so on – the sands were shifting. The corporations needed to find a way of staying in touch without sacrificing control of their product.

In 1992, MCA closed what proved to be a landmark deal with Andre Harrell, former colleague of Russell Simmons and, later, head of his own Uptown Records. MCA had, in the 1980s, risen to the position of market leader in black music, squeezing Motown from the top spot and acquiring a reputation, principally through its head, Jheryl Busby (who was later to become president of Motown after its takeover by MCA and others in 1988 and its subsequent sale to PolyGram in 1993). After creating a black music division at A & M Records in the early 1980s, Busby moved to MCA where he was given authority to set up a black music division that would sign its own artists and handle its own promotion, marketing and advertising. Under Busby, MCA signed, developed and worked with New Edition, Bobby Brown and Gladys Knight, among others. Virtually every album by these artists sold more than a million copies.

MCA had done well out of the popularity of black music. *Black Enterprise* writers Rhonda Reynolds and Ann Brown estimated that, collectively, the black genres (including rap, r'n'b, gospel and reggae) accounted for 24 percent of all music sales (1994). Even if we deduct the 3.3 percent contribution of jazz, which has never been an exclusively black musical form, this still leaves a significant 20.7 percent. In its efforts to stay ahead of the field, MCA focused on Uptown Records, a small independent label that boasted then up-and-coming artists, like Mary J. Blige and Heavy D and the Boyz. The seven-year deal was worth a shocking $50 million to Harrell. Shocking that is by 1992 standards, when the idea of sinking money into a relatively untested independent led by a young man – Harrell was 31 at the time – seemed iffy. MCA did not complain. Indeed, the deal became something of a model. (As we saw in Chapter seven, Harrell later moved from Uptown to head of Motown.)

Two years later, one of Harrell's producers at Uptown, Sean "Puffy" Combs, repeated the trick. He struck a deal with Arista and BMG worth $10 million over three years that committed him to deliver three albums a year from his Bad Boy Entertainment. Combs, then 24 years old, had recently left Harrell's company. In the first year of the deal, Bad Boy launched two million-selling acts, Craig Mack and Notorious BIG. Arista extended a similar deal to LaFace Records, headed by

Antonio "LA" Reid and Kenneth "Babyface" Edmonds, which was estimated to be worth $10 million and provided for the setting up of a studio in Atlanta, Georgia. Acts such as Toni Braxton ($200 million and then some in record sales) and TLC – whose album *CrazySexyCool* sold seven million copies, making them a bigger-selling female act than even the Supremes – amply justified the outlay (TLC had sold a total of 17.5 million albums and singles by the end of 1996). But, this was an exceptional deal in that LaFace received a roughly equitable division of profits projected at $100 million over five years and half-ownership of the masters.

All this signalled a willingness on behalf of the big corporations to invest money in smaller labels in the expectation of medium-term rewards. The corporations risked money; the labels risked autonomy. After Harrell's move to Motown, MCA retained the master tapes, the roster of artists and, perhaps most importantly, the Uptown name. Harrell, reflecting on his period as the Uptown boss, announced to *Newsweek*'s Johnnie Roberts: "I had fake control" (1995: 48).

Yet neither side to the arrangement complained too hard. "We create the pie and get to keep the crust," said Harrell (1995: 50). People like Harrell, Combs and Reid were hailed as the new moguls of black music, the "Big Willys." Certainly, they prospered; though perhaps not as greatly as the figures suggest.

Typically, a 1990s-style deal with an independent label would implicate the major corporation in a time-specific arrangement: the bigger company would demand product at a certain rate from the smaller company, which it would undertake to distribute and, under some agreements, to market. In return, it paid out a lump sum or an annual allowance. Let us say, a working allowance of a million dollars was provided to the label. An additional recording fund of, say, $300,000 was allowed for each artist on the roster. Promotion and marketing would add more cost. For example a video could cost up to a million dollars and marketing it a further $100,000 at late-1990s prices.

None of this money was given out of the goodness of the corporation's heart: it was strictly investment and every nickel was expected to be paid back out of sales. By the estimates of Reynolds and Brown: "On a basic low-end deal, the black label wants to make 16% to 20% of the retail music sales. The label signs an artist and forks over 10% to 14%, then keeps the remaining 4% to 6% as profit" (1994: 89). The label, or "sub-label," existed on the slim profit margin. When all this is considered, the deals do not look so fabulous: of the $15–17 a consumer paid for a cd, the artist got a little more than $1.50 and the label got about 50 cents, but only after all the front money received from the major corporation had been paid off. The pressure to keep up sales was immense.

The benefits to the label are obvious: exposure to a wider market, better distribution and promotion, and the possibility of big money should sales stay up. The Warner-Interscope fiasco illustrated the costs. Independent labels in the 1990s were hard pressed to manufacture, distribute, market, sell and collect on a record beyond the level of a 100,000 units or so. So, the prospect of a bigger organization handling the noncreative aspects of this was clearly attractive.

More generally, the trend encouraged entrepreneurship among African Americans and created at least some millionaires and many more others who could boast the title "President and CEO." It also offered a low-risk strategy for would-be music moguls: the capital put up by the corporations was effectively an interest-free loan. And, should sales live up to expectations, the label would be in a strong position to renegotiate an extension of the arrangement under improved terms.

"But not everyone can achieve a high level of success," according to Tariq K. Muhammad, who writes for *Black Enterprise*. "Thus, for every successful sub-label that has generated enough sales to renegotiate their deal into a more favorable joint venture arrangement, there are probably 10 or more sub-labels in 'plantation-like' situations" (1995: 76). The same writer also speculates on the wider implications of making more money available in this way to black entrepreneurs: "It has exacerbated an existing problem – the lack of cooperation and unity among African Americans in the industry." Like crabs in a barrel trying to escape, black entrepreneurs were prepared to crawl over each other as the major corporations dangled money before them. Muhammad refers to "a new system of exploitation" in which a few spectacularly successful music entrepreneurs obscured the real struggle that lay beneath them.

The black culture industry operates just as any other industry in advanced capitalist societies. In the 1990s the major music corporations' acquisition strategy is but one part of a wider process of aggressive globalization that takes place between a variety of entertainment and electronics conglomerates. As Stephen Lee writes in his informative article "Re-examining the concept of the 'independent' record label": "The consolidation of film, television, recording, publishing, electronics, computers, advertising and talent brokering has resulted in a group of powerful oligopolies that broker cultural materials in much the same way any other commodity would be sold" (1995: 16).

Lee's case study of the independent Wax Trax label shows how small labels in the early 1990s were increasingly unable to maintain independence in the face of market pressures. Their fate is often to operate independently for a short period before collapsing, or to sell to a bigger company. Sometimes, the limit of the owner's aspirations is to sell out at a profit and become a titular CEO but an effective employee of a major corporation. So it is with the new heads of the black culture industry: media moguls by name, millionaires by bank balance, but paid staff nevertheless. And, for every Andre Harrell or Puffy Combs, there are countless other failed or failing record label owners who will never come close to touching the hem of greatness.

_____

In his essay on the African American film-maker Oscar Micheaux, J. Ronald Green writes: "Black musicians, preachers and writers showed there were different ways to make improvisational music, oral jeremiad, and narratives that could both be understood by their own cultures and later be celebrated by Eurocentric cultures" (1993: 35). He adds that: "The contribution of these forms to art and to pleasure has been the greater for their ethnic authenticity." There seems to be a contradiction here. In the process of reaching the stage at which they were appreciated by "Eurocentric cultures" – by which I take Green to mean whites – the music at least has lost whatever "ethnic authenticity" it once had.

One of the arguments of *The Black Culture Industry* is that what we popularly accept to be black culture is, on closer inspection, a product of blacks' and whites' collaborative efforts. As we saw in examining the transfer of blues from a country music played by blacks and whites to a recorded art form reflecting the black experience, the unseen influences of whites were decisive. No less so in many of the other cultures that have been turned into commodities, principally for the white market. Black culture is not devalued because it is a hybrid. But we should not neglect the conditions under which the hybridity is allowed to occur. Historically, those conditions have been more conducive to the prosperity of white entrepreneurs than that of black artists; though black capitalists have emerged since the 1960s.

There is great commercial value in promoting a product as if it were "authentic," but it is difficult to demarcate between authentic and inauthentic. Deborah Root argues: "Authenticity is a tricky concept because of the way the term can be manipulated and used to convince people they are getting something profound when they are just getting merchandise" (1996: 78). So effective has it been as a selling point that Root, in her revelational *Cannibal Culture*, refers to a "commodification of authenticity." In this case, the purported authenticity attributed to so much of what is received as black culture might be regarded as a definition imposed by those who profit most from it. The ethnic authenticity about which Green enthuses may not exist outside of the industry that promotes and exploits it.

On the account presented here, its primary role has been in assuaging white guilt. The paradox or "dilemma" is addressed, if not solved. There is an almost addictive remuneration from integrating black culture into the mainstream. Not only to whites: in a context in which many of the rewards are not readily available to blacks, there is atonement of sorts in seeing one's culture represented in mainstream media. Shohat and Stam, in discussing identifications with films, use the term "compensatory outlet" and suggest there is a process like transferring "allegiance to another sports team after one's own has been eliminated from the competition" (1994: 351). If you do not believe your group is getting enough breaks, it is at least some recompense to see representations of that group in the popular media.

Of course, not *all* black people use this interpretation, nor do *all* whites sit back in satisfaction at the dilemma's bogus resolution. At least not in a conscious, deliberate sense. Yet there is another sense: as carriers and creators of culture, we learn through association: for all our commitment to independence of thought and speech, we are not free-standing indviduals, but creatures of our particular environments. Our thoughts and commitments are products, just as we are products of the social contexts in which we are raised and in which we operate. A discourse of rules, codes, conventions, practices, routines and customs makes it possible for us to be who we are. In other words, we are able to realize ourselves only in our commerce with others.

Whether they like it or not, whites are parties in a certain kind of discourse that has rendered black people subalterns, lowly ranked groups without any meaningful voice. African Americans have been virtually silenced, their political views and artistic endeavors made irrelevant or smirked at. Even now, we might argue that concessions need to be made before African Americans are allowed to make their imprint. In a memorably vulgar epigram from a May 1995 interview with Kevin Powell, bell hooks reminded *Vibe* magazine readers of the continuing presence of the racial hierachy: "Black people get to the top and stay on top only by sucking the dicks of white culture."

Black artists' admission into the cultural mainstream is conditional. Historically, artists have either conformed to whites' preconceptions of what blacks were or should be like, or they have been denied commercial success. In some cases, properties have been imputed to black performers that at least made them seem to fit whites' expectations. The case of Michael Jackson shows that these are not either/or alternatives. White culture has enforced a definition of its normality by admitting only black interlopers who lived up or down to its images: others, who possessed exotic or peculiar gifts but at a cost to their full humanity. The symbolic eunuch has been welcomed by white culture, as has the exotic temptress. Despite their testosterone-pumped posturing and scornful dismissal of all things feminine, the gangsta rap artists of the 1990s were emasculated players in a white psychodrama. Like other members of the black entertainment elite, their role was a tightly defined one: amuse, play music, kill each other, if you will; make like you hate whites and enjoy scaring them. "The successful black people zoo" is hooks' term for this state of representational captivity.

It has been possible to succeed without resort to type. Many a black actor or singer, male and female, has managed to resist the pressures to conform, though, as we have seen, the likes of Dorothy Dandridge and Lena Horne were eventually squeezed into marginal roles. It is also interesting that Dandridge's co-star in *Porgy and Bess*, Sidney Poitier, avoided stereotypes in search of more nuanced roles and was, in the late 1960s, rebuked by many blacks for assimilating. We have also seen how Diana Ross' transition to stardom was meticulously calibrated with the mood of the time. In the late 1990s, any number of black overachievers in the entertainment business shun two-dimensional images in favor of more complex parts. Yet, there are always counterweights. For every Denzel Washington, Whitney Houston or Luther Vandross, there is an Eddie Murphy, Whoopie Goldberg or Snoop Doggy Dogg. This kind of ambivalence is actually functional: it is a reminder that a minority of "nice ones" can always make it.

In his preface to Fanon's *Wretched of the Earth*, Jean-Paul Sartre wrote that "the European has only been able to become a man through creating slaves and monsters" (1968: 26). Black people have served as a kind of mirror to whites, but not one that gives a true image: more like a warped, polished surface that provides a distorted representation. Much of whites' self-image has been constructed as a response to what they believe blacks are not. If whites understand themselves to be superior, intellectually and culturally, then images of blacks have signified ignorance and barbarity. It has been vital to maintain those reflections, no matter how hideously inaccurate. One way has been to create a context in which blacks have had little choice but to act up to whites' expectations. We have seen evidence of this in virtually every chapter of this book. Black people, especially those conspicuously engaged in entertainment, have been reminders to whites of what they are *not*. As we noted in the first chapter, the very category of whiteness was invented in counterposition to blackness. In simple terms, without black people, there were no whites; no "others," no "us."

I opened this book with a remark about difference and about how whites have moved from fearing the cultural and physical differences they recognized in African Americans. What people define as difference and how they interpret that difference changes from context to context, from one historical epoch to another, depending on the specific calculus of power and knowledge that holds sway. Today, we live in a market: the scope of commodification is now so wide that everything, including difference, can be reshaped into a package that can be bought and sold. As Root observes: "The apparent seamlessness between culture and the marketplace means that anything can come under the purview of capital" (1996: 86). Industries have developed around youth, sports, even emotions – as the near-universal popularity of Prozac suggests. This has been facilitated by the emergence of what Michael Read calls *Super Media*, "the apex of development of media and culture" (1989: 19).

No sooner is a film released than we are invited to buy the soundtrack, visit the web site, take the downloads, enter the competitions, read the books, study production notes, wear the apparel; when we see the movie, we are tempted by popcorn, soda pop and trailers of upcoming films. We return home to watch television, where a complementary process begins and we become captivated by a new set of invitations, all of which involve parting with money. Our days are spent, our lives are lived buying products; and the advent of digitalization means that we have no need to leave our homes.

When we do, we clothe and accessorize ourselves in products bearing the names and logos of the companies that exploit our weakness for commodities: T-shirts plastered with DKNY, Armani motif'd eyeglasses, personal stereos with Sony's insignia, knockoff Rolexes that look "authentic." These are not just products: they are commodified values. And we do not just buy them: we collude with the manufacturers to become ambulant advertisements. It is as if we are proud to exhibit our own exploitation. "I paid $300 for a shoulder bag worth a tenth of that and it has the Vuitton design to prove it." Of course, the bag is not worth only a tenth of its price because it is not just merchandise: it is a desirable commodity. The value of something depends on whether that something can be turned into a commodity. That includes cultural products.

It is not only romantic, but foolish to believe that African American culture exists outside this process. Nor should we imagine that this is a new phenomenon: as we saw in Chapter three, the appropriation of cultures associated with blacks began in the early years of the nineteenth century, as soon as whites realized the commercial possibilities in them. Now, the heirs to the industry crudely inaugurated by the promoters of minstrel shows own record label or chairs in corporation boardrooms. Like W. C. Handy, who operated in the early 1900s, some are African Americans themselves. But, there are equally permanent features of the black culture industry: it is still owned by whites, has a predominantly white market and, if the argument advanced here is accepted, has functions that are rarely, if ever, discussed. I will close with a résumé of its principal one.

I have often thought that *An American Dilemma* was a misnomer. After all, a dilemma suggests a choice between two equally unacceptable alternatives and what Gunnar Myrdal was really trying to convey was that no choice was necessary. The practical reality of contemporary America, with its obdurate racial hierarchy, is at odds with its official commitment to democratic egalitarianism in which basic rights are inviolable. There is never any doubt about America's option. What Myrdal was actually describing was "An American Paradox": a contradiction between rhetorical freedom and actual oppression.

More than fifty years after Myrdal disclosed the paradox in 1944 and assembled copious data to support his finding, America still struggles unavailingly with its most intractable and embarrassing problem. The unemployment rate for black males is more than twice that of their white counterparts. Even black men with jobs and higher education do not, for the most part, receive the same pay as white men. Among recent college graduates with one to five years on the job, black men earned less than 88 percent of the amount earned by white men. The leading cause of death among black males between the ages of 15 and 24 was homicide. In the 1990s, book after book has documented the persistence of stubborn racial inequalities. Michael Dawson's *Behind the Mule*, Paula McClain and Joseph Stewart's *"Can We All Get Along?"* and Joe Feagin and Hernán Vera's *White Racism*, to name three titles, all tell a similar story of continuing discrepancies in employment, political representation and housing.

No nation has been as tortured by racism as the United States. In the late 1950s, its civil rights movement brought both agony and redemption as previously undisturbed institutions were challenged, then broken. The attempt to bring together ideal and reality took the form of legislation guaranteeing the rights stipulated in the US constitution – that hallowed document designed in the spirit of revolutionary France and Tom Paine's vision of a federalist-republican England.

Whatever flights of fancy whites may have about the advances made over the past three decades, they are brought to earth with a bump when the views of black Americans are solicited. As Eddy Harris writes, in his *South of Haunted Dreams*: "To be black is always to be reminded that you are a stranger in your native land. To be black is to be surrounded by those who would remind you" (1993: 102).

The integration of what passes as African American culture may be a type of resolution; one that affords whites the benefits of identifying with blacks and welcoming them without actually doing much about the fundamental inequalities that remain. Cornel West uses the term "redemptive culturalism," to describe the view that culture can yield political redemption for black people (1993: 66). There is appeal in the idea that cultural change can be an agent of more wide-reaching social changes. But, we should at least allow the possibility that black culture is, to borrow from chemistry's lexicon, amphoteric – capable of acting both ways. The spread and acceptance of African American inspired music, particularly over the past thirty years, may have come not as an agent, but *instead* of social change.

If there is black culture, it is more likely to be discovered in the kinds of attitudes, customs, values and language uncovered by John Langston Gwaltney in his study *Drylongso: A self-portrait of black America*. The "core black culture" documented by anthropologist Gwaltney bears no resemblance to the genres that have been industrialized and reach us via the channels of the corporation-owned media. Black culture in his conception is nourished by the minor everyday thoughts and practices of people, their mishaps and achievements; the disarray and organization that characterizes any living culture. Cultures cannot be force-grown, but spring seemingly unaided from tiny seeds of experience.

Culture is a dangerous and, in some ways, daunting subject. Offending someone's mother is often dealt with less severely than offending that person's culture. Yet, we often seem to forgive the commodified versions. I recall sitting in a cinema in Kingston, Jamaica, watching the movie *Marked for Death* in which Jamaicans were depicted as belief-beggaring stereotypes. The crowd roared approvingly with laughter, while I cringed. As an Englishman, I should be insulted by fluffy notions of my countryfolk as silly-asses with "Golly gosh" and "Oh, rather!" accents. Still, I can endure the likes of *Four Weddings and a Funeral* without getting upset and reminding all around me that this is the same culture that brought the world Sade and Seal. It is as if we accept the distortions as long as they are perpetrated in celluloid, particularly in the pursuit of mammon.

The iconography of black culture is full of Gangstas, Shafts, and Black Venuses. As black people make headway socially, as they have since days of civil rights, the culture attributed to them has attracted interest from all quarters. Elements have been picked up and changed into products, which have in turn stimulated greater interest. The dynamic that keeps the cycle going is likely to continue. As a consequence, black culture, or at least a commodified version of it, will be sought after, acquired and appreciated by a widening audience. But, there are other consequences, as I have shown in this book. One of them is an alleviation of the white guilt that Malcolm X once recognized as the bitterly relentless force that drives racism.

While we may enjoy black culture in all its saleable forms, we should remind ourselves of the misanthropic opportunism that brought it to our ears and eyes. In black culture, we can find a history of American perfidy, American violence, American oppression and American racism, all captured for our delectation in a way that provokes reflection without spurring us to action. For all the resistance promised by those who valorize "cultural redemption," black culture provides more comfort than challenge and, for this reason, must be approached with the same kind of skepticism that once greeted the minstrels, themselves empowered by the money they earned yet constrained by the very environment in which they prospered. The same might be said of all those associated with the black culture industry.

Bibliography

Adorno, T. (1991) *The Culture Industry*, London: Routledge.

Allen, T. (1994) *The Invention of the White Race*, vol. 1, New York: Verso.

Andersen, C. (1994) *Michael Jackson: Unauthorized*, New York: Simon & Schuster.

Baker, H. (1987) *Modernism and the Harlem Renaissance*, Chicago: University of Chicago Press.

Baker, H. (1987) *Blues, Ideology, and Afro-American Literature*, Chicago: University of Chicago Press.

Baker, H. (1993) *Black Studies, Rap and the Academy*, Chicago: University of Chicago Press.

Barlow, W. (1989) *"Looking up at Down": The emergence of blues culture*, Philadelphia: Temple University Press.

Bennett, L. (1993) *The Shaping of Black America*, New York: Penguin.

Berman, P., ed. (1994) *Blacks and Jews: Alliances and arguments*, New York: Delacorte Press.

Berman, P. (1994) "The other and the almost the same", *Society*, September/October, pp. 4–16.

Bernal. M. (1987) *Black Athena: The Afroasiatic roots of classical civilization*, vol. 1, New Brunswick, NJ: Rutgers University Press.

Bernard-Donals, M. (1994) "Jazz, rock'n'roll, rap and politics", *Journal of Popular Culture*, vol. 28, no. 2 (Fall), pp. 127–38.

Berry, C. (1987) *The Autobiography*, London: Faber & Faber.

Berry, J. (1986) *Up from the Cradle of Jazz*, Athens: University of Georgia Press.

Bogle, D. (1980) *Brown Sugar: Eighty years of America's black female superstars*, New York: Harmony.

Bogle, D. (1988) *Blacks in American Film and Television: An encyclopedia*, New York: Garland.

Booth, S. (1991) *Rythm Oil* [sic], London: Jonathan Cape; New York: Pantheon.

Boskin, J. (1986) *Sambo: The rise and demise of an American jester*, New York: Oxford University Press.

Bradford. P. V. and Blume, H. (1992) *Ota Benga: The pygmy in the zoo*, New York: St Martin's Press.

Carmichael, S. and Hamilton, C. (1967) *Black Power: The politics of liberation in America*, New York: Vintage.

Cashmore, E. (1992) "The new black bourgeoisie", *Human Relations*, vol. 45, no. 12, pp. 1241–58.

Chapelle, T. (1991) "The movement of Spike Lee" *The Black Collegian*, vol. 21, no. 4 (March/April), pp. 56–62.

Cone, J. (1991) *The Spirituals and the Blues*, Maryknoll NY: Orbis.

Cross, D. (1993) *It's Not About a Salary: Rap, race and resistance in Los Angeles*, New York: Verso.

Dawson, M. (1994) *Behind the Mule: Race and class in African-American politics*, Princeton, NJ: Princeton University Press.

Du Bois, W. E. B. (1989) *The Souls of Black Folk*, New York: Bantam.

Dubner, S. (1992) "From rap to riches", *New York*, vol. 25, no. 50, pp. 69, 71.

Fanon, F. (1968) *The Wretched of the Earth*, New York: Grove.

Fanon, F. (1986) *Black Skin, White Masks*, London: Pluto.

Feagin, J. and Vera, H. (1995) *White Racism*, New York: Routledge.

Fernando, S. H. (1995) *The New Beats*, Edinburgh: Payback Press.

Frazier, E. (1957) *Black Bourgeoisie: The rise of the new middle class*, New York: Free Press.

Frederickson, F. (1987) *The Black Image in the White Mind: The debate on Afro-American character and destiny, 1817–1914*, 2nd edn, Hanover, NH: Wesleyan University Press.

Friedlander, P. (1996) *Rock and Roll: A social history*, Boulder, CO: Westview Press.

Gabler, N. (1988) *An Empire of Their Own: How the Jews invented Hollywood*, New York: Anchor Doubleday.

Gates, H. L. (1988) *The Signifying Monkey: A theory of African-American literary criticism*, New York: Oxford University Press.

George, N. (1988) *The Death of Rhythm & Blues*, New York: Pantheon.

Giles, J. and Samuels, A. (1994) "Straight out of Compton", *Newsweek*, vol. 124 (October 31).

Gilroy, P. (1993) *The Black Atlantic*, London: Verso.

Glasgow, D. (1980) *The Black Underclass*, New York: Jossey Bass.

Glickman, S. (1995) "Prince", pp. 185–89 in S. Bourgain (ed.) *Contemporary Musicians: Profiles of the people in music*, vol. 14, Detroit: Gate Research.

Golkin, P. (1989a) "Blacks, whites and blues: The story of Chess Records" part one, *Living Blues*, September/October, pp. 22–32.

Golkin, P (1989b) "Blacks, whites and blues: The story of Chess Records" part two, *Living Blues*, December, pp. 25–29.

Gordy, B. (1994) *To Be Loved: The music, the magic, the memories of Motown*, London: Headline.

Green, J. R. (1993) "'Twoness' in the style of Oscar Micheaux", pp. 26–48 in M. Diawara (ed.) *Black American Cinema*, New York: Routledge.

Griffin, A. G. (1992) "Seizing the moving image", pp. 228–33 in M. Wallace and G. Dent (eds) *Black Popular Culture*, Seattle, WA: Bay Press.

Guralnick, P. (1986) *Sweet Soul Music: Rhythm and blues and the southern dream of freedom*, London: Virgin Books.

Gwaltney, J. L. (1993) *Drylongso: A self-portrait of black America*, New York: The New Press.

Hacker, A. (1992) *Two Nations*, New York: Scribner's.

Hannaford, I. (1996) *Race: The history of an idea in the West*, Baltimore, MD: Johns Hopkins University Press.

Harris, E. (1993) *South of Haunted Dreams: A ride through slavery's old back yard*, London: Viking.

Hatch, D. and Millward, S. (1990) *From Blues to Rock: An analytical history of pop music*, Manchester: Manchester University Press.

Henderson, D. (1983) *'Scuse Me While I Kiss the Sky: The life of Jimi Hendrix*, New York: Bantam.

Henderson, E. (1996) "Black nationalism and rap music", *Journal of Black Studies*, vol. 26, no. 3, pp. 308–40.

Herrnstein, R. and Murray, C. (1994) *The Bell Curve: Intelligence and class structure in American life*, New York: Free Press.

Herskovits, M. (1941) *The Myth of the Negro Past*, New York: Harper & Brothers.

Hirschberg, L. (1996) "Does a sugar bear bite: Suge Knight and his posse", *New York Times Magazine*, January 14, pp. 26–40, 50–55.

Hirshey, G. (1994) *Nowhere to Run: The story of soul music*, New York: Da Capo Press.

hooks, b. and West, C. (1991) *Breaking Bread: Insurgent black intellectual life*, Boston, MA: South End Press.

Hoskyns, B. (1988) *Prince: Imp of the perverse*, London: Virgin Books.

Hoskyns, B. (1996) *Waiting for the Sun: The story of the Los Angeles music scene*, London: Viking.

Jennings, J. (1994) *Blacks, Latinos and Asians in Urban America*, Westport CT: Praeger.

Jensen, A. (1969) "How much can we boost IQ and scholastic achievement?" *Harvard Educational Review*, vol. 39, no. 1 pp. 1–123.

Jones, L. (1995) *Blues People*, Edinburgh: Payback Press.

Kushnick, L. (1981) "Racism and class consciousness in modern capitalism", pp. 191–216 in B. Bowser and R. Hunt (eds) *Impact of Racism on White America*, Beverly Hills, CA: Sage.

Lee, S. (1995) "Re-examining the concept of the 'independent' record label: The case of Wax Trax records", *Popular Music*, vol. 14, no. 1, pp. 13–31.

Levine, L. (1978) *Black Culture and Black Consciousness*, New York: Oxford University Press.

Lewis, D. L. (1981) *When Harlem Was in Vogue*, New York: Knopf.

Lidz, F. (1990) "From hair to eternity", *Sports Illustrated*, part 73 (December 10), pp. 88–103.

Lieberfeld, D. (1995) "Million-dollar juke joint: Commodifying blues culture", *African American Review*, vol. 29, no. 2, pp. 217–21.

Locke, A. (1969) *The Negro and His Music*, New York: Arno Press

Lorez, J. (1995) "Def Jam 10-year anniversary special", *Blues and Soul*, no. 701, pp. 26–30.

Lupica, M. (1991) "The sporting life", *Esquire*, part 115 (March 3), pp. 52–54.

Mabry, D. (1990) "The rise and fall of Ace records: A case study in the independent record business", *Business History Review*, vol. 64 (Autumn), pp. 411–50.

McClain, P. and Stewart. J (1995) *"Can We All Get Along?" Racial and ethnic minorities in American politics*, Boulder, CO: Westview Press.

McClintock, A. (1995) *Imperial Leather: Race, gender and sexuality in the colonial conquest*, New York: Routledge.

McDuffie, M. (1991) *Prince: Alter ego*, London: Titan.

Malcolm X. (1971) *The End of White Supremacy: Four speeches*, ed. Benjamin Karim, New York: Arcade.

Marable, M. (1984) *Race, Rebellion and Reform*, Basingstoke, Hampshire, UK: Macmillan.

Marcus, G. (1976) *Mystery Train: Images of America in rock'n'roll music*, New York: Dutton.

Mercer, K. (1994) *Welcome to the Jungle: New positions in black cultural studies*, New York: Routledge.

Miller, W. (1968) *Martin Luther King, Jr.*, New York: Avon.

Moses, W. (1993) *Black Messiahs and Uncle Toms: Social and literary manipulations of a religious myth*, 2nd edn, University Park PA: Pennsylvania State University Press.

Muhammad, T. K. (1995) "The real lowdown on labels", *Black Enterprise*, vol. 26, no. 5 (December) pp. 74–78.

Murray, C. S. (1989) *Crosstown Traffic: Jimi Hendrix and the rock'n'roll revolution*, New York: St Martin's Press.

Myrdal, G. (1995) *An American Dilemma: The Negro problem and modern democracy*, London: Transaction.

Newfield, J. (1995) *Only in America: The life and crimes of Don King*, New York: William Morrow.

Nilsen, P. (1993) *Prince: A documentary*, London: Omnibus Press.

Orth, M. (1995) "The Jackson jive", *Vanity Fair* (September), pp. 48–53.

Patterson, A. (1992) *Spike Lee*, New York: Avon.

Pieterse, J. (1992) *White on Black*, London: Yale University Press.

Read, M. (1989) *Super Media: A cultural studies approach*, Newbury Park, CA: Sage.

Regen, R. (1990) "Neither does King", *Interview* , vol. 20 (October 10), pp. 104, 115–18.

Reynolds, R. and Brown, A. (1994) "A new rhythm takes hold", *Black Enterprise*, vol. 25, no. 5, pp. 82–89.

Ritz, D. (1991) *Divided Soul: The life of Marvin Gaye*, New York: DaCapo.

Roberts, J. (1995) "A piece of the action", *Newsweek*, vol. 125, no. 25 (December 18), pp. 48–53.

Rogers, D. (1982) *Rock'n'Roll*, London: Routledge & Kegan Paul.

Root, D. (1996) *Cannibal Culture: Art, appropriation and the commodification of difference*, Boulder, CO: Westview Press.

Rose, T. (1994) *Black Noise: Rap music and black culture in contemporary America*, Hanover, NH: Wesleyan University Press.

Rosen, S. (1995) *The Artist Formerly Known as Prince*, Chessington, Surrey, UK: Castle Communications.

Ross, D. (1993) *Secrets of a Sparrow: Memoirs*, New York: Villard Books.

Said, E. (1993) *Culture and Imperialism*, London: Vintage.

Samuels, D. (1991) "The rap on rap", *The New Republic*, November 11, pp. 24–29.

Segal, R. (1995) *The Black Diaspora*, London: Faber & Faber.

Shelley, J. (1996) "Def ambition", *Guardian Weekend* (April 27), pp. 36–42.

Shohat, E. and Stam, R. (1994) *Unthinking Eurocentrism: Multiculturalism and the media*, New York: Routledge

Sidran, B. (1995) *Black Talk*, Edinburgh: Payback Press.

Sitkoff, H. (1981) *The Struggle for Black Equality*, 1954–1980, New York: Hill & Wang.

Smedley, A. (1993) *Race in North America: Origin and evolution of a worldview*, Boulder, CO: Westview Press.

Spinelli, J. (1991) "Shadow boxing", *Sports Illustrated* (November 4), pp. 73–86.

Takaki, R. (1990) *Iron Cages: Race and culture in 19th century America*, New York: Oxford University Press.

Takaki, R. (1993) *A Differerent Mirror: A history of multicultural America*, Boston: Little, Brown.

Taraborrelli, J. (1991) *Michael Jackson: The magic and the madness*, New York: Birch Lane Press.

Tocqueville, A. de (1946) *Democracy in America*, New York: Oxford University Press.

Toll, R. (1974) *Blacking Up: The minstrel show in nineteenth-century America*, New York: Oxford University Press.

Toop, D. (1984) *The Rap Attack: African jive to New York hip hop*, London: Pluto.

Vaughn, C. (1992) "Russell Simmons' rush for profits", *Black Enterprise*, vol. 23, no. 5, pp. 66–74.

Vincent, T. (1995) *Keep Cool: The black activists who built the Jazz Age*, London: Pluto Press.

West, C. (1993) *Keeping Faith: Philosophy and race in America*, New York: Routledge.

White, C. (1984) *The Life and Times of Little Richard, The Quasar of Rock*, New York: Harmony Books.

Wierviorka, M. (1995) *The Arena of Racism*, London: Sage.

Williams, J. (1987) *Eyes on the Prize: America's civil rights years, 1954–1965*, New York: Viking Penguin.

Wilson, M. (1987) *Dreamgirl: My life as a supreme*, New York: St Martin's Press.

Wilson, M. and Romanowski, P. (1990) *Supreme Faith: Someday we'll be together*, New York: HarperCollins.

Index

NOTES

NOTES

NOTES